Mat McLachlan is one of Australia's leading battlefield historians and media presenters in the history space. He is the author of *Walking with the Anzacs, Gallipoli: The Battlefield Guide* and *The Cowra Breakout,* and the founder of Mat McLachlan Battlefield Tours, which sends thousands of Australians to visit battlefields around the world each year.

As a media presenter, Mat is a regular on TV and radio and in print. His *Living History* podcast reaches more than 30,000 Australian history enthusiasts each week, and he produces the *BattleWalks* and *Pete & Gary's Military History* podcasts. Mat also produces and presents history documentaries for various networks. He appears regularly as a history expert on all major Australian television and radio networks, and reaches over five million people on YouTube each year. He lives in Sydney with his wife and children.

Also by Mat McLachlan

Walking with the Anzacs
Gallipoli: The Battlefield Guide
The Cowra Breakout

KRITHIA

THE FORGOTTEN ANZAC BATTLE OF GALLIPOLI

MAT McLACHLAN

hachette
AUSTRALIA

Published in Australia and New Zealand in 2024
by Hachette Australia
(an imprint of Hachette Australia Pty Limited)
Gadigal Country, Level 17, 207 Kent Street, Sydney, NSW 2000
www.hachette.com.au

Hachette Australia acknowledges and pays our respects to the past, present and future Traditional Owners and Custodians of Country throughout Australia and recognises the continuation of cultural, spiritual and educational practices of Aboriginal and Torres Strait Islander peoples. Our head office is located on the lands of the Gadigal people of the Eora Nation.

 A catalogue record for this work is available from the National Library of Australia

ISBN: 978 0 7336 4910 3 (paperback)

Cover design by Luke Causby / Blue Cork
Cover and internal photographs courtesy of the Australian War Memorial unless otherwise specified
Map by Laurie Whiddon, Map Illustrations
Typeset in Simoncini Garamond by Kirby Jones
Printed and bound in Australia by McPherson's Printing Group

 The paper this book is printed on is certified against the Forest Stewardship Council® Standards. McPherson's Printing Group holds FSC® chain of custody certification SA-COC-005379. FSC® promotes environmentally responsible, socially beneficial and economically viable management of the world's forests.

Contents

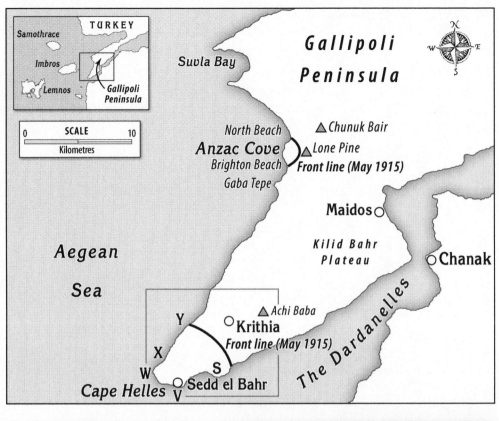

TURKEY

Samothrace

Imbros

Lemnos

Gallipoli Peninsula

0   SCALE   10
Kilometres

*Gallipoli
Peninsula*

Suvla Bay

North Beach
Anzac Cove
Brighton Beach
Gaba Tepe

△ *Chunuk Bair*
△ *Lone Pine*
Front line (May 1915)

Maidos ○

*Kilid Bahr
Plateau*

Chanak ○

*Aegean

Sea*

△ *Achi Baba*

Y

○ **Krithia**
Front line (May 1915)

X

S

W

Cape Helles

V

○ **Sedd el Bahr**

The Dardanelles

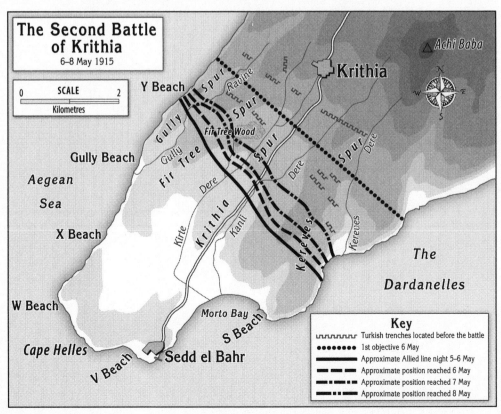

The Second Battle of Krithia
6–8 May 1915

0   SCALE   2
Kilometres

△ *Achi Baba*

Y Beach

Gully Spur

Ravine

Spur

Fir Tree Wood

Spur

Krithia

Gully Beach

Gully

Fir Tree

Gully Dere

Spur

Dere

Dere

*Aegean

Sea*

X Beach

Kirte Dere

Krithia Dere

Kanli Dere

Kereves Se.

Kereves

W Beach

Cape Helles

Morto Bay

S Beach

V Beach

Sedd el Bahr

*The

Dardanelles*

Key

〜〜〜 Turkish trenches located before the battle
•••••• 1st objective 6 May
▬▬▬ Approximate Allied line night 5–6 May
▬ ▬ ▬ Approximate position reached 6 May
▬·▬·▬ Approximate position reached 7 May
▬··▬··▬ Approximate position reached 8 May

A NOTE ON NAMING CONVENTIONS

Turkish/Ottoman: The military forces at Gallipoli historically and colloquially referred to as 'Turkish' are more accurately described as 'Ottoman'. In 1915, the Ottoman Empire stretched from the Red Sea to the Black Sea and, although the bulk of its soldiers came from what is now Türkiye, its military forces also included troops from today's Syria, Iraq, Saudi Arabia, Yemen, Israel, Palestine and elsewhere. Although modern historians have embraced the term 'Ottoman' to refer to this ethnically and culturally diverse group, historical sources almost universally use the term 'Turkish'. This presents a problem in a book that is written using a combination of modern narrative and historic quotes so, for simplicity, I've made the decision to use the term 'Turkish' throughout the book, so that the narrative and quotes use the same terminology. It's a nod to readability over technical accuracy and not intended to diminish the substantial contribution of troops from other parts of the Ottoman Empire, which was essential to victory in the Gallipoli campaign.

ANZAC/Anzac: The spelling and use of the word 'Anzac' has caused confusion and arguments since it was first used in 1914. The term was originally coined to describe the combined Australian and New Zealand military force that would eventually fight at Gallipoli – the Australian and New Zealand Army Corps. The original abbreviation was 'A & NZ Army Corps', which was then shortened to 'A&NZAC' and inevitably to 'ANZAC'. But as early as the opening months of the Gallipoli campaign, the term was evolving from an acronym to a proper noun (with an upper-case 'A' and the rest of the word lower-case). The sector in which the Australians and New Zealanders were fighting was called 'Anzac' to distinguish it from the British sector of Helles, the beach where the troops had come ashore was officially designated 'Anzac Cove' and the men who were fighting at Gallipoli referred to themselves as 'Anzacs'.

After the war, other Anzac-related terms entered the Australian dialect including 'Anzac Day', 'Anzac Memorial' and 'Anzac biscuits' as proper nouns. The established convention in English is that words that begin as acronyms often evolve to proper nouns (or simply nouns) with common usage (such as Qantas, scuba, radar, etc.). Therefore, the only time 'ANZAC' should be spelt with all-capitals is when referring to the original military force that served at Gallipoli – the Australian and New Zealand Army Corps. All other uses of the word should be spelt 'Anzac'. In this book, if it's not immediately obvious that the acronym is the correct choice, I've gone with the proper noun. 'Anzac' is much less jarring in a sentence than 'ANZAC'.

Similarly, I've used the (technically redundant) term 'the ANZAC Corps' as opposed to the correct but potentially confusing 'the ANZAC'.

Topographical features: During the campaign, the rugged terrain at Gallipoli was known by both English and Turkish names. For the sake of clarity, I've used the more commonly known English place names in this book, even to refer to sites before they were so named. The best example is Anzac Cove, a name I've used while describing Turkish operations there before and during the landing. If a feature had a Turkish name, I've included it at the first reference but then use the common English name thereafter.

Personal accounts: A key feature of this book is telling the story through the words of the men who lived through it. Many of these accounts were written as diary entries in battered notebooks or on scraps of paper, and the writing was necessarily abbreviated. In the interests of clarity, I have edited some accounts for readability without altering the intended meaning.

PROLOGUE

Lance Corporal Harry Kelly lay prone in the dirt. He tried to flatten himself into the hard earth, as if through an act of will he could sink through the crusty surface and find some blessed protection from the bullets flying around him. Behind him was a trench, which he had clambered out of only seconds before. In front of him was a bare plain, which seemed to extend all the way to the horizon, rising slowly in the distance to a stubby and ugly hill. The plain wasn't entirely featureless; it just felt that way. Harry had noted crude clumps of scrub scattered across the landscape before he went to ground. But what scant vegetation there was provided little concealment and no cover – the worst of both worlds – and the scrubby brush was thorny and unfriendly.

Two or three bullets smacked into the ground to Harry's left and he pressed his face even further into the baked ground. Dirt went up his nose and into his eyes and he inhaled coarse dust as he drew in a ragged breath. But he didn't care. He'd put up with *anything* just to be spared this brutal fire.

The noise of rifle and shellfire was all-consuming but, through the din, Harry could hear, off to his left, the dreaded

1

tap-tap-tap-tap of a Turkish machine gun. Harry had spent enough time in the front lines to recognise a good gunner when he heard one. This Turk wasn't spraying bullets – he was being murderously methodical, picking targets and then sending three or four bullets toward them in short bursts. This was a bad sign. The care with which the Turkish gunner was handling his weapon suggested he wasn't feeling any pressure, which meant the New Zealand soldiers who were supposed to be attacking him weren't advancing. The left of the Allied line must have been as stonewalled as Harry's battalion was in the centre.

A bullet smacked into a rock a few feet in front of Harry's head and ricocheted away with a shrill whine, like a snapped violin string. It smacked into someone behind him with a sickening wet thump, the unique sound of lead meeting flesh that Harry had become all too familiar with in the past two weeks. He didn't know who had been hit and didn't care, but the fact that the man wasn't screaming didn't bode well for his longevity. When a hit was fatal, men went down with a low groan, not a scream.

Harry's rifle was in his right hand but, in his exposed position, the weapon was purely ornamental. There was nothing to shoot at and, even if there was, only a madman would raise himself into a shooting position in this fire.

Above the noise, Harry could hear shouting. 'Corporal! Corporal!' The voice was plaintive, so Harry could tell it wasn't an officer trying to give him an order. It was a private desperate for help. 'What do we do now?'

'Keep your bloody head down!' Harry yelled in reply. It was a pointless statement – not a man was moving but Harry couldn't think of anything else to say. And even if he could, he was in no position to offer direction or comfort to the man – just three days earlier, Harry had been a private himself. The promotion had come not because Harry offered exceptional leadership skills on the battlefield – but because all the other lance corporals in his platoon had been killed or wounded. The couple of years Harry had spent in a militia unit before the war made him the most experienced man left but Harry struggled to work out how his skills at marching and peeling spuds would equip him to lead men in battle. Christ, he hadn't even had time to sew his lance-corporal's chevron onto his tunic sleeve.

Maybe it was the desperate tone in the man's voice that spurred Harry into action but he decided he should at least try to get a better idea of just how much trouble they were in. He didn't dare lift his head; instead, he cautiously eased his face out of the dirt and turned a few degrees so he could look to his right. His platoon had been advancing across a narrow spur that fell away to a rough valley on his right. He couldn't see much, but on the opposite slope he could make out men advancing in a rush. A flash of red on their trousers told him who they were – French Zouaves from the colonies of Africa. Their colourful uniforms might have looked resplendent on a parade ground, but on a battlefield they stood out like blue-and-red beacons. Harry saw several men go down as shrapnel shell burst in an ugly brown-black cloud above their heads. Hopefully enough Zouaves would survive to capture the Turkish line and the blokes currently shooting in Harry's direction would have something else to occupy them.

Harry turned his head to the left. His view was impeded by a clump of gorse but he could see a few men lying still in the dirt not far from him. The first bloke was obviously dead – half his head was blown away – but he couldn't tell what state the others were in. A bit further on, two men huddled together, pressed close. They were obviously mates and seeking comfort from each other but Harry knew what a tempting target they would make if the Turks spotted them. He thought of yelling at them to spread out, but what was the point? Even if they heard him, they would ignore him, and he was buggered if he was going to go over and sort them out. One of the men was holding something in front of his face – for a minute, Harry had the crazy thought that it was an umbrella. But then he realised what it was – a shovel. It was a silly thing to do – the thin metal was never going to stop a bullet – but Harry could relate to the sentiment. Any cover was better than none on this killing field.

'Australians!' Someone was shouting again – this time, the voice was authoritative and could not be ignored. 'Which of you men are Australians? Come on, Australians!' Harry didn't know who the officer doing the shouting was but he knew what it meant. Unthinkably, Harry and the men around him were being ordered to stand up, to walk forward into the maelstrom and to face the full force of the Turkish onslaught head on.

For a moment, Harry considered playing dead before waking up to himself. He gripped his rifle, said a prayer into the dusty earth, and rose gingerly to a half-crouch, bracing for machine-gun bullets to tear into his chest at any moment. He felt a bizarre surge of elation when he wasn't instantly killed. All around him, carnage unfolded. How the hell had it come to this?

1.

THE NEW ZEALANDER

The day of 3 August 1914 was a bank holiday in New Zealand and 24-year-old Cecil Malthus, a teacher from Nelson at the top of the South Island, was spending it larking around with friends. It was a cold day but the sun was shining, so Cecil and his mates headed off for a hike up Dun Mountain. The views were breathtaking and the banter flowed between the chums as freely as the icy water in the mountain's creeks. After several hours of tramping, the group stopped for a break beside a waterfall at a clearing in the bush. A roaring fire soon warmed cold hands; the young men shuffled their frozen feet and waited for the billy to boil. Naturally, the conversation turned to sport. The group of mates all played on the same rugby team and they lightly ribbed each other about their skills on the field. That drew laughter, which hung in the air briefly before fading into the mountain mist. Despite the lightheartedness, the group had more serious issues on its mind.

Eventually, Cecil broke the silence. 'Who among you is going to enlist?' he asked. War hadn't come to New Zealand yet but it felt inevitable, and his question prompted an animated conversation about the coming storm – it was all anyone had been talking about for the past month. 'It was agreed that it was the urgent duty of every able-bodied man to consider the question of enlisting,' Cecil later wrote, 'and that self-interest would be no excuse for staying at home.'[1] The consensus among his mates was that the Germans would be easily overthrown. 'Such optimism ... seems hard to explain,' he wrote. 'But we were a self-confident nation in those days.'

Two days later, Cecil heard the news he had been expecting – Britain and Germany were at war and New Zealand was climbing into the ring right beside them. Cecil and his mates had made up their minds – they were going to enlist. 'Without a pang, without doubt or hesitation,' he wrote, 'we dropped the life that had absorbed us. No resolve or decision was involved. It just had to be that way. And so the great adventure began.'

Cecil wasn't alone in his determination to join the war effort. A long queue snaked into the Nelson enlistment office. On signing up, he was assigned to the Canterbury Infantry Battalion, one of four newly formed units of the fledgling New Zealand Expeditionary Force (the others were the Auckland, Otago and Wellington battalions, with accompanying units from the Mounted Rifles, artillery and various support units). Volunteers from the Nelson district were gathered together and on 15 August sent to the main training centre at Christchurch by sea. The recruits were given little notice of the move and were miffed to be ushered onto the waiting ship in the dead of night, giving them no opportunity to farewell loved ones. 'Friends and relatives woke to find us vanished,' Cecil later lamented. 'For many of them it was goodbye forever.'

On arrival in Christchurch, the early thrill of adventure soon gave way to the drudgery of daily army life. Long marches and feints with the bayonet became the order of the day. No-one was really sure what sort of warfare they would encounter so they trained for everything. Instruction on new technologies such as machine guns and hand grenades took place alongside the old standards of army life – hygiene, physical fitness and platoon drill. For the green recruits, eager to get stuck into the Germans, the training seemed to drag on for an eternity. The griping reached fever pitch when the force was shipped to Wellington. There was no room for the new arrivals in the region's camps, so the troops, all 1300 of them, plus 350 horses, were forced to live on the ship, coming ashore each day for training and manoeuvres. Life on board was hot, cramped and monotonous. The men slept in three tiers of bunks that had been jammed into the ship's hold as tightly as possible, and the improvised mess hall could only be reached by a perilous climb down a roughly fashioned wooden stairway. Eventually, the overcrowding became unbearable and space was found ashore for the mounted troops – for the sake of the horses, not the men.

Among the other New Zealand battalions bogged down by the tedium of training was the Wellington Battalion, commanded by Lieutenant Colonel William Malone, one of those larger-than-life characters that the Gallipoli story throws forth in abundance. Originally from the UK, Malone had lived in New Zealand since he was twenty-one and had worked as a constable and farmer in the Taranaki region of the North Island. He was an upstanding member of his community and studied law by night while working as a farmer during the day. As well as becoming a prominent local solicitor, he was a member of the council and several boards before enlisting in the military at the time of the Boer War. By 1910, he was a lieutenant colonel and commanding officer of the 4th Battalion, Wellington (Taranaki) Rifle Volunteers. At the outbreak of the First World War, he was appointed to command the Wellington Battalion and, despite being fifty-five years of age and the oldest man in the battalion, he was also one of its fittest. He was a demanding and powerful character, with a fastidious mind and an infamously short fuse. Although frustrated with the inefficiencies of military bureaucracy, the army was where he was meant to be. He looked forward to leading his battalion into battle.

> I feel very well. This life suits me, mind and body. It is a man's life. I wonder if I shall come back or leave my bones in Europe but I am content. I am in God's hands and no death can be better.[2]

By this stage, Cecil and his comrades in the New Zealand forces had been in uniform for two months. There was a genuine concern that the whole show would be over before they had even left New Zealand. The newspapers carried little else but news about the war, and daily tales of derring-do from exotic-sounding places like Mons, the Marne and Le Cateau raised the enthusiasm and impatience of the recruits to be a part of it. When the time came, they would be ready. Most newly enlisted men had done time in militia or cadet units before the war, and their officers, sergeants and corporals had largely been drawn from New Zealand's existing territorial army, giving the whole force a level of experience that greatly aided the training process.

By the time they left Wellington, the motley group of civilians had been shaped into an efficient fighting force and had attained a level of efficiency that New Zealand would struggle to maintain in new recruits for the rest of the war. Early recruiting officers had only wanted the best men and rejection rates had been high. Those men who did make it through were generally fitter and better educated than those who followed later on – these men were New Zealand's brightest and best, and they knew it. 'I have never known finer comrades than in those early days, rough bushmen and men of all work as they largely were,' Cecil later wrote. 'There was hardly a man in our platoon with whom one could not be on terms of friendly good fellowship.'

In a reflection of the 'Pals Battalions' being formed in Britain, men who had enlisted in the first wave in New Zealand were grouped into units with other men from their district, and Cecil was assigned to the 12th (Nelson) Company of the Canterbury Battalion. Several of his mates had enlisted with him and, in an odd coincidence, he found himself serving alongside a group of old boys from Nelson College, where he had briefly taught before enlisting. Although only a couple of years older than his former pupils, Cecil naturally tried to act as a father figure to them – but they were having none of it. 'They were young, irrepressible madcaps,' he later recalled with a touch of nostalgia, 'determined to snatch what compensations they could from all our tribulations.' The unlikely group became firm friends. Cecil drew special attention to several of his chums in his diary, in a list that reads like a casting call from a pantomime: Bert Warnock, Porky Littlejohn, Buck Whiting, Harold Ching, Smiler Pike, Hartley Palmer, a talkative Italian named Loo Vannini and three resplendently named brothers, Roy, Dudley and Patrick D'Arcy-Irvine. The eclectic mob was commanded by a well-respected group of officers. One in particular, Second Lieutenant Alexander Forsythe, a 28-year-old jeweller with a broad Scottish accent and a quick wit, was a favourite among the men. Another man who earned special mention in Cecil's letters home was his platoon sergeant Billy Williams, a Cockney who seemed to delight in causing misery to his charges. According to Cecil, Williams was 'small, shrewd, monkey-faced, with a long upper lip, but he has not a trace of humour and is only unintentionally funny. He keeps up a self-important dignity by roaring out orders and treating us like dirt.' But like all good sergeants, Williams was intent on shaping his platoon into an efficient fighting force – and the results could mean the difference between life and death on the battlefield. In spite of their griping, the men knew it. 'Billy has been the most important person in our young lives during the last ten weeks,' Cecil wrote. 'Without such training we would never be fit for the life in the trenches. Without it perhaps we would never have developed the comradeship which is the finest thing war has to offer.'

When word finally came that the force would be sailing for Europe, it came fast. Once again, the men were marched onto ships at short notice with no time for farewells. At dusk on 16 October, the first contingent of the New Zealand Expeditionary Force (known as the Main Body) steamed out of Wellington Harbour. The small fleet made a fine sight as the ten transports fell into two lines astern and four warships (two New Zealand, one Australian and one Japanese) took station on the four sides of the convoy. The fleet turned into Cook Strait and steamed northwest past the top of the South Island as the sun hung low in the sky. It was a stunning evening and the decks were crowded with soldiers. Few spoke. It was near on dark when the ships passed the aptly named Farewell Spit on the very northern tip of the island – right on cue, the lighthouse on the promontory lit up as they sailed by. It was the last glimpse they would catch of their homeland. Cecil turned and walked slowly down the creaking stairway into the gloom of the ship's hold.

— —

The long voyage didn't warrant much space in Cecil's diary, which is decidedly odd considering how much drama unfolded in the ten weeks he was at sea. The ten New Zealand transports steamed to Hobart and then onward to Albany in Western Australia, where they were joined by the twenty-eight transports and two fast cruisers carrying the Australian contingent. On 1 November, the convoy set sail for Europe. No-one knew it yet, but the group of men that would soon and forever be known as the Anzacs had just come together for the first time.

On 9 November, the convoy was cruising off Direction Island, in today's Cocos (Keeling) Islands group, when a distress call came in from the island's wireless station. A party of Germans had landed from the cruiser *Emden* and was attempting to disable the station. 'Instantly we saw the powerful cruiser *Sydney* dashing off at full speed,' Cecil later wrote. 'The little Japanese cruiser followed, and slowly, regretfully returned when ordered to do so.' (In spite of Cecil's slightly condescending recollections, the 'little Japanese cruiser' was in fact the battlecruiser *Ibuki*, which was larger and more heavily armed than *Sydney*.) Cecil and his comrades didn't see the naval battle that took place but they soon heard about it over the ship's wireless: *Emden* was a smashed wreck and had been run aground on the island; *Sydney* had suffered only minor damage. It was the first action of the new Royal Australian Navy.

Over the rest of the voyage, the tedium of life on board the overcrowded ship and the uninspiring diet encouraged the soldiers to seek distraction. The ingenious employment of a fishhook on a string gave Cecil and his mates both a break from the boredom and a supplement to their rations. They used it to pinch supplies from the canteen by snagging them and hoisting the booty through an open skylight. The lark came to an abrupt end when they were nabbed by the military police but the bars of chocolate they had managed to snatch more than made up for the couple of hours of deck scrubbing they received as punishment.

Late in the voyage, the ship was due for a brief stop in Colombo. Every man and horse on board was desperate to get off the cramped and sweaty vessel, and to stretch the legs on dry land. The news that no-one would be allowed to leave the ship was greeted with a near riot. Cecil recalled the men assembling in the mess hall after the ship had put to sea again, and that it was:

> dimly lit, hazy, frightfully hot, smelly and sweaty, so that even the time it took to swallow dinner was a sore trial to the patience. So it happened that when the orderly officer appeared that day with the traditional 'Any complaints?' he was greeted with an almost unanimous roar of anger, and the next moment was hit fair in the face with an old hunk of cheese.

The men were threatened with 'calamitous penalties if the offender did not own up, but the secret was well kept and the affair blew over'.

And so Cecil and his hardy band of mates journeyed on, their bellies unsated but their spirits high, their destination and their fate uncertain.

— • —

The long and uncomfortable journey finally came to an end for the ragged new antipodean force on 3 December. But the joyous news that they would soon be stretching their legs on dry land was somewhat tempered by the discovery that the land would not be the bucolic fields of France but the sands of Egypt. Cecil didn't recall hearing the announcement that the Ottoman Empire had joined the war on the side of the Germans but he saw the results first-hand: the Suez Canal was a vital British asset that had to be protected from the Turks. After steaming through the canal in darkness, the force was disembarked at Alexandria and then herded onto rough and rickety rail carriages for a long, sweaty journey to Cairo. Most of the troops had never been much further than Christchurch or Adelaide, and the new arrivals found the chaos of the city overwhelming. They pitched their tents within earshot of the city's din in a dustbowl called Zeitoun. Today, it's been absorbed by the endlessly expanding Cairo but in 1914 it stood removed and offered little but sand, flies and misery.

Life in this new desert army was about as far from the heroic tales portrayed in the newspapers as the troops could imagine. Thirty-five kilometre marches under full pack and scorching sun were commonplace and meals consisted of dry biscuits and oily bully beef, probably the worst combination of food for parched men in a desert environment. An occasional orange purchased from local vendors provided the only relief from this nauseating menu. At night, the men slept in bell tents on dirt floors as hard as concrete. This was not the war they had signed up for.

— —

Cecil pressed himself hard against the earth bank and tried vainly to get some respite from the incessant desert wind. It was 2 February 1915 and he and his mates had been doing hard graft for several days. A week earlier, his company had been ordered to leave camp and catch a train northeast to the shores of Lake Timsah, to help guard the Suez Canal against Turkish incursions. After leaving the train, the Kiwis were faced with yet another dreaded desert march and, this time, they were carrying their full battle kit. 'We had to struggle over several miles of deep sand, against a hot and heavy gale, and in full marching order, which was now a terrific weight,' Cecil recalled. 'The ammunition and blanket made a great difference, and we even carried bundles of firewood.' As they topped a rise, they saw the Indian brigade they were supporting advance in extended order against Turkish lines on the far side of the canal. It was the first combat any of them had seen and the young Kiwis were transfixed. There were no practice manoeuvres or feints with the bayonet here – these men were being shot at and being hit. Turkish shrapnel shells burst in ugly grey-brown clouds above the distant figures. Cecil saw several of them crumple to the ground and not get up again.

By nightfall, the New Zealanders had reached the bank of the canal, although this offered little shelter from the wind. The sand was everywhere, getting into everything; Cecil tried to eat some rations and got a mouthful of the hated stuff for his troubles.

He pulled his blanket up to his ears and did his best to snatch some sleep. He was just nodding off when his whole world exploded. The platoon to his left had opened fire, and it seemed every man in the line was firing his rifle. The chatter of machine guns joined the chorus and, through it all, Cecil could make out the low drumbeat of exploding artillery shells.

He risked a glance over the bank and saw, away to his left, a small armada of pontoon boats attempting to cross the canal. He could just make out the shadowy figures of their Turkish crews paddling furiously as the rifle fire swelled. Whether the Turks were being brave or foolhardy Cecil couldn't tell, but the result was the same either way. The New Zealanders began to find the range and bullets smacked into boats and bodies. The Turks cried out in terror and reversed course, racing toward the far bank as men fell all around them. The survivors hit the shore and made a mad dash from the boats to the safety of the bank. Few made it.

Turkish marksmen began to reply to the rifle fire and bullets thudded into the near bank. Cecil saw a small group of men from the platoon on his left exchanging shots with the Turks and recognised one of them as Private Bill Ham. He was a young bloke who had lived near Cecil on the South Island and they had enlisted around the same time. Ham was shouting something and then went down hard, shot through the throat. He was still alive – frothy blood gurgled from the ugly wound – but he was obviously in a bad way. The stretcher-bearers dragged him away from the bank and to the field hospital, but he died the next day. 'There may have been some proud consolation for his people,' Cecil later wrote, 'in the fact of his being the first New Zealand casualty of the war.'

Dawn revealed the horror of the battlefield. Battered pontoons were scattered on the far bank; mangled corpses lay in grotesque piles on the shore or bobbed in the water. The Turks were still active and, although they didn't present good targets, Cecil got his first taste of combat as he and his platoon took pot shots at any man who showed himself. It wasn't clear if they hit anyone. Mid-morning, enemy artillery fire began. Shrapnel shells burst overhead, spraying their deadly payload in clouds of dust around the New Zealanders, and Cecil pressed himself into the bank. 'I don't mind saying I was horribly frightened,' he said, 'and dug into the sand like a rabbit.' The gunfire drew nearer and the pine trees behind the line were thrashed and stripped by the fire. Billy Williams, the platoon sergeant, patted Cecil on the shoulder as he moved along the line, encouraging the men to hold their nerve and keep their heads down. Williams cried out in pain and grabbed his shoulder as a shrapnel ball tore into him – he hit the ground in a cloud of dust and swear words. A stretcher-bearer dragged him away.

Then, just as quickly as it had arrived, the shellfire slackened. A Royal Navy warship came racing along the canal, guns blazing, and silenced the Turkish guns. As the ship passed Cecil's position, a rifle shot rang out from the far bank and the sailor on lookout duty in the crow's nest fell dead. A shot from the ship's 12-inch guns sorted out the sniper in a bloody instant.

It had been an eventful few days. Cecil's company had a new sense of purpose and self-belief as they were relieved from the line and sent back to camp. The rest of the battalion was desperate to hear about their brush with the enemy – the stories stretched on long into the night. The New Zealanders had met their enemy and not been found wanting – when the next opportunity came, they would be ready.

— —

Life soon returned to normal for the Nelson Company. Once again, their days were filled with the monotony of training. By now, the New Zealanders had merged with the Australian forces, and this new formation – the Australian and New Zealand Army Corps – was preparing for something big. Rumours were swirling that the whole force would soon be sent to a new front and a sudden increase in rations (clearly an attempt to use up stores before a big move) did nothing to dampen the scuttlebutt. No-one was sure when the move would take place, but an astonishing lack of security meant that the destination was all but certain. Cecil wrote in a letter home on 4 March that he would soon be leaving for the Dardanelles and the information was apparently considered so widely known that it was passed unedited by the army censor. 'This Dardanelles affair,' Cecil wrote, 'is a very daring undertaking, with tremendous possibilities. If successful it will undoubtably shorten the war, so I am all for it.' It is telling that so much was being discussed about the Gallipoli campaign weeks before it was even launched. If a lowly New Zealand private in a camp in Egypt knew all about the upcoming offensive, then the Turks certainly did as well.

In preparation for the coming offensive, the ANZAC Corps took part in its largest-ever training exercises – division-sized manoeuvres involving more than 12,000 men, with all required to practise their intricate role in this complicated desert ballet. Cecil was enthusiastic but exhausted by the end of it, thoroughly ready to embark on the next phase of his adventure.

By early April, the battalion's commanders were warning the men to be ready to leave any day and promising that heavy action was not far off. Sergeant Billy Williams had recovered from his wounds received at the canal and was back bossing the men around. Several men who were considered below standard were removed from the ranks – weeded out to ensure the battalion was at maximum proficiency. The heat, dust and flies were becoming unbearable and every man was itching to make a move.

Finally, on 9 April, news came that the entire force would be shipping out of Egypt. Cecil packed his meagre belongings, took one last look at the barren, dusty camp and started walking. In spite of the hardships it had forced on him, he was uneasy about leaving camp – God only knew what awaited them on the battlefield. 'If we were not so excited,' he wrote home, 'we would almost feel some regret at our departure.' Trains took the men to Alexandria, where ships waited to transport them to a place and a fate they could scarcely imagine. The Anzacs were on their way to Gallipoli.

2.

THE ENGLISHMAN

Eighteen-year-old Joe Murray did his best to keep quiet. He sneaked in the back door of his family's modest home in Burnopfield, County Durham, but his mother was waiting for him. 'Where have you been until this late hour?' she asked.

'Just to the pictures, Mum.' Joe couldn't face telling her the truth. Eight years earlier, his oldest brother Tom had left home to join the navy and that news had prompted twenty-four hours of uninterrupted tears from his mother. There was no way Joe could reveal that he had just come from the recruiting office after signing up to the Royal Naval Division. He might not get accepted anyway – he had to return later that week for a medical examination and there was no telling how that would go.

At the outbreak of war, the navy had found itself with too many volunteers and not enough ships to put them on. The Royal Naval Division (RND) was formed as a repository for the excess men – although part of the navy, the division would fight as infantry. As an added bonus, the division enabled the navy to conduct its own limited land operations without needing to call on the army for support. Each battalion of the RND was named after a hero of British naval history.

Joe was stout and strong. He had left school at twelve to work in the local coalpit so his fitness shouldn't have been much cause for concern. But in October 1914, the war was only eight weeks old and the recruiters were picky. They only wanted the brightest and best, and men were frequently rejected for trifling medical issues. Joe needn't have worried – a few days later, after standing naked and awkward with a crowd of other enlistees and receiving a cursory medical examination, he made the thirteen-kilometre trek home to announce to his family that he had joined the RND. His father was astounded. 'He remained quiet for a moment and then shook me by the hand for the first time in his life. My childhood had terminated and in a few brief moments I had become a man.'[1] His mother, as expected, was inconsolable and let go a full broadside about how foolish Joe was being. She stated plainly that, as Tom was already serving, the family had done enough. 'Do not worry, Mother,' Joe told her. 'I shall come back safely enough, I am positive of that.'

The following week, Joe was saying his farewells and fighting to get to the train station under a crush of well-wishers who had turned out to see him off. Someone produced an accordion and, before long, the merry band was singing as it escorted him to the train. Joe was apparently quite a popular lad.

Someone made an impromptu speech which ended with the request that all present should shake hands with the conquering hero and the lassies must kiss him for luck ... The hand-shaking, back-slapping and kissing went on; I know some of the lassies had several goes in the queue but, be that as it may, it was not until all were satisfied or exhausted or both, the train and I could escape. Dozens of them wanted to come with me ... but I would not allow this.

On arrival in London, Joe joined a motley assortment of new recruits. Training for war was a mundane ordeal of marches and drills that sapped body and spirit. The tedious training stretched into weeks and then months. Joe had been allocated to the Hood Battalion of the RND, named for Admiral Samuel Hood, who had earned fame in the eighteenth century for chasing pirates and French frigates around the Caribbean. Presumably, the battalion's founders hoped that a bit of the old admiral's glory would rub off on the new recruits – but there was little glory or inspiration to be found in the endless hours of drudgery in the training camp. As Joe recalled:

> Now that I was on draft I had to be frequently told the old story 'You're in the Navy now and not behind the plough'. I think this must be in Kings Regulations as every instructor uses it at the first possible opportunity. Personally I had never been behind the plough and was beginning to think that I was totally unsuited to serve behind the mast. Everything we knew we were told to forget. We were no longer individuals with free minds but numbered images without power of speech or reason. I was beginning to lose faith and it struck me forcibly that if I was to fight for my country I would have to fight myself first.

Joe gives the impression in his diary that he was an easygoing chap but the constant haranguing from petty officers and bullying from fellow sailors in the training camp drove him to a minor breaking point. One evening, after Joe had performed less than admirably at the shooting range, he joined a raucous crowd of young sailors at an amateur boxing match in the drill hall basement. 'It was a real slaughter-house at times but we all enjoyed it,' he said. One of the boxers, who had spent several minutes forcefully rearranging the facial features of his opponent, spotted Joe in the crowd and amused the onlookers by likening his opponent's punches to Joe's shooting: off target and not very effective. Joe's response was unequivocal:

> After his bout he suggested he would like to give me a lesson in straight-shooting. I, to the crowd's obvious delight, accepted the challenge. I fooled about for the first round until I got the measure of him. When the bell went for the second round I set about him in earnest. I clouted him unmercifully. A lovely upper-cut to his chin lifted him clean off the floor and that was that. 'Would any of you other sharp-shooters like to show me how to box?' There were no offers.

Joe doesn't acknowledge it but there was no doubt another reason for his pent-up anger. He had just found out that his brother Tom was dead.

Tom's ship, HMS *Good Hope*, had been sunk in a lopsided encounter with the powerful German East Asia Squadron in the waters off Coronel, Chile. HMS *Monmouth* had also been sent to the bottom beside her, and all 1600 men on both ships had been lost. It was the first British naval defeat in more than a century and a humiliation for the entire nation.

When Joe heard the rumours that both ships had been lost with all hands, he held out irrational hopes that Tom might have survived as part of a shore party or that he was bobbing about the southern Pacific in a life-raft but, when no good news came, his mood darkened. And it wasn't just his fellow recruits who faced his wrath; it was also the Germans.

> An eye for an eye, a tooth for a tooth: this would be my motto from now on, come what may. I cared not for any instructors; they could bully, ridicule and scoff – I would

not hear them. My object was quite clear in my mind. Tom was the elder son and I the youngest. In the ordinary course of life the elder takes care of the younger but war upsets reason and routine. I worshipped him though he did not know it. To me, everything he did was manly and honest. There would come a time when I could avenge him.

As much as Joe longed to get stuck into the Germans, the tedium of training was unrelenting. The recruits' spirits were briefly raised by the thought they were embarking overseas when the entire Hood Battalion was ordered to cram onto a train at King's Cross Station. But instead of heading east toward the Channel, they steamed west into the sodden backcountry of Dorset. It was December and the site of their new camp was cold, bleak and lonely. Joe was bitter about it: 'Some desk-bound War Office General had, out of sheer spite, decided that we should be spirited away to the most isolated wilderness in the country.'

Every soldier, in every diary, gripes about the hardships and monotony of training, and Joe Murray was no exception. But it does seem that the men of the Hood Battalion had ample reason to complain – their training did appear to go on for an inordinately long time, under conditions that would try the toughest new recruit. As related in Joe's diary, the Dorset chapter of the Hood Battalion's story was a seemingly endless ordeal of mud, physical exhaustion, bullying and privation. By the time it finally concluded, the men of the battalion were desperate to be sent to the front.

The only reprieve for the young sailors during the two-month ordeal was six days of leave over Christmas. Joe was apprehensive about returning home. The boy his family remembered was long gone and he wasn't sure how he would relate to them. He was also troubled by the effect his sudden return home would have on his grieving parents – the family had long since given up hope that Tom was still alive. His anxiety is seemingly demonstrated by the short shrift he gives the Christmas break in his diary – apart from mentioning that his father was disappointed he hadn't arrived in his navy uniform, Joe effectively skips over the entire week and mentions little about his experiences at home. It's possible nothing of note occurred but it's unusual for Joe not to recount this important last meeting with his family before heading off to the war (in contrast, he allocates a full page to describing the send-off he received from family and neighbours when it was time to return to camp).

Once back with his battalion, Joe was thoroughly sick of training and itching to get stuck into the Germans. By this stage, he was supremely fit and healthy but thoroughly disillusioned with life in the camp.

We marched anywhere and everywhere, stopping now and then to do a bit of bayonet practice – naval style, of course. Then more marching and squad drill – 'Right wheel, left wheel, on the left form platoon, right incline, left incline, about turn, halt, order arms, slope arms, by the right quick march'. It was heartbreaking. The same movements over and over again all day and every day. Rushing here and there, lying down in the mud and then standing in the freezing wind and rain, it all appeared to be so useless.

But finally, blessedly, on 8 January, they received orders that the battlefield would soon be their new home. The following day saw the battalion in new, clean uniforms, with equipment spit-and-polished, lined up in perfect rows in a grassy field. Obviously, something big was about to happen but no-one could predict just how big it would be. A bugle blared and King George V rode onto the field to inspect the men. Winston Churchill, the father of the RND, was with him. Joe was less interested in the pomp and ceremony than he was in what it foretold: 'it conveyed to those who understood procedure that this was the final inspection before we proceeded overseas.'

After the parade, the news was confirmed when their commanding officer informed them that they would soon sail for the Mediterranean to force the Dardanelles. (It's worth pausing here to reflect on the significance of that announcement. It says a lot about the overconfidence of the Gallipoli planners that they were happy to telegraph their intentions to a bunch of junior sailors – and the world – so long before the campaign began.)

Joe and his mates began to get their affairs in order. The anticipation of finally going to war sent the rumour mill into overdrive but the men were also becoming philosophical about their time on the training field:

> The days came and went and every day had its quota of rumours: 'Leaving at the end of the week' – 'Operation cancelled' – 'Going to France after all'. Each rumour was said to come from an impeccable source. Camp life in England was – like the month – drawing to a close and, looking back on it, it had not been so bad really.

Despite Joe's attempt at magnanimity, life in the camp had been close to insufferable – the recruits had good reason to feel aggrieved. But perhaps their griping would have been somewhat stifled, their curses muttered a little less fervently, had the men of the Royal Naval Division known what was waiting for them on the battlefield.

– —

Joe was roughly awakened by a boot to the ribs. He was lying on the deck of the troopship *Grantully Castle*, desperate to get some respite from both the heat and the stench of the crammed quarters below deck. The kick he received wasn't unexpected – Joe had requested that one of the sailors on watch wake him when the ship entered the Strait of Gibraltar. Tom had told him stirring tales of sailing past the famous Rock of Gibraltar and Joe was determined not to miss it. Easier said than done – it was 3 am and the rock formed barely a shadow in the inky night. But still – Joe was satisfied with this hazy glimpse and, with luck, would see it in daylight on the return journey.

The Hood Battalion had been at sea for about a week, leaving wintery England far behind. Now that they were approaching the Mediterranean, 'the weather was glorious with the warm sun and the sea calm as a millpond. It was good to be alive.'

The troopship had been joined by two French warships and, as the small convoy steamed into the Grand Harbour at Malta, the ship's band rolled out both 'God Save the King' and 'La Marseillaise'. The brief stay in Malta allowed for a decent stretch of the legs and for the men to breathe some fresh air. Less than a day later, the convoy was steaming again and this time the destination was the island of Lemnos – less than eighty kilometres from the Dardanelles. Mudros Harbour was crammed with warships, both British and French – something big was in the air.

The battalions were soon ashore, skirmishing and marching. Joe was transfixed by the timeless tranquillity of Lemnos; the comparison to the rain-soaked Britain he had left behind less than a fortnight ago was striking.

Time had stood still on this island. I observed a Greek using a wooden plough drawn by two oxen and making a really good furrow, but the pace was slow. It was nice to be on dry land again; one felt more free and was able to move about. Somehow the air was different and the sun was hot. There was no shade anywhere.

Joe and his RND chums spent a busy and sweaty week on Lemnos. It wasn't hard to guess what would soon be expected of them – every day they practised landing on an enemy shore.

Each day the routine was much to the pattern of the first day. We went over the side by way of rope ladders and into the ships' boats, rowed ourselves ashore, scrambled out and lined the beach to attack the mythical enemy. After we had cleared the beach we got back into some sort of formation and marched inland followed by supposedly friendly Greek inhabitants offering for sale chocolate, oranges and figs. This was comical as neither oranges nor figs grew on the island; they must have been brought from the Turkish mainland.

The irony was lost on no-one that if local fruit vendors knew the British were here and practising a landing, the Turks must know as well. The element of surprise was quickly evaporating.

After a week of mock landings and feints against an imaginary enemy, the Hood Battalion was beginning to feel that the curse of training was never-ending but when the call to battle came, it came fast. At 5 pm on 18 March, as the men were settling down to prepare an unappetising dinner, they were ordered to pack kits and double-time for the dock. Within the hour, they were crammed onto a troopship and steaming out of the harbour. The destination was clear – they were heading for the Dardanelles and an imminent landing.

The following morning, the men of the battalion were ordered to line the rails in full battle order, with bayonets glistening in the morning sun.

In full view of the Turks, we expected the order to disembark at any moment … For two hours we remained on view, watching and wondering. No doubt the Turks were also wondering exactly where and when we would strike; as invaders it was for us to choose the time and place. There was not much choice of a landing place but, even so, the decision was ours. The Turks had to remain where they were, ready to defend their homeland.

But, once again for the men of the Hood Battalion, disappointment and frustration were the order of the day. Instead of a landing and a fight for glory, the men watched the enemy coast fade from view as the ships turned and began steaming back to Mudros. 'We had come over 2000 miles, opened the gate and strolled up the garden path,' Joe recalled with more than a dash of dejection. 'The door stood wide open but we did not enter but turned and left.' He didn't know it at the time but the navy had just been pummelled by the Turkish forts that lined the straits and the insidious mines that lurked beneath them. Three British and one French ship had been lost and the will of the navy to force the straits unaided had sunk with them. 'The Gallipoli Peninsula must be occupied but the navy could not go it alone.'

For the next two weeks, the battalion was shuttled around half the Mediterranean. A stint in Port Said, Egypt, brought unpleasant memories of the tribulations of the Dorset training camp but this time sand and heat replaced mud and snow. A spell of guard duty on the Suez Canal came with its own dangers – one of Joe's comrades was paralysed in a swimming accident and another died from heat stroke, losses that added to the collective frustration of the men at being denied the chance to fight.

In mid-April, the battalion was marched onto yet another troopship and steamed (again) for Lemnos. Their hopes for battle were confirmed when the battalion was addressed by their colonel. 'In a few days' time we are going to land on the Gallipoli Peninsula,' he told them. 'The eyes of the world will be upon us and the whole course of the war will depend on the success of our efforts. We *have* to succeed and take Constantinople from the Turks.' Joe was excited at the news but the feeling was tempered by a sense of foreboding. 'Now we knew officially where we were going,' he later wrote. 'We had known unofficially before we left England; the whole world must have known.'

And with that disconcerting thought, Joe headed to his bunk where an uneasy night's sleep awaited him.

— —

Joe awoke as a thunderous barrage rocked the ship. He rushed to the deck to find the transport surrounded by warships, each spewing smoke and fire as they bombarded the Turkish coast. It was clear that the landing was finally underway but, despite the large number of troopships all around them, no men appeared to be going ashore.

The Royal Naval Division had been assigned to a flotilla that had steamed north along the Turkish coast to feign a landing at Bulair, the narrowest neck of the peninsula. After watching the warships bombarding the shore until the afternoon, Joe was given the opportunity to participate in the feint in a much more proactive way than he had hoped for. Joe had been 'volunteered' to join a group of thirty men who would row ashore to enhance the ruse that a landing was taking place in the north of the peninsula.

> We were the bait and were to attract the enemy's attention so that they would be left in no doubt that this was the spot chosen for a landing ... At nine in the evening the 'suicide'

party – as we were called – were given as much steaming hot cocoa as we could drink … A wit referred to it as 'The Last Supper'.

At 10 pm, Joe and his small group boarded boats and headed silently for the shore in the perishing cold. 'The oars cut the water as if they were handled by ghosts – not a sound, not a single light anywhere.' The men were nervous and uncertain about their role – no-one had told them if they were actually supposed to land. If they were, what use would thirty men be against a Turkish army that was primed and waiting?

As they neared the shore, Joe swung his rifle into firing position and readied himself to hit the shore. But there was no landing. Instead, the boats began doing laps just off the coast, their payload of men sitting freezing and exposed as fire from the warships lit up the shoreline and threw distorted shadows on the cliffs. 'We just pootled around the coast, trying to attract attention,' Joe later recalled of the bizarre non-landing. 'That's what puzzled me. I thought to myself "well, now we're here, we're off the coast, we're within shooting distance, we've got a hundred rounds of ammunition wrapped round our necks; why the devil did we bring our rifles if we didn't fire them?"'

Eventually, the boats swung about and began the long row back to the ship. The sun was rising as the men clambered back on board, cold, hungry and confused. It had been an unsatisfying introduction to warfare but the ruse had appeared to work. Joe later learned that hundreds of Turks had been held in the Bulair area, ready to repulse a landing that never came.

For the next few days, the men of the Hood Battalion were ferried up and down the coast of the Gallipoli peninsula. No-one seemed to know where they should be sent. They arrived off the Anzac sector as shrapnel shells burst in white puffs above the ridgelines.

There was an awful lot of men on the beach. And there was a lot of shells bursting amongst the men on the beach. On the flanks there were some fellows, I remember seeing a whole crowd of them, trying to go up this sort of a ridge, because there were ridges on both sides. And then you could see men coming back. But there seemed to be an awful lot of confusion on the beach.

The ships sailed on and they were soon off Cape Helles, at the southern toe of the peninsula. Their comrades from Britain had come ashore here on the day of the landing but, at first glance, the fighting appeared as stalled as it had been at Anzac. 'At Cape Helles, there was no beach for them to get on! There was only five or six yards of beach, with men climbing all over the cliffs.'

They stood off the cape for most of the day, as warships pounded the shore. The next morning, they were back at Anzac. 'The situation on shore looked much the same as yesterday; rifle fire and continuous shelling.' The men of the RND were seasick and anxious. They longed to get ashore and join the fighting. Frustratingly, the ships turned and sailed south again for Cape Helles.

But this time, for the men of the Hood Battalion, there would be no bobbing around impotently offshore, no straining to view the distant beachhead, no speculating about who was winning and who was losing. Joe Murray and the men of the Hood Battalion were going ashore; they were late arriving but they were eager to get into the war. They had no way of knowing what exquisite horrors awaited them.

3.

THE AUSTRALIAN

Life as a working man in Victoria's Yarra Valley was tough in the early twentieth century. The velvety green paddocks that run sedately down to the lush banks of the Yarra River were mostly given over to sheep and timber. Just about everyone was a farmer or a sawyer, and all were cut from the same rough cloth. Nineteen-year-old Harry Kelly certainly fitted the mould – he was short and stocky, and his hands and arms bore nicks and scars from years of working in the sawmill at Launching Place, named for the bend in the river where freshly cut logs were launched into the Yarra to be floated sixty kilometres downstream to Melbourne. On his enlistment papers, Harry listed his occupation as 'puller out', which basically involved handling the cut timber once it had been run through the saw, a dangerous job that required strength, timing and courage. The local paper, the *Healesville and Yarra Glen Guardian*, was replete with grisly stories of severed fingers and mangled limbs that illustrated in more detail than anyone ever asked for the cost of a lapse in concentration in an Edwardian sawmill.

After life in the mill, the potential perils of the battlefield mustn't have seemed too bad. Harry headed to the enlistment office in Carlton with his mate Bert Rowland within two weeks of the start of the war. Both were assigned to the newly raised 7th Battalion of the 2nd Brigade, a wholly Victorian unit that consisted of the 5th, 6th, 7th and 8th battalions. The 7th Battalion was commanded by the ineffable Lieutenant Colonel Harold 'Pompey' Elliott.

Two weeks later, Harry and Bert were in a training camp in Broadmeadows, surrounded by equally enthusiastic but inexperienced recruits. They became firm friends with two in particular, Harold 'Nick' Nicholls and Jack Dixon. Harry found himself the de facto corporal of a detachment of recruits – he had done a few years in the 58th Battalion of the Citizen Forces and had worn his old uniform to the camp; the only person there, apart from the instructors, who wasn't dressed in civilian clothing. Each recruit was issued with 'towels, under clothing, shaving material, tents, blankets, waterproof sheets and straw, but nothing to put the straw in'.[1]

The first week in camp was defined by hard graft, as the raw recruits were drilled and paraded in the frosty clutches of a Victorian winter, sustained by an unappetising diet of bread, jam, tea and rough-cooked army stew. The young men had ample cause for dejection but they seemed to keep their spirits up. The issuing of rifles and identity discs reminded them that this was a serious business. Harry was happy to be allocated to the same tent as Bert. Both men were used to roughing it and, all things considered, life wasn't too bad. 'Things were beginning to get squared up a bit,' Harry recalled, 'but the stew did not seem to improve.'

As the weeks progressed, the training got tougher. The expectation that the war would be short and the Australian contribution to it would be relatively small meant that standards were high. There were frequent parades in front of the doctor and the less-hardy recruits were unceremoniously dumped from the battalion. Marching and physical drill soon gave way to proper soldiering and the fledgling 7th Battalion was put through its paces in mock assaults all over the countryside. Harry was mildly derisive of this 'sham fighting' but took some pleasure in knocking off wildflowers and caterpillars at close range with the blast from the blank cartridges in his rifle. He had a few run-ins with his commanding officers (once for the seemingly innocuous offence of calling a mate a '____ fool' – Harry doesn't stipulate whether the epithet was 'bloody', 'damn' or something stronger) but for the most part he was a good soldier. The constant training was starting to wear thin, however. 'Things went on fairly smoothly in the camp but we were all beginning to get sick of the sight of Broadmeadows.' During these weeks, a common sight in the camp was sanitary and water wagons emblazoned with the words of the Shepparton manufacturer 'Furphy'. Soldiers gathering near the wagons to use the latrines or fill water bottles naturally shared gossip and rumours – it wasn't long before these snippets of misinformation became known as 'furphies'.

On 17 October, the tedium of camp life was broken when Lieutenant Colonel Elliott announced that the battalion would be embarking for active service the following day. 'The cheering was deafening,' but the short notice came as a rude shock – most men would not have the chance to farewell their families. In one of the strokes of good luck that seemed to define Harry's early military career, his father and brother had set up a fruit stall outside the camp, so he was able to say goodbye to them and a small band of friends and family before the battalion departed.

After a sleepless night, the men of the battalion gathered in the pre-dawn light, ready for whatever adventure awaited them on the battlefield.

We marched to the station carrying our sea-kit bags and rifles and while we were leaving the camp one of the bands played *Rule Britannia*, the onlookers cheering until we were right out of the campground. Trains were all in readiness to convey us to the Port Melbourne railway pier and all seemed to be smiling with the thought that we were at last getting away from the dummy warfare. Hats were waved and cheers broke forth as the train pulled out from Broadmeadows station and singing continued until we reached Port where we were ordered to remain quiet.

The battalion marched up the gangway to the troopship *Hororata*, strung their hammocks and stowed their equipment. Harry and a few mates then went up on deck to see if any well-wishers were waiting to give them a send-off on the dock. There was no-one there but 'a couple of sentries with fixed bayonets and a man with a moving-picture machine'. Harry and his comrades didn't realise it but they were part of the first Australian contingent to embark for the war, and the press was keen to capture their departure on film. Several photos of the men of the 7th Battalion boarding the ship still exist today – Harry is in there somewhere.

Harry was happy with his new surroundings and made special note in his diary of the quality of the food.

The *Hororata* was a nice clean vessel of 9591 tons on her maiden trip, but with two battalions (6th and 7th – over 2000 men), and about sixty horses on board, there was not much room for one to move about. Our next meal was also very fair, and we thought now that we had at last got away from our own cooks and their spoiled dinners.

The ship overnighted at anchor in Port Phillip Bay and the men slept well in their hammocks, wrapped snug in new blankets.

We all rose fairly early next morning to have a good look at the sight that some of us would never see again, and at about nine o'clock she pulled up her anchor and set sail down the Bay. At last we were on our way to our unknown destination.

As the ship left Melbourne behind and steamed west into the Great Australian Bight, diversions on board began to wear thin. In the cramped confines of the transport, there was little opportunity for organised training so the commanders simply gave up on it and encouraged the men to maintain their fitness in whatever way they could. There were only so many games of cards the men could play or books they could read before boredom set in, and to Harry's horror an old nemesis reappeared in the ship's mess.

Our regimental cooks were now ordered to assist the ship's cooks with the meals, much to our disgust, for no sooner were they working than we got back to our stews, worse even than they had been at Broadmeadows. Our first meal after our cooks got to work was sausages and nobody but the cooks knew whether they were boiled, fried or stewed or dished up in their raw, mouldy and green state. We did not feel much like looking at or smelling it before pushing it down our throats, [not] eating it being out of the question.

Harry kept his spirits up by doing an hour's exercise on the deck each day and enjoying a beer with his mates in the evening.

A week later, the ship arrived at King George Sound in Albany, Western Australia, where it would join the rest of the convoy that would convey the first contingent of Australian and New Zealand troops to Europe. The anticipation of being able to leave the ship and stretch the legs was short-lived; the men were informed that there would be no shore leave. In the week that the ship was anchored at Albany, Harry's only respite ashore was a brief excursion to collect water from the pier. The only event of interest seems to have been the mysterious disappearance of Sergeant Jack O'Meara in the dead of night.

Search parties were quickly organised, one of which was led by Sergeant George Greig, a longtime cadet and militia man who had been working on Melbourne's trams when war broke out. He had enlisted within a couple of weeks and joined the 7th Battalion, and was swiftly promoted due to his military experience and apparently domineering personality. When O'Meara disappeared, Greig was one of the first people called into the search party. He spent a rough afternoon in a rowboat scouring the choppy waters of the sound.

At 12pm we formed a search party and got permission to use the life boat, and 2 other sergeants and myself went out and searched the coast, but after a 3 hour search we returned to the ship without a clue. We had a very rough time in the boat.[2]

Rumours spread that O'Meara had deserted, or been murdered, or was kidnapped by German spies, but the reality was rather less melodramatic. A court of inquiry later concluded that Sergeant O'Meara had fallen overboard after a drinking session and had drowned. He was among the earliest Australian casualties of the war. O'Meara's body was never found and today he is commemorated at the Victorian Garden of Remembrance in Springvale.

Life on board the ship in the harbour was cramped and monotonous. One day the 7th Battalion was inspected by the brigadier, but Harry reported in characteristic fashion that 'he did not stop long for everybody was complaining of the food we were given to eat'. But in spite of the tribulations, there was little griping. Every day, more troopships arrived in Albany's broad harbour and the men on *Hororata* began to understand the magnitude of the operation in front of them.

By Sunday, 1 November, the convoy had been joined by the vessels carrying the New Zealand contingent and there was little space left in the harbour for more ships. 'At 6.25 on the morning of November 1st, in bright sunlight, with the harbour glassily smooth, the [escorts] *Minotaur* and *Sydney* up-anchored and moved out between the sun-bathed hills to sea.'³ The transport vessels followed in three lines and the armada steamed toward the open sea.

From Harry's perspective, a long sea voyage was the ultimate hardship. Not only was the food atrocious but, after four days at sea, the ship's supply of cigarettes ran out, forcing the soldiers to roll their tobacco in any bit of scrap paper they could lay their hands on. To top it all off, the only supply of water on board was condensed sea water, which was 'anything but pleasant'. Harry wasn't the only one struggling with the tedium of the trip.

> Nearly any day we would see a couple of men settling an argument with the gloves and there used to be some good goes. Otherwise things were pretty quiet and as we were only travelling at a very slow pace we thought we would never reach a port where we would be able to buy some smokes.

Things changed in a hurry when the troops spotted the *Sydney* steaming off at speed to do battle with the German raider *Emden*. Harry swore he could hear gunfire in the distance – unlikely given how far the convoy was from the action – but even bad food and dodgy cigarettes were forgotten when news reached the convoy of *Emden*'s demise. 'Cheer after cheer rang forth, the bands struck up some of their liveliest tunes and every countenance seemed to be beaming with delight. Australia had at last got a chance of proving her worth in the Great War.'

A few days later, the ships arrived at a picturesque port in Colombo, in modern-day Sri Lanka, where Harry 'got a close view of the *Sydney* and by her somewhat battered appearance, we could see that she had partaken of a pretty lively engagement'.

Once again there was no shore leave, but the troops were able to buy quantities of cigarettes from local traders who paddled out to the ships in ramshackle boats. The Anzacs amused themselves by tossing coins into the water for the locals to chase. They witnessed 'some very clever diving, but of course they were being pretty well paid for it … I never saw one of them fail to get a coin.'

The convoy sailed on and called briefly at Aden, Yemen, 'a very desolate place, far different from the pretty sights we had seen at Colombo'. It was about this time that Harry and his comrades received the startling news that their destination would not be Marseille and the battlefields of France but the far less appealing Egypt. Instead of *vin blanc* and *belles filles*, they would now face sand, heat and a newly antagonised Turkish army, which had recently joined the war on the side of Germany and had its heart set on capturing the Suez Canal.

On 2 December, the convoy entered the famous canal. 'Right along it on both sides were stationed many English and Indian troops.' The convoy finally reached Alexandria, its final destination, on 3 December. The troops had been trapped on board the ship for seven weeks and were desperate to get ashore, stretch their legs, find some entertainment beyond cards and books and, above all (at least to Harry), 'to buy ourselves a decent meal'.

––

Although Harry Kelly griped in his diary about the tribulations of training back in Australia, he saved his most disparaging remarks for Egypt. He hated the place from the moment he arrived and wasn't swayed in his opinion for four months. He called it the 'land of the filthy' and despised pretty much everything he encountered, from the food to the people, whom he referred to in a creative range of racist epithets. For Harry, life in the training camp at Mena was a disconsolate mix of gruelling military training, 'which none of the First Contingent, left living, will ever be likely to forget', and dissatisfying leave in the grimy streets of Cairo.

The relationship between the Anzacs and the locals was strained, to say the least, but if Harry's diary is anything to go by, the residents of Cairo were justified in their enmity. Each soldier was granted leave two or three times a week, and so every night bored and rowdy Anzacs descended on the town en masse. There had been little opportunity to spend their wages during the long sea voyage, so Harry and his mates were cashed up and looking to make the most of it. Their first destination was always a restaurant where, in addition to bargaining as low a price as they could for their food, they would 'pinch their knives, forks, spoons, salt and pepper castors, and anything that we could hide; not that we really wanted them but we felt that we were getting some of our own back'.

After dinner, the unruly troupe would head out for an amble around the city, 'which in some parts was really pretty, but in most places was frightfully dirty, and if we were not looking where we were going, we were very apt to fall over one of those dirty, evil-smelling natives asleep on the footpath'. Other diversions appear to include the temporary theft of donkeys for impromptu races through the narrow streets or stifling giggles as a local funeral procession passed by.

The funerals were very funny. The deceased is placed in a coffin which has handles by which it is carried and legs to stand it on when the carriers get tired. The common native never uses a hearse, and they march along the street singing in their language, which sounds to one who does not understand it to be the same thing over and over again. On their arrival into the cemetery they do not lower the coffin into a grave, they just turn the body out onto the ground and build the earth over it, and then there is generally a row over who is going to carry the coffin back.

Even the grandeur of the pyramids didn't prompt much praise from Harry. He and a mate paid a local guide to escort them into the tombs by candlelight, 'which was not at all pleasant but of course very interesting … I was not sorry to get out into the fresh air again.'

The rest of December was spent training and parading in Mena and marauding in Cairo. Christmas came with a special treat: the YMCA put on a Christmas feast that Harry considered 'one of the best dinners' he had ever sat down to.

On 29 December, the battalion was addressed by former prime minister and Australia's first High Commissioner in London, Sir George Reid. His words were intended to be stirring but were not well received by the men, who were forced to parade in stifling heat for two hours.

He could not say enough in our praise, but we took it like all other speeches made to us, growling because we had to stand and listen to the same old story: that we were very fine soldiers and Australia was proud of us, and that we were going to prove ourselves worthy of her praise, and all those things that we had learned by heart before leaving Australia.

Alongside Reid was the commander of the British forces in Egypt, General Sir John Maxwell, who also failed to impress the Anzac troops but would later earn notoriety by crushing the rebellion in Dublin in 1916.

The new year arrived without fanfare but with a surfeit of marching. In early February, the battalion was ordered to pack camp and was bundled onto trains for the long and hot ride to the town of Ismailia. The Turks had launched an attack on the Suez Canal, and British, Indian and New Zealand troops were heavily engaged in defending it (this was the same action that Cecil Malthus, the New Zealand private, was fighting in). The Australian 7th and 8th battalions were being sent in as reserves and the men looked forward to their first taste of action. Soon after arriving, Harry encountered a Turkish prisoner who had been captured during the assault; this was his first look at an enemy he would come to know all too well. Harry wasn't impressed. 'He looked as though he had had a pretty rough time of it and his uniform looked as though it was made out of anything that he could lay his hands on.'

The next day, Harry and half his company were ordered to board a tug that would carry them along the canal to the town of Serapeum, where they would enter the trenches and relieve the New Zealanders. Finally, it seemed, the men would see some action.

> We were stationed among some trees along the bank of the Canal but the only fighting that we had was with some very strong forces of mosquitoes who attacked us on all flanks. We did not see any of the enemy that we came here to fight, excepting a few who had been shot before our arrival here and had not yet been buried.

Harry and his platoon spent the next couple of days toiling away on trenches that would collapse as soon as they were dug into the soft sand, and complaining about the heat and mosquitoes. The anticipated clash with the enemy never came.

Before long, they were back at Ismailia and embroidering elaborate tales of combat and courage to impress their mates who had stayed back in camp. The Australians returned to Mena, where camp life in the desert quickly deteriorated to the same dreary routine as it had been before they'd left. Nerves began to fray. Arguments flared up over trivialities and often ended in fights. The patience of the Anzacs was wearing thin.

The only moment of levity came when the battalion was paraded before Lieutenant Colonel Elliott in mid-February. One man turned up without his hat and was berated by Elliott for having lost it. Elliott told him he had to get a hat; he didn't care where it came from. The following day, 'the Colonel's own hat was pinched while he was at lunch' and wasn't seen again.

Later in the month, the 3rd Brigade left Mena, leaving the rest of the Australians to speculate on where they were being sent and what it meant for their chances of going into combat. Unsurprisingly, rumours began to fly: 'They were going to France. Or to Gallipoli. Or back to the Canal. Everybody that spoke of them knew where they were going, but no two knew alike.'

By March, the regimen of route marches and rifle drill seemed never-ending, the heat and dust unrelenting. Harry celebrated his twentieth birthday 'with one of the hardest day's drill I have ever had. Leaving camp at seven o'clock we were out digging trenches until dinnertime, returned for lunch, then out again at four o'clock and remained out all night digging trenches and making night attacks, returning in time for breakfast.' A few days later, the battalion was inspected by Sir Ian Hamilton, commander of the entire Mediterranean

Expeditionary Force, and, once again, his words failed to impress, being dismissed by Harry as 'a lot more bluff'. The men of the Australian Imperial Force (AIF) were extremely fit and toughened by the hardships of their desert training but were nearing the end of their tether.

Charles Bean painted a picture in the Australian official history of a military force that was barely under control:

> Matters were swiftly coming to a point when discipline in the A.I.F. must either be upheld or abandoned. Besides the high spirit of the troops there existed a very different cause of trouble. A much graver class of crime was appearing – heavy drinking, desertion, attacks upon natives, in some instances robbery. In an extraordinary proportion of cases the serious trouble came from one class of man – the old soldier. A large number of these men were not Australians, though a set of Australian criminals and sharpers was added to them. The Australian name was suffering heavily from their drinking and slovenliness.[4]

By this stage, New Zealand officers were ordering their men to have nothing to do with the Australians, and to demonstrate by their neatness and sobriety that they were a different type of soldier from their rowdy Anzac cousins. Unsurprisingly, this did little to strengthen ties between the Australians and the Kiwis in the lead-up to the Gallipoli campaign. The low point in Australian ill discipline came when more than 300 men were arrested for being absent without leave in Cairo. Had they been British soldiers, they likely would have been shot for desertion; this was not an option for Australian authorities but they still took severe action. The men were discharged from the army and shipped back to Australia in disgrace. The situation was so bad that newspapers were asked not to report on the real reason the men had been sent home, but the incident stoked further resentment in the troops who remained in Egypt.

Something had to give and, on the night of Good Friday, it did so, spectacularly and violently. Harry Kelly wasn't directly involved but, like everyone in the AIF, he heard the full story of the night of rampage in the Haret el Wasser red-light district.

> There had been a brawl in Cairo. In a part, known as the Wassa, noted for its immorality, some of the soldiers were throwing out all sorts of furniture from some very high buildings into the street and, placing them all in a heap, set them on fire. The fire brigade arrived but their hose was cut to pieces. The English military police, known as the red caps, on account of the caps they wore trimmed with red, were discharging their revolvers very freely into the mob, but it was a long time before order had been maintained and not before several of the men had been wounded. At last things were quiet and the men returned to their different camps.

In the decades since the war, the 'Battle of the Wazza' has come to be regarded as a bit of harmless fun, Anzac troops letting off steam and causing the sort of mischief they have long been respected for. But in reality, the riot was a festival of destruction, looting and violence that should be regarded as one of the most shameful chapters in Australia's First World War story.

Casualties from the riot amounted to more than a few men wounded. Cecil Malthus, the young New Zealander, claimed that he witnessed 'a poor Arab boy run over by a car full of mad Australians and instantly killed'.

Blame for the riot was laid squarely at the feet of British military police, or on the prostitutes spreading venereal disease (an argument that conveniently ignored their customers), or

Australian commanders who hadn't provided enough leisure diversions to the bored and frustrated men.

Regardless of legitimate causes or blame-shifting excuses, one thing was certain: the reputation of the AIF had been severely tarnished and would take a long time to recover.

Once the excitement of the Wazza riot had died down, the Anzacs got back to the job of soldiering. On 3 April, the 1st Brigade marched out of Mena and Harry and his comrades in the 2nd Brigade were ordered to pack up and be ready to follow them 'at a moment's notice'. To Harry's frustration, that 'moment' was a long time coming; it wasn't until 8 pm the following evening that the battalion was finally ordered to leave camp. The 7th Battalion 'marched into Cairo, singing the whole journey', and crammed onto a train that took them to Alexandria. Now that the Anzacs were on the move, they were moved quickly – they marched from the train straight onto a troopship and, within hours of being given orders, were jammed into the hot and airless hold. Then the frustrations piled up again. The ship left the dock but, instead of heading to sea, she dropped anchor just far enough offshore to dissuade any potentially reluctant warriors from jumping overboard and swimming for it. There she remained for three days, until the anchor chains clattered, the boilers groaned and the creaking old girl, her hold bursting at the seams with enthusiastic young men, set course for Lemnos and the war.

The ship arrived in Lemnos a few days later and Harry was pleased to see the men of the 3rd Brigade waiting for them. He didn't know it at the time but the 3rd Brigade had been tasked with being the first unit ashore in the upcoming landings – its members needed every extra day of training they could get before the big day. For their part, Harry and the 2nd Brigade remained on board their ship for the next couple of weeks, growing impatient at the lack of activity. They only went ashore once, for a few hours of skirmishing and to practise a dummy landing on a friendly shore. Harry came through the training unscathed, until he had the completely alien experience of treading on 'some little thing with points sticking out of it like a porcupine' while taking a dip at the beach. It was a sea urchin, and he was still painfully plucking quills out of his foot days later, when word came that they were shipping out.

> We were not sorry, for the good food had run out and we were now living on bully beef stews. We were told that we were to land at Gallipoli but we did not mind where we were to land so long as we got some real fighting to do for we were all heartily sick of dummy warfare.

He didn't know it but Harry was going to get his wish, and more besides. Waiting for him just over the horizon, poised and ready, was the Turkish Fifth Army and more 'real fighting' than he could ever have imagined.

4.

THE WAR IN 1915

By the start of 1915, the war had been raging for five months and was a very different beast from the one everyone had expected it to be. German ambitions for a swift and victorious march on Paris had been stymied by heroic Belgian and French resistance and the timely arrival in northern France of the small but lionhearted British Expeditionary Force.

For their part, the Allies were forced to abandon their vain hopes of overwhelming the Germans and bundling them out of France and Belgium. The war of movement that defined the early weeks of the war quickly evaporated as the opposing armies sought respite from shrapnel and bullets by digging in. By the end of 1914, both sides faced an unbroken line of trenches that stretched from the Belgian coast to the Swiss Alps, and the situation dreaded by all military planners – stalemate.

On the Eastern Front, the Russians were reeling after successive blows from the Germans. Early Russian successes against the Austro-Hungarians in 1914 were quickly forgotten under the weight of a German onslaught that was bolstered by fresh troops transferred east from the stalemate on the Western Front. Despite their vastly superior numbers, it appeared in early 1915 that the Russian soldier was no match for his German adversary.

On the Western Front, the first winter on the battlefields was an ordeal that few men were prepared for or would ever forget. The transition from open warfare to fixed trenchlines in 1914 had come about so quickly that the trenches were poorly sited and constructed. As more and heavier artillery guns arrived at the front, the flimsy trenches were smashed, and men found themselves occupying a series of muddy ditches as the biting chill of winter descended on them. As fighting died down during the long and dark winter months, the priority became to solidify the trenchlines and to improve living conditions for the soldiers forced to occupy them. This meant digging, and lots of it.

Even though there were no major attacks taking place, the risk of death was constant. Men were blown apart by shells or buried by their blasts in cloying mud. And a new scourge was beginning to make its presence felt on the battlefield – the sniper. Both sides hand-picked their best marksmen and equipped them with specially modified rifles to pick off enemy soldiers too inattentive or reckless to keep their heads below the parapet. A British infantryman described the unrelenting horror of life in the trenches in the early days of 1915.

> Poured with rain all day and night. Water rose steadily till knee deep when we had the order to retire to our trenches. Dropped blanket and fur coat in the water. Slipped down as getting up on parapet, got soaked up to my waist. Went sand-bag filling and then sewer guard for two hours. Had no dug out to sleep in … In one place we had to go through about two feet of water. Were sniped at a good bit … Roache shot while getting water and Tibbs shot while going to his aid (in the mouth). He laid in open all day, was brought in

in the evening, unconscious but still alive. Passed away soon after.[1]

As the bitter winter finally began to ease in March 1915, the British went on the offensive. At the northern French town of Neuve-Chapelle, British and Indian troops launched one of the largest offensives on the Western Front to date. The Battle of Neuve-Chapelle was both an experiment in new tactics and a planned blueprint for future attacks. This was the first 'set-piece' battle the British would launch in the war – a planned offensive against fixed enemy positions.

The planners of the battle had an inkling of how the war was going to play out, and it was clear that artillery would be the key ingredient for success. At Neuve-Chapelle, 530 guns fired more shells in the 35-minute opening barrage than in the entire three years of the Boer War. The shock of this opening hurricane bombardment overwhelmed the German defenders and the four attacking divisions successfully captured the German lines. But holding them was going to be another story – the Germans counter-attacked and the British held on for several days, but were eventually forced to fall back with heavy loss. Nothing material was gained from the battle, but the 13,000 casualties taught the British some painful lessons. The most obvious was that fixed enemy positions could only be overcome if the attackers were supported by a huge quantity of artillery – quantities that only months earlier would have seemed preposterous. The Australian official history summed up the inarguable requirement for attacking troops to be protected by artillery:

In recent fighting in France the Germans had prepared the way for advances of infantry by systematically destroying with shellfire the opposing trenches, while the French as regularly protected their assaulting troops by placing in front of them a curtain of shellfire as they advanced. By March, 1915, the British also had amassed sufficient shells to pulverise the German trenches on a narrow front at Neuve-Chapelle; and, though the annihilating bombardments and elaborate 'barrages' of later years were still undeveloped, commanders were leaning more and more upon their artillery in almost all tactical difficulties. Crudely stated, the general notion was that no trenchline well furnished with machine-guns could be approached by infantry until the guns had been destroyed or silenced by artillery fire.[2]

Neuve-Chapelle also demonstrated that, for an attack to have any chance of success, the attackers needed to outnumber the defenders by a large margin. Even though the British attacked with twice the number of men as the Germans had in defence, as soon as German reinforcements arrived and evened the numbers, the attack faltered. Accurate intelligence was vital. Without knowing precisely how many Germans they were facing or where they were entrenched, the British couldn't effectively overcome them. But above all, Neuve-Chapelle showed what a brutal task it was going to be to force the Germans from their newly won ground. Any attack in this war was going to be costly and success would rely on careful planning and innovative thinking. Sadly, all these lessons would be ignored in the forthcoming Gallipoli campaign and the men in the front line paid for this lapse with hardship and blood.

Given the wholly unanticipated and alien circumstances of trench warfare, it was inevitable that Allied commanders would get creative with their plans to break the deadlock. Presented with such a formidable and seemingly insurmountable challenge, ideas that would be considered risky, or even harebrained, in more conventional circumstances received disproportionate attention from Allied military leaders in 1915. This was really the genesis of the Gallipoli idea. With armies going nowhere in the west and the Russians struggling in the east, it was understandable that the Allies would start thinking outside the box.

The key architect of the Gallipoli campaign has often been presented as Winston Churchill, in 1915 First Lord of the Admiralty, but he was hardly alone in his desire to find a creative solution to break the stalemate on the Western Front. Regardless of whose idea it was, Churchill couldn't launch a campaign on his own initiative; the decision to fight at Gallipoli was a collective one from the government and military decision-makers.

Principal among those was the decidedly odd Lord Horatio Herbert Kitchener, a cross-eyed, sexually ambiguous relic from the nineteenth-century wars in Sudan and South Africa. But he was also a national hero – his stern pointing finger on posters declaring that Kitchener 'Wants You' for his New Army prompted hundreds of thousands of young men to enlist in the first year of the war. In 1915, he was Secretary of State for War and effectively ran much of the war effort single-handedly. As a key member of the War Council, he originally protested that Churchill's plans for Gallipoli were too risky, but as Allied fortunes faltered in early 1915, the War Council approved plans for a limited offensive operation against the Turks.

Kitchener had no hesitation in appointing his number-one man, Lieutenant General Sir Ian Hamilton, to command the expedition. Historian Peter Hart makes the excellent point that 'sometimes an officer is judged only on the final act of their career'[3] – this assessment applies to Hamilton more than just about anyone. By every measure, he was an outstanding soldier, having served in the military for forty-one years by the time of the First World War. He had fought in a dozen wars and smaller campaigns, had been recommended twice for the Victoria Cross and had succeeded at all levels of command. At the start of the First World War, the Germans considered him the most experienced general in the world. But he was also indecisive and strangely deferential to his subordinates; his appointment to command the invasion of the Gallipoli peninsula was a bridge too far for him. He had served as Kitchener's chief of staff in the Boer War and, rather than forging a strong professional relationship between the two men, this experience seems to have resulted in a strange and completely unworkable relationship more akin to that between a schoolboy and a headmaster than two military commanders.

If Hamilton's relationship with Kitchener was odd, his interactions with his immediate subordinate, Major General Sir Aylmer Hunter-Weston, were downright bizarre. Hunter-Weston was commander of the British 29th Division that would play a key role in the attack at Gallipoli. Hamilton held the outdated notion that a commander planned a battle like firing a bullet from a gun – he should do everything possible to ensure the planned battle was carefully aimed in the right direction, but once the trigger was pulled, he had no control over the direction of the action. Hamilton was a good soldier and often had a better grasp of the strategic situation at Gallipoli than Hunter-Weston did. But time and frustrating time again, he left the practical decision-making to Hunter-Weston and refused to intervene as things went wrong. This attitude would contribute materially to the failure of the campaign.

From the outset, Hamilton clearly held doubts about the task he had been set. It's a well-worn anecdote but bears repeating: when he departed for Gallipoli, Hamilton made only two purchases – a Colt automatic pistol and a notebook. As an anecdote to illustrate how slapdash the enterprise was from its earliest days, this one stands unrivalled.

The pistol was clearly for offence: every soldier needs a weapon, although an operation would have to go severely wrong if the commanding officer found himself needing to use a sidearm. The notebook was for defence. Hamilton intended to document every decision, order and communiqué; he knew that if the campaign went wrong, he would be the scapegoat. He must have smelled something in the wind, for he began to prepare his defence case long before he got anywhere near the peninsula. The result is a diary that is remarkable for its defensiveness, caution and paranoia. This isn't a whimsical collection of random thoughts – it's a defence case intended to stand up in court. He had come up with the idea following a series of Royal Commissions that followed the Boer War – the 'sleuth-hounds following the criminals', as he derisively referred to them. Effectively, Hamilton's campaign diary is an exercise in arse-covering and no arse needed more covering than his after the bloody debacle he would oversee at Gallipoli.

And so, with a half-baked plan, a commander unsuited to the task, an under-strength and under-equipped force of inexperienced soldiers, a preposterous lack of information about where they were going and who they would be fighting, and a fierce resolve to ignore lessons learned in previous battles, the great Gallipoli adventure began. What could possibly go wrong?

5.
LANDING AT HELLES: THE TURKISH PERSPECTIVE

Major Mahmut Sabri peered through his binoculars at the choppy waters of the Aegean, willing the morning mist to lift so he could get a better view of the sea and anything that lurked upon it. He could just make out the cloud-shrouded lump of Imbros, an island on the horizon, but apart from that the murky waters refused to reveal their secrets. It was early on the morning of 24 April 1915 and he was anxious. The battalion he commanded, the 3rd Battalion of the Turkish 26th Regiment, had only arrived in this sector of Cape Helles the previous day and his men were scrambling to come up to speed with the unwieldy defensive positions they had inherited. And somewhere out there lurked the Allied fleet.

The Turkish defenders at Cape Helles were ludicrously overstretched. British intelligence had predicted before the landings that the Turks would need a full division to adequately guard the beaches of Helles. In reality, there was only one division, the 9th, in the entire southern half of the peninsula, an area of more than 200 square kilometres that stretched from Anzac Cove all the way to the southern toe at Cape Helles. The Turkish plan relied on defence in depth; the coast would be screened with a thin layer of forward posts, which would hold back an enemy landing as long as they could, while the bulk of the Turkish forces would be held inland to reinforce where needed. This gave the Turks the flexibility they desperately needed to defend the peninsula – there were simply not enough men to cover every landing point and the troops that were available couldn't be everywhere at once. As soon as it was clear where the Allies were landing, waves of Turkish reinforcements would rush to counter-attack.

Sabri's thousand-odd men had been tasked with forming the forward outpost of the entire southern end of the peninsula, an area that stretched to over seven kilometres of wind- and water-battered coastline, and which was broken by several long sweeps of sandy beach and dozens of sheltered coastal coves. Any of these could offer a tempting target for an Allied landing. Sabri had placed his headquarters a kilometre inland, really as close to the coast as he dared, in the hope that he would at least be able to provide his tiny coastal force with some direction should the Allied landing fall on them.

There were few settlements in the area. Right on the southern tip of the peninsula was Sedd el Bahr, a small village and fort that overlooked the shimmering waters of the Dardanelles. Six kilometres up the peninsula and a couple of kilometres inland from the coast was the village of Krithia, which had been established by the Athenians 2500 years before the First World War. It was so old, in fact, that when Claudius Ptolemy described it in 138AD, he called it an 'ancient town'. It had been ruled by everyone from the Persians to the Ottomans but had always been populated by Greeks; the name comes from the Greek word *krithos*, meaning 'barley', and it was aptly named. The inhabitants were mostly farmers who, in addition to barley, grew tomatoes, poppies and olives in the surrounding fields. By 1915, the whitewashed village was home to about 3000 people. There was a church, a school and a row of white windmills. The village was overlooked by a dumpy hill known as Achi Baba, which stood two kilometres to the northeast. The Turks didn't know it but the village of Krithia and the summit of Achi Baba would form the key British objectives on the day of the Gallipoli landing – and the costly efforts to capture or defend them would determine the outcome of the campaign.

All told, this was a lot of territory for a single battalion to guard. As if their puny numbers weren't challenge enough, Sabri had been faced with an even greater problem: he and his men knew nothing about the ground they would have to defend. For reasons that have never been fully explained, on 23 April, the commander of the Turkish 9th Division, Colonel Halil Sami, swapped the position of the 25th Regiment, which for weeks had been preparing defences along the coast, with the 26th Regiment, which had been training in the reserve area. It's possible that Sami wanted the vital coastal defences commanded by the officer he trusted most, the 26th's stoic Major Hafiz Kadri, but why he didn't simply swap regimental commanders, rather than the entire regiments, is a mystery. The result was that the 25th Regiment was suddenly snatched from the defensive positions it had spent weeks preparing and ordered to the rear, and the 26th now found itself garrisoning an imposing stretch of coastline that was completely alien to it. Even the move to the coast was an ordeal. The 26th had come under a heavy naval bombardment during its march into the lines and had lost a number of good men before it had gotten anywhere near the coast. It was forced to shelter near Krithia until nightfall screened it from the guns of the Royal Navy. It was well into the early hours of 24 April when it arrived at its new post in the shallow trenches of Cape Helles.

Even then, the work of the regiment was only just beginning. The sister regiment it had replaced might have been familiar with the lay of the land, but constructing adequate defences to safeguard it had proved too much. Instead of a strong network of trenches and redoubts, Sabri found only half-dug positions protected by thin coils of barbed wire.

The fortification of the area consisted of a series of trenches along the beach. The barricades in the west [overlooking W Beach] did not have much resistance because they were made of sand. Although two or three lines of barbed wire were being built in front of the trenches, these had not yet been completed.[1]

It was clear these pitiful defences would never be enough to hold back an Allied landing, particularly once the guns of the Royal Navy began to do their deadly work. Sabri ordered his men to bend their backs to strengthen the fortifications and passed on a stern order from his divisional commander to get the construction work done, by day and by night. 'The proximity of an enemy battleship and destroyers and their use of searchlights for illuminating will not be a reason for delays in work. When the spotlights are on you should lie down, when they're off care should be taken to work in silence.'[2]

Not only were the forward defenders dangerously exposed, they would effectively be cut off from their commanders once the shooting started. Only one telephone cable connected the battalion to its regimental headquarters, which had been hastily laid above ground, and there were no cables at all connecting it to the battalions on either side.

One of the most dangerous aspects of the late swapping of the regiments was confusion about where the unit's supporting machine guns should be deployed. Turkish orders that survive are contradictory but it seems that the previously well-sited machine guns of the 25th Regiment were withdrawn to the rear area with the regiment when it was pulled out of the front line. But for some reason, the machine guns of the 26th Regiment failed to arrive with the rest of the unit. It appears that a machine-gun section from the 27th Regiment was sent to the Helles sector but was posted inland from the beaches and was not active during the landings. Regardless of the reasons, and contrary to popular perception (from both later histories and the memories of the veterans who landed on the beaches of Cape Helles), the result was that no Turkish machine guns would be defending the beaches on the day of the landings. The Turkish infantrymen would have to rely on their rifles – and a strong dose of good luck.

As far as the Turkish commanders were concerned, their frontline troops weren't completely unsupported. The 9th Division was equipped with an artillery detachment that, although lacking in heavy guns, would be deadly against enemy troops hitting the beaches in slow, open boats. But no-one could seem to agree on where the batteries should be placed, or what they should be ordered to do. They couldn't be positioned overlooking the beaches – the naval bombardment that would accompany any landing would smash them in the opening minutes. They therefore needed to be dug in on the eastern slopes of the peninsula, where they would be shielded from Allied guns but could still pour indirect fire onto the beaches. But the division's commander made the job of the artillery virtually impossible when he decided to have an each-way bet. Remembering the hammering that the Turkish forts lining the straits had taken in the naval battle of 18 March, he ordered his artillery to prepare for two eventualities. If the Allied navy attempted to force the straits again, the guns should target the ships. If, however, the Allies tried to land on the coast, the guns should target the beaches. The contradictory instructions left the Turkish gunners with the worst of both worlds – their light artillery pieces would be relatively useless at sinking ships, but in order to cover the waters of the straits, they were forced to move their batteries well away from the beaches. The upshot was that during the landing, the Turkish artillery was unable to provide much support. 'The bitter reality was not that the batteries did not perform their duties but the organisational role in deployment and management of the artillery was neglected ... For that reason it was not possible to use the full mass of firepower effectively.'[3]

Given what the British who landed at Cape Helles were to face, the absence of enemy artillery was a blessing.*

As the sun set on 24 April, Sabri issued a final order to his men in the front line, preparing them for the assault he suspected would soon fall on them. Not only had he dispersed his troops cleverly, he also gave them clear orders that were designed to maximise the effect of his small band of defenders. In addition to instructing the men to collect water and ammunition, he also instructed them to hold their nerve. 'Faced with the enemy landings,' he said, 'there will be no rush and intense fire will be opened once the sloops approach 200–300 metres to the shore.'[4]

It had been a busy day for the Turkish defenders. Now naval gunfire, which to this point had been sporadic, began to increase – it was clear the Allies were softening up key targets. The landing was coming.

---

*   One artillery weapon that was employed to defend the beaches was the Nordenfelt 37-millimetre autocannon, an enlarged version of a Maxim machine gun that fired explosive projectiles. The Turks entrenched a small number above V and W beaches as part of their forward defences. Known as the 'pom-pom' due to its distinctive slow rate of fire, British accounts frequently describe coming under its fire during the landings.

— —

In the late hours of 24 April, Turkish observers saw destroyers and torpedo boats from the Royal Navy edging closer to shore. The ships began firing half-heartedly at W Beach. Turkish labour units, who had been beavering away laying barbed-wire entanglements on the shoreline, were ordered to withdraw. They had done all they could but time was up. The defences, as improvised as they were, would have to do.

The sporadic fire continued for a couple of hours. The Turks were unsure if it was the precursor to a landing or simply an opportunity to soften up a few choice targets. Given the surfeit of landing options open to the Allies, the Turks were cautious about being lured into a trap and suspected that the increase in fire might have been a feint to distract them from a landing elsewhere on the coast. But as the naval fire directed at the toe of the peninsula intensified, Turkish commanders began to suspect that they would soon be facing an amphibious assault. Turkish reports indicate that at about 3.20 am, a sizeable naval force was spotted off the coast – it suddenly opened a heavy barrage, guiding the fire with spotlights from the destroyers. Curiously, this bombardment is not mentioned in the British official history. Regardless, the Turks were now on full alert. Any illusions they had had about a feint were quickly dispelled. The British were coming.

· At 4.50 am, the sporadic fire swelled to a roar as more than 300 guns in the fleet let rip on the landing beaches. Sabri rushed to the top of a hill near his headquarters and was greeted by a vision of hell: ships of all sizes spewing fire, and shells crashing down on the shallow trenches above the beaches. Explosions tore the earth and great clouds of ugly black and red smoke roiled across the battered shoreline. The hastily dug trenches had always seemed insubstantial; now, under the weight of this massed fire, they seemed ludicrously inadequate. How could any man possibly survive this hellish barrage?

> The sections and formations of the battalion on the shore line seemed to have disappeared under an incredible cylinder of fire … Some trenches, which were dug to preserve life, served as graves. At the same time, the injured, those who were capable of walking, began to move towards the first aid areas.[5]

For the poor Turkish infantrymen in the front line, this was like nothing they had ever been through. They pressed themselves as deep into the dank soil of the trenches as they could, and prayed for the barrage to end. It was hell on earth, but for the most part the Turkish defenders held fast under the torrent of shells. Sabri could be forgiven for skirting with hyperbole as he later recalled their bravery:

> Despite seeing many of their friends being buried under the earth by their side, and some of them seeing heads and legs fly in the air, they did not contemplate the superior power and ammunition of the enemy. They waited patiently for the time they could use their weapons and occasionally looked out of the trenches to see whether it was time to fire them yet. Those who survived the flattening of the trenches settled in the ditches made by the missiles and built new barricades.[6]

A few minutes before 6 am, the barrage finally lifted. Turkish heads now began popping up all along the line. The sight that greeted them was extraordinary: thousands of men, tiny as ants at this distance, were scrambling down the sides of the big ships at the back of the fleet and clambering into smaller boats.

Suddenly, strings of small boats – one observer counted more than forty – began to make for shore. As instructed, the Turks held their fire but it was a severe test of nerves. An occasional artillery shell from a distant battery burst in a frothy column among the boats but, apart from that, the landing beaches remained eerily quiet.

Above V Beach (Ertugrul Koyu to the Turks), the defenders were astounded to see a strange, dark shadow looming out of the murky light and heading straight for shore. It was a ship. The *River Clyde*, an old collier, was steaming slowly, comically slowly, toward the eastern end of the beach, accompanied by four small steamboats. When about 400 metres from the shore, it suddenly let loose a covering barrage with machine guns bolted to its foredeck. Machine guns on the steamboats joined in the fusillade and, once again, the beleaguered Turkish defenders in their shallow trenches found themselves caught under a murderous fire. Many who had survived the naval bombardment were now hit by bullets and the battered trenchlines did little to shield them.

But just as it reached its crescendo, the machine-gun fire began to slacken; the *River Clyde* speared into the shallows and grounded on a rocky spit. An ungainly cluster of boats weaved and bobbed around its hull and, for the time being, the Turks were at a complete loss as to what was going on with it.

But as this drama was playing out, Turkish attention was drawn to the main sweep of beach. The small boats carrying the first wave of the landing force began to hit the shore. Turkish patience had paid off – by holding their fire until the very last moment, they now had prime targets to shoot at, and at the short range, they couldn't miss. The Turks opened up a barrage of their own with every rifle in the line. The British troops in the open rowboats were defenceless as they covered the last forty metres to the beach. Bullets smacked home against wood and flesh. Men cried out in shock and sheer frustration as a stream of lead was directed onto them. Many cried out in agony as the bullets found their mark. In the battered trenches on the clifftops, Turkish officers were disciplined and ruthless. They ordered entire platoons to fire on each boat in turn, methodically working it over until every man in it lay still. Their shooting was so coordinated that many British survivors on the receiving end mistook it for machine-gun fire.

The landing quickly turned to pandemonium. Crewless boats laden with corpses bobbed and lurched in the surf line, forcing those behind them to take evasive action as they desperately tried to get to shore. Unwounded men tumbled over the sides of the boats to escape the hail of bullets – the lucky ones smacked down on wet sand and scrambled desperately for a low bank above the beach, the only shred of cover on the otherwise desert of sand. The unlucky ones went over the side too early, were dragged underwater by the weight of their gear and met a lonely and panicky death on the seafloor. As each Turkish marksman found and picked off his target, the water turned red with blood and screams drowned out the din of rifle fire.

> There were twenty-five in my boat, and there were only three of us left. It was sad to hear our poor chums moaning, and to see others dead in the boat. It was a terrible sight to see, the poor boys dead in the water; others on the beach roaring for help but we could do nothing for them.[7]

This was sheer, bloody murder – and it wasn't supposed to be like this. Further along the coast at Anzac Cove, a combination of the element of surprise and the completely unintended but ultimately fortuitous bunching together of the landing force meant that the first Australian waves came ashore on a virtually undefended strip of sand and landed with light casualties.

But at Helles, the landing areas were obvious and well-guarded, and the British came ashore straight into the maw of the Turkish defences. Except for the absence of machine guns, the British ordeal bore more in common with the trials their comrades on the Western Front were enduring than the relatively unopposed operation of their antipodean cousins at Anzac.

As the hapless British infantrymen continued to land, and continued to die, activity around the *River Clyde* began to draw the attention of the Turks away from the main landing. The ungainly armada of small craft had sorted itself out after a fashion and now extended in a rough line from the *Clyde* to the shore. Pontoons, which had been lashed to the sides of the ship, were being frantically positioned in the water. Troops were scrambling all over the boats and pontoons attempting to lay boards that could form a makeshift bridge from ship to shore. As if the scene couldn't get more astonishing, as soon as the pontoon bridge was in place, gangways were lowered and streams of troops came rushing out of doors in the hull of the ship. In a grotesque nod to the ancient city visible on the far shore, the British had devised their own Trojan horse. The first wave of more than 2000 men, who had endured a rough and cold crossing in the spartan hold of the *Clyde*, now began to pour out of specially cut 'sally ports' in the sides of the ship.

It was bewildering. It was farcical. It never had any chance of success. The Turkish defenders had looked forward to meeting the British landings with brutal force but even they couldn't quite believe what juicy targets they were being presented with. A seemingly endless stream of men rushed out of the sally ports in single file, lumbered down the rickety gangways and began a slow, arduous and perilously exposed crossing of the bobbing pontoon bridge toward the shore.

Turkish riflemen took a calculated risk and rushed forward, abandoning the relative safety of their trenches to gain a better shooting position above the *Clyde*. They opened fire in unison, concentrating their fire on the gangways and the lurching pontoon bridge. Men fell by the dozen, and then by the hundred. The pontoon bridge in particular was a deathtrap and the handful of men who survived the charge down the gangways dived for safety in the bottom of the adjacent boats. Petty Officer David Fyfe watched the ghastly spectacle from the deck of the *River Clyde*:

> We could hear splash after splash as the gallant fellows fell dead from the gangway. A few however reached the nearest barge, raced across her open deck and crouched for shelter in the adjacent open boat. One after another the devoted fellows made the dash down the deadly gangways until a considerable number gathered in the bottoms of the open boats or were lying prostrate on the deck of the barge. Then the order was given and up they leapt and rushed for the rocks while a hail of rifle and machine-gun fire beat upon them. Wildly they leapt from boat to boat in that gallant rush while we on the ship cheered wildly at the sight, until they reached the last boat, when they leapt down into the water and started wading towards the rocks that were their goal, holding up their rifles high above their heads. But to our horror we saw them suddenly begin to flounder and fall in the water, disappearing from view and then struggling to the surface again with uniform and pack streaming, only to go down again, never to reappear as the hailing bullets flicked the life out of the struggling men … We almost wept with impotent rage.[8]

The landing from the *River Clyde* was a murderous disaster but it could have been so much worse. Had the Turks had even a single artillery battery within sight of V Beach, the

Clyde would have gone from Trojan horse to sitting duck and would surely have been wiped off the face of the earth, along with the more than a thousand men still sheltering in its cramped interior. As it was, the commanders on board called a halt to the slaughter and ordered the men who had not yet attempted the suicidal dash to remain where they were. As the day progressed, a few more half-hearted attempts would be made to get the men ashore, but they were all abruptly aborted after suffering the same fate at the hands of Turkish marksmen as the troops in the first wave. The ordeal faced by the men still crammed into the airless hold, who had watched their comrades cut down as they scrambled out of the sally ports, and who were now forced to wait in deadly limbo as bullets pinged off the steel hull, doesn't bear thinking about. The whole *River Clyde* debacle was summed up by the Turks as a 'bankrupt operation'.[9] Not only had the landing from the *Clyde* been a colossal failure, it had also enabled the Turks to respond more quickly and to better concentrate their forces; by investing in such an expensive gamble, the British had demonstrated conclusively that their main landing effort was taking place at Cape Helles.

The Royal Navy continued to pound the cliffs above V Beach and machine guns on the *Clyde* continued to chatter away, but by 9.30 am, the British attempt to land at V Beach was effectively over. The survivors who had made it across the sand huddled in terror beneath the bank above the beach and waited for death or darkness to end their ordeal, whichever came first. Of the 700 or so men who had attempted to land, probably only 200 were now ashore and unwounded. A single, bedraggled Turkish company had managed to impede a landing by an entire British brigade. At specific points, the British reverse had been astonishing: below the village of Sedd el Bahr, at a place dubbed The Camber, a British company of more than 200 men had launched a diversionary landing and been held up for hours by *nine* well-placed Turkish defenders.

Confident that he was facing the main British effort, Sabri called up his reserve company to reinforce the line and, for the first time in hours, was able to breathe a little easier. The Turks now had about 300 men guarding the beach and village. For the time being, their line was secure.

The afternoon at V Beach passed with an absurd absence of activity. Below the sandy bank, the survivors hunkered; in the brimful bowels of the *Clyde*, they sweltered. Turkish rifles cooled with the evening air. Everyone waited for nightfall.

While the British troops at V Beach had been learning the brutal lessons of the effects of bullet on flesh, less than two kilometres northwest, another stalwart British battalion was faced with a similar ordeal. W Beach (Teke Koyu to the Turks) was a wide sweep of sand about 350 metres long and dominated by sloping cliffs. As at V Beach, it was relatively lightly defended; a single Turkish company of fewer than 150 men guarded the entire beach. But they were entrenched much more strongly than at V Beach and had the terrain on their side. From their dress circle above the beach, the Turks had clear observation and even clearer fields of fire. They had coiled several barricades of barbed wire on the sand and in the water. Hidden mines with tripwires lurked beneath the waves. Had the Turks been armed with even a single machine gun, W Beach would likely have been impregnable.

Faced with the daunting task of landing here was the 1st Battalion of the Lancashire Fusiliers, one of the most distinguished regiments in the British military and one that could trace its origins back nearly 250 years to the obscure Nine Years' War of the late seventeenth century. The Turks who faced them had been stunned by the severity of the naval bombardment but, as with their comrades across the peninsula, they bounced back with impressive speed and coolness. Although British naval gunners had deluged the landing beaches with shells, they had been hampered by the flat trajectory of their fire, which was poor at smashing shore defences, and also by a lack of visibility. The Turkish trenches were hard enough to spot from the land; from the ocean, they were practically invisible. The navy also made its job even more difficult by anchoring too far out to adequately spot their targets; once their barrage began to throw up dust and smoke, their fire had to rely more on guesswork than steady aim.

The result was that, even though the Turkish defences above W Beach were pummelled, they were not destroyed. As soon as the guns fell silent and lines of rowboats could be seen making for the beach, the Turks wasted little time in shaking off their thumping headaches to reoccupy the broken ground. The barbed wire along the beach was likewise dishevelled but still intact. The bombardment had ended ten minutes before the landing troops were due to hit the shore – this gave the Turks all the time they needed to get ready. They held their nerve with aplomb, even when machine guns on the naval cutters began peppering the cliffs with lead. As the Lancs rowed into the shallows, most of their boats grounded on rocks and, at less than a fifty-metre range, the Turks saw their chance. They opened up with every rifle they had.

The Lancs had watched the bombardment with awe and delight as the cliffs were seemingly churned to dust, so they were shocked by the ferocious fusillade that greeted them as their rowboats grounded in the shallows. They were still a disconcertingly long way from the safety of the beach and their boats were going nowhere, so they did the only thing they could: they plunged into the shallow water and began wading ashore. Captain Richard Willis was in the first wave:

The timing of the ambush was perfect; we were completely exposed and helpless in our slow moving boats, just target practice for the concealed Turks, and within a few minutes only half of the thirty men in my boat were left alive. We were now 100 yards from the shore, and I gave the order 'Overboard'. We scrambled out into some four feet of water and some of the boats with their cargo of dead and wounded floated away on the currents still under fire from the snipers. With this unpromising start the advance began. Many were hit in the sea, and no response was possible, for the enemy was in trenches well above our heads.[10]

Just when it seemed things couldn't get any worse, the Lancs reached the barbed wire and were forced to lay in the surf line and try to cut through the entanglement with handheld wire-cutters. The Turkish wire, thick as a man's thumb, didn't yield willingly to the puny cutters and, for several terrifying moments, the British were trapped on the beach. Throughout it all, the Turks brought a torrent of fire down on their heads. Captain Willis later recalled the horrific scene:

We toiled through the water towards the sandy beach, but here another trap was awaiting us, for the Turks had cunningly concealed a trip wire just below the surface of the water and on the beach itself were a number of land mines, and a deep belt of rusty wire extended across the landing place. Machine-guns, hidden in caves at the end of the amphitheatre of cliffs enfiladed this [in reality, the Turks had no machine guns at W Beach and were defending only with rifles, but to the beleaguered men of the Lancashire Fusiliers, who were on the receiving end of their concentrated fire, the distinction made little difference]. Our wretched men were ordered to wait behind this wire for the wire-cutters to cut a pathway through. They were shot in helpless batches while they waited, and could not even use their rifles in retaliation since the sand and the sea had clogged their action. One Turkish sniper in particular took a heavy toll at very close range until I forced open the bolt of a rifle with the heel of my boot and closed his career with the first shot, but the heap of empty cartridges round him testified to the damage he had done.[11]

Through sheer determination, the Lancs began to cut and blunder through the barbed wire, the rusty barbs tearing uniform and flesh. The men began to pour through the gaps and took shelter in the lee of the cliff. Having gained a measure of respite from the deadly fire, they probed left and right, and began to scale the sloping cliffs on each flank, using rocks and scrub for cover. As they reached the top, the Turks realised they were outflanked and began to pull back. By 8 am, W Beach was tentatively secured.

But the cost had been atrocious. Of the nearly 1000 Lancashire Fusiliers who had hit the beach, 426 had been killed or wounded. Major General Hunter-Weston recognised just what a tough nut W Beach had been to crack, and reportedly declared that 'every man should have a VC if they had their rights'.[12] In an unusual arrangement, he nearly got his wish – six Victoria Crosses were awarded for the action and the survivors were asked to nominate the men they felt deserved them most. In an awkward way, the 'six VCs before breakfast' were to be seen as having been bestowed on the entire battalion. In another nod to the bravery of the unit, Hamilton rechristened W Beach as 'Lancashire Landing', the name it held for the rest of the campaign.

North of W Beach, the coastline extends in an unruly tangle for more than six kilometres to the plains of Krithia. For most of this distance, the shoreline is downright hostile to military manoeuvres, with scrub-choked slopes plunging directly into the sea. There was nowhere along this stretch of fierce coast for the British to land so the Turks had thinly garrisoned it with observation posts, with virtually no combat infantry in the whole area. Even if they had wanted to guard it more heavily, they simply couldn't have – they had run out of men. 'For a regiment assigned with the duty of responding to all of the surrounding enemy landings,' the history of the Turkish General Staff drily notes, 'it was impossible to spread out any further.'[13]

Sabri was, therefore, astounded to learn that British troops were coming ashore at not one place here but two. In probably the only inspired part of Hamilton's plan, the British had launched two aggressive, and completely unexpected, flanking manoeuvres. At X Beach, a kilometre and a half north of W Beach, at a spot known to the Turks as Ikiz Bay, a single Turkish squad of nine men found itself facing a landing by more than 600 British troops on a rugged strip of sand only seven metres wide. The job of the defenders became even more difficult when the battleship *Implacable* parked itself only 450 metres offshore and tore the living hell out of the cliffs with a hurricane of point-blank 12-inch gunfire. The battered Turkish squad couldn't be expected to do anything more than fire a few scattered shots before scarpering but, unbelievably, it held its ground and peppered the British landing force with fire. It was never going to hold up the landing (and the Turks didn't actually succeed in hitting anyone) but the unexpected opposition created delays and doubts in the minds of the British, who convinced themselves that they were facing a much larger force than they actually were. They came ashore without a single casualty but with an abundance of caution, and tentatively edged forward as the Turkish defenders pulled back.

The delaying tactics had been crucial and created in British minds 'an alarm at the unknown … putting the enemy in doubt as to whether or not the terrain on which they had landed was deserted'.[14] As the British inched slowly forward, Turkish opposition grew noticeably stiffer. Sabri had thrown every man in the area into the fight, but the British advance seemed unstoppable. Just as all seemed lost, the figurative cavalry arrived. In a rare display of initiative, a Turkish lieutenant threw his reserve company into the fight above X Beach without orders, bolstering the Turkish line and preventing a British breakout. Sabri rushed to the sector to see what was going on and got a bullet in the thigh for his troubles. He ordered the men still remaining to fight to the death.

The British force, despite outnumbering the Turks by more than sixty to one when it had landed, now dug in after an advance of less than 800 metres. It eventually linked up with the troops who had advanced from W Beach. The British now had a coherent line but it was going nowhere.

If the surprise flanking attack at X Beach had signalled trouble for the Turks, the second surprise landing nearly spelled disaster. A couple of kilometres north of X Beach is a rubbly strip of sand backed by a sheer, scrub-covered slope. It is barely worthy of the name and yet was dubbed Y Beach by the British. From the Turkish perspective, there was no possible hope that the enemy would stage a landing here – the 'beach' was entirely isolated and so tiny as to barely exist. Even today, it is exceedingly difficult to locate, from both sea and land. The spot meant so little to the Turks that they didn't even bother giving it a name and left it completely undefended. A couple of isolated platoons were scattered around the general area but the nearest Turkish rifleman was at least a kilometre away from Y Beach.

Y Beach might have been a tough spot for the British to land, but the one thing it did have in its favour was proximity. Once the treacherous slope had been scaled, the objective of Krithia lay across open plains only two kilometres away. At Y Beach, Hamilton was going to play his trump card.

It's difficult to give an account of the landings at Y Beach from a Turkish perspective, simply because there were no Turks around to give any perspective on it. At 5.30 am, the Royal Navy bombarded the undefended cliffs and more than 2000 British troops came ashore completely unmolested. Within the hour, they had scaled the slope and were looking out on open ground to Krithia in the near distance and the imposing hump of Achi Baba hill, the British objective, beyond. There was not a soul to be seen. This was more like a countryside picnic than a war – scouts were sent out who gamely wandered about the landscape seeking someone to shoot at. They made it as far as Krithia – actually entered the village – without suffering as much as a stubbed toe. They returned to their lines above Y Beach to report that the entire area was completely deserted. The Turks, for their part, were so stretched by the ferocious fighting unfolding on the other landing beaches that they didn't even know the British had landed at Y Beach. Krithia lay completely open, and with it the chance to sweep up the peninsula in one fell swoop.

But the British at Y Beach were paralysed by indecision. Although Hamilton had been enamoured with his *coup de main* at Y Beach, Hunter-Weston was not having a bar of it. When several messages from the Y Beach force desperately seeking instructions landed on his desk, he swept them aside without responding. The situation might have been saved by assertive leadership on the ground, but this was also sadly lacking. Worse still, the instructions issued to the Y Beach force had been inexcusably vague and its commanders squabbled over whether they were supposed to advance immediately on Krithia or try to link up with their comrades further south. In the end, they did neither and simply dug in at the top of the slope immediately above the beach. They had advanced less than 200 metres.

It was not until 4 pm, more than nine hours after the force had landed, that the Turks suddenly noticed that the best part of an enemy brigade was camped out adjacent to the most important objectives at Helles. They couldn't quite believe their luck – they should have been completely outflanked and fighting for survival by now. The Turkish official history referred to the British failure to seize the initiative as 'a great chance lost'.[15] But, unlike the British, once the Turks saw an opportunity, they pounced on it.

Although ludicrously outnumbered by the large British force frantically digging in above Y Beach, Turkish reinforcements were both courageous and clever in their movements against their enemy. The Turkish attacks were coordinated and vicious in the fading evening light. Wave after wave of troops launched themselves out of the shadows, getting to within metres of the terrified British defenders before falling back. Not all these encounters went according to plan, as recounted in a British diary:

> Several times the enemy approached within ten yards of our position … so close did the enemy reach to our lines that in one place a German officer walked up to our trench and said, 'You English surrender, we are ten to one.' He was thereupon hit on the head with a spade.[16]

When an attack failed to break through on the left, the Turks would attack on the right. And then in the centre. The Brits didn't know where the next attack would come from or how long it would last. And in spite of relying on machine guns and the ominous fire of the warships for defence, British casualties began to pile up. In the whirlwind of indecision that had gripped them since they had come ashore, the Brits had paid scant attention to adequately digging in. They now found themselves desperately trying to hold a line that consisted of little more than half-dug scrapes, less than fifty centimetres deep. This was no place to hold back a determined enemy – and the Turks were using every dip and roll in the landscape to deadly advantage. Snipers picked off British officers, support troops kept up a murderous fire with bullet and bomb, and assault troops threw themselves against the line incessantly.

The first Turkish attack was launched at 4 pm. And then another two hours later. Turkish reinforcements continued to arrive and, by 7.15 pm, they received a reprieve as the guns of the Royal Navy fell silent for the night. At 9 pm, the Turks went in again, this time supported by machine guns. Each time, the British line held but holes were beginning to appear, and British nerves were fraying. The situation was compounded by a ludicrous mix-up with the allocation of British weapons. Most of the troops were armed with the modern Lee–Enfield rifle but some units carried the older variant, which used a different type of ammunition. On more than one occasion, the British defenders found one part of the line shooting furiously while another was ominously silent as its men desperately scrounged for ammunition.

It wasn't just the men on the front line who were cracking under the strain. Just after midnight, the Y Beach commander, Lieutenant Colonel Godfrey Matthews, reported that his situation was 'serious'. British commanders asked for an appraisal from the navy and received a reply that the situation appeared hopeless. A frantic gaggle of men, growing larger by the hour, could be seen tumbling down the cliff and back to the beach. Officers on the shore were signalling to the navy to send in cutters to remove the men – whether this was a reasonable request to remove just the wounded or a panicky call to evacuate the whole force is unclear. During the night, Matthews twice cabled Hunter-Weston, pleading for reinforcements. Both cables were ignored.

Somehow, daylight saw the desperate and delirious British troops still holding their shallow line. They had lost more than 600 men to the ferocious Turkish attacks and those left were barely holding on. But it was a false dawn. Any hope of the British regaining their composure and holding their line quickly evaporated as the first broadsides from the navy began to pound the Turkish positions. A salvo from one of the warships fell short and exploded among the British defenders. This was more than the men could stand and fear gave way to genuine panic. The trickle of men heading back to the beach grew to a stream. A young officer on the right flank, isolated and desperate, sent a message to the navy pleading for his exhausted force to be evacuated, and the navy dutifully despatched a small fleet of cutters to the rescue. The sight of men re-embarking was too much for the stretched and shellshocked main force, and word quickly spread that an evacuation had been ordered. Before it could be stopped, a disorderly and completely spontaneous withdrawal began, as unwounded stragglers climbed into boats alongside the wounded.

While Matthews and his men continued to resist on the clifftop, below them on the beach the situation was unravelling. At 7.25 am, a panicked officer on the beach sent a signal to the ships pleading for them to 'send all boats at once. We are outnumbered. Hurry.' Minutes later, someone else signalled, 'we are driven on to the beach. I will give you the order when we are clear of the crest,' and ten minutes later another signal read, 'send boats to Y Beach. Position desperate.'[17]

On the clifftop, yet another Turkish assault had been beaten back and Matthews took the opportunity to walk around his line. To his horror, the trenches on his right flank were completely deserted. Realising that his position was now hopeless, he signalled Hunter-Weston that he could not hold on without reinforcements and began to pull back his remaining men to the top of the slope above the beach. Looking down and seeing that half of his force was already in boats and on its way back to the ships, he accepted that the writing was on the wall and ordered the remaining men to join their comrades and evacuate the beach. By 11.30 am, without impediment from the exhausted Turkish troops, the last British troops climbed into boats and the high hopes and golden opportunities of the brief Y Beach adventure drifted away on the wind.

Throughout the final hours of panic and drama, the Turks had been effectively silent, too exhausted by the night's bitter combat to attack again, and too reluctant to face another inevitable pounding from the ships' guns. They had effectively given up at Y Beach and couldn't believe their luck that the British had withdrawn; they wasted little time in redeploying their forces into the maelstrom raging around the beaches further south. The Turks abandoned the battlefield so completely that a group of British sailors who went ashore late in the afternoon to look for wounded spent an hour exploring the former British lines without being fired on.

The British troops who had landed at Y Beach had spent twenty-nine hours ashore, a decent amount of that time without being opposed by the Turks. By the time the last British boot stepped onto the deck of a navy ship, a third of the 2000 men who had gone ashore had been killed or wounded. Despite the village of Krithia lying invitingly undefended in front of them, despite initially not being opposed by a single Turkish soldier, and despite outnumbering those who were in the immediate area by more than twenty to one, the Y Beach force only managed to advance a couple of hundred metres before fleeing with their tails between their legs. It was a dispiriting and undignified saga. Throughout the entire ordeal, Matthews had not received a single reply from Hunter-Weston to his increasingly desperate messages. As poorly as it had performed, the Y Beach landing force had been effectively abandoned from the moment it hit the shore.

And it wasn't just his subordinate officers that Hunter-Weston had ignored. Hamilton had watched the successful landing at Y Beach from the deck of his flagship with glee – this was his masterstroke (he called it his 'special child'[18]) and it had started better than he could possibly have imagined. But once again, his deferential and decidedly unmilitary relationship with Hunter-Weston reared its head. Noting that the unopposed force at Y Beach was a glittering opportunity, Hamilton had cabled Hunter-Weston to politely enquire if it would be too much trouble to perhaps get a few reinforcements ashore at Y Beach to exploit the gains. After forty-five minutes of heavily pregnant silence from Hunter-Weston, he messaged again and received a vague reply that landing troops at Y Beach would interfere with naval arrangements. Bizarrely, Hamilton left it at that. The next morning, he had a front-row view of the panicked retreat from Y Beach, and was shocked by the sight. He had no clue if the disorderly evacuation he was witnessing had been ordered by Hunter-Weston but was too polite to find out, and too preoccupied with good manners to interfere. 'My inclination was to take a hand myself in this affair,' he wrote in his diary, 'but the Staff are clear against interference when I have no knowledge of the facts – and I suppose they are right. To see a part of my scheme, from which I had hoped so much, go wrong before my eyes is maddening!'[19] Maddening indeed, but perhaps if Hamilton had been more of a general and less of a gentleman, the campaign might have gone very differently.

From the Turkish perspective, the first day of the campaign was a mad scramble to allocate insufficient resources to the places they were most needed. As one crisis was dealt with, another sprang up, and the tireless Turkish infantryman found himself caught up in a bloody whirlwind of savage, close-quarter fighting and desperate route marches. But, despite the odds against them, it was working. Astute Turkish leadership recognised and extinguished every bushfire as it ignited and had a knack for having the right men in the right place at the right time. With their paucity of troops, the Turks could never expect to hold the British on the beaches, much less drive them into the sea, but they were making the expected easy jaunt across the Helles plains a vicious ordeal for their enemies, with every inch of ground won with blood and pain. And most importantly, the stoic Turkish defence was soaking up the one resource the British could not replenish – time. As each hour ticked by with distant British objectives remaining disconcertingly out of reach, more Turkish troops streamed into the line. The British were faced with a compounding conundrum – the more time it took to gain a piece of ground, the larger the job would be to capture the next one.

By the time the sun set on the first day of the Gallipoli campaign, Allied and Turkish troops were scattered across the peninsula like pieces on a draughts board. Neither side had anything like an established front line; instead, a thousand tiny battles commanded by captains and sergeants had been fought throughout the day, and both sides were physically and emotionally shattered.

But in reality, this was what the Allies should have expected. If Hamilton's plans seem over-complicated, they were. Not only had he completely squandered the element of surprise, as a final gift to the Turkish defenders he had also settled on a landing plan that relied on wishful thinking more than military sense. The Allies gave away their initial advantage in numbers by landing piecemeal complements of troops at isolated points all over the peninsula. The British landed on five beaches at Cape Helles, the French landed a diversionary force at Kum Kale on the Asian shore, the Anzacs landed at Anzac Cove and another diversionary feint was made at Bulair. Not only did this whittle away the Allies' numerical superiority, it also dangerously dispersed their forces. The landing beaches were too far away from each other to be mutually supporting – each landing party found itself engaged in its own desperate, and completely isolated, battle. Had the Allies concentrated their forces at either Helles or Anzac, they would have swept the Turkish defenders away in the opening hours. As it was, they held little more than a beachhead at every place they had come ashore. The entire peninsula still lay in front of them and with it, every Turkish battalion in the area. In a single day, the Gallipoli invasion had turned from a surgical strike to a heavyweight brawl. If the Allies didn't regroup quickly, they would be out on their feet.

6.

LANDING AT ANZAC: THE TURKISH PERSPECTIVE

Deputy Officer Muharrem was paralysed by indecision. As commander of the forward Turkish platoon on Hain Tepe hill (which would come to be known as Plugge's Plateau to the Anzacs), he was the forward man, in the forward-most trench at the very tip of the Turkish spear defending the Gallipoli peninsula. As he peered out on the inky sea from his grandstand position above a small cove (known to the Turks as Ari Burnu but soon to be rechristened Anzac Cove), he was shocked to see an armada of ships not far offshore. He didn't know it but more than an hour earlier, this armada had been spotted by sentries from the higher ridges behind him – but his senior officers could not agree on exactly what they were looking at and whether it represented a threat. One of these officers, Captain Faik, summed up the initial confusion:

> I went to a new observation point and kept watching. This time I saw them as a great mass which, I decided, seemed to be moving straight towards us.

Faik immediately telephoned divisional headquarters and spoke to the second-in-command, who asked how many of the ships were warships and how many were transports.

> I replied, 'It is impossible to distinguish them in the dark but the quantity of ships is very large.' With that the conversation closed. A little while later the moon sank below the horizon and the ships became invisible in the dark. The reserve platoon was alerted and ordered to stand by. I watched and waited.[1]

For the previous two weeks, Allied vessels had steamed innocuously up and down this stretch of coast. Turkish commanders eventually decided that tonight was no different and that there was no imminent danger from the Allied fleet. They were so confident in this assessment that they made the grave error of not informing the men in the front line that an enemy force was potentially massing in front of them, so when Muharrem spotted a flotilla of small craft detaching from the ships and heading straight toward him, he didn't know what to do about it.

Like his comrades twenty kilometres away at Cape Helles, Muharrem was guarding a long stretch of coast with a paper-thin force. On stretches of shoreline where there should have been hundreds of men, the Turks had to make do with dozens. The best Muharrem could do was to allocate soldiers in groups of two or three to forward observation posts, with more solid trenchlines in key positions that could be manned at the first sign of an attack. As the Anzac covering force approached the beach, the observation posts fell back as instructed. But here the plan fell apart. Instead of ordering his platoon to rush forward and occupy the main trenchline on Ari Burnu knoll, a manoeuvre they had practised dozens of times before,

Muharrem froze, ordering his men to remain where they were in the support trenches on Plugge's Plateau. The result was that the first Australians nearing the shore were not greeted with a torrent of fire from well-positioned and entrenched defenders on the cliffs above them (as is so often described in accounts of the Anzac landing), but instead received only a sprinkling of fire from Turkish sentries who were too far away to do them much damage. A handful of unlucky Anzacs was hit in the boats but, within minutes of reaching the shore, the vast bulk of the first wave had landed unhindered, and was racing for the safety of a scrubby cliff that backed the beach. Not only were the Turkish defenders too far away to adequately defend the cove, but by not occupying the forward ground, they had also gifted the Anzacs a superb piece of cover as they came ashore – the dark hump of Ari Burnu knoll effectively obscured most of the narrow beach from Turkish eyes and rifles on Plugge's Plateau.

The Turkish defenders were now in a precarious position. They knew that hundreds, potentially thousands, of enemy soldiers were streaming out of boats on the narrow strip of sand below them, but they had no way of stopping them, or even of reporting their presence to other troops behind them. A small group of Turks from the northern end of the cove belatedly occupied the forward trenches on Ari Burnu but, to their horror, found themselves completely isolated and coming under fierce fire from the beach below. A few dashed for safety up a communication trench that led to Plugge's Plateau, but the braver souls stayed put, and died where they stood as the Anzacs swept over them. Other Turkish outposts further along the cove fired a few desperate shots as the boats hit the beach, and then ran for their lives up Shrapnel Valley. Few of them survived the dash.

From his grandstand position on Plugge's Plateau, Muharrem was witnessing a scene from his nightmares. All along the shoreline, khaki-clad figures scrambled up from the beach, scaling cliffs and charging into gullies. He watched a few isolated Turkish posts trying to hold out but all were quickly engulfed by the khaki wave. A few Australians fired shots as they went, but most of the killing was done with the bayonet. The occasional muffled scream could be heard in the chill air – these, too, were quickly snuffed out. The men of his platoon could do little to hold back the invaders. They were hit one by one and the survivors pulled back across the plateau. Muharrem was yelling orders, trying to keep a semblance of order in his panicked force, when he went down hard, shot through the shoulder. Two men dragged him to safety minutes before the Anzacs swarmed over the plateau.

By now, more than half the men in the Turkish platoon on Plugge's Plateau had been killed or wounded. Those who were still alive had seen enough and made a desperate dash across a narrow strip of land known as the Razor Edge to temporary safety with their comrades on higher ground. Bullets screeched past them as they retreated, and several found their mark with a sickening thud. The Australians were hot on their heels.

> Four or five men who were reaching the summit at that moment made for the Turks, who ran across the small plateau. One was nearly caught, when an Australian stepped from behind a bush and bayoneted him in the shoulder; the other was shot on the farther edge of the summit, where he rolled down a washaway in the steep side and hung, dead, in a crevice of the gravel.[2]

As the Turkish defenders pulled back to higher ground on Second Ridge, they were reinforced by other platoons, but these early hours of the first day of the campaign were defined by indecision and mistakes from the Turkish junior commanders.

The First Contingent: Men of the 7th Battalion march down the Port Melbourne pier to embark on HMAT *Hororata* (left), before sailing for Egypt, 19 October 1914. Private Harry Kelly is somewhere in this group.

The Architect of Disaster: General Sir Ian Hamilton (front left) departs after inspecting a unit of the Royal Naval Division at Gallipoli. His overly complicated plans and peculiar relationships with both his superiors and subordinates would spell disaster for the men under his command at Krithia.

The New Zealand Colonel: Lieutenant Colonel William Malone skilfully commanded the Wellington Battalion at Gallipoli. He had little time for inefficiency or Australians, and his acerbic diary entries make frequent mention of both.

AWM G01374

The Forgotten Ally: More than 80,000 French soldiers served at Gallipoli and 15,000 of them died there, more than all the Australian and New Zealand dead combined. This French artillery piece is well supplied with ammunition, in stark contrast to British guns.

AWM G00957

The Anzacs Land at Helles: Australian troops disembark on a flimsy pier beside the *River Clyde* at V Beach on the morning of 6 May 1915. The *Clyde* was used as a 'Trojan horse' during the landings of 25 April, a bloody debacle that cost hundreds of British lives.

The New Camp: Anzac troops dig in behind muddy earth walls at Cape Helles, 6 May 1915. The men are under Turkish observation and fire from the high ground on the horizon. The village of Krithia and the front line are in the middle distance.

The Father of the Anzac Legend: Charles Bean, official war correspondent and later founder of the Australian War Memorial, in the front lines on the Krithia battlefield. At great personal risk, Bean reported on the disaster at Krithia as it unfolded.

The Frontline HQ: Major Gordon Bennett (left) in his advanced headquarters on the Krithia battlefield. During the advance Bennett led with skill and bravery, and was one of the few Australian officers to come out of the battle unscathed.

The Killing Field: The open ground crossed by the Australians during their bloody advance at Krithia, photographed by Charles Bean when he returned to Gallipoli in 1919. The rough hump of Achi Baba hill, the Allied objective, can be seen on the right.

The New Front Line: Australians occupying their new front line the morning after the battle. Fir Tree Spur, where the New Zealanders advanced, is in the background.

The Dead: The battlefield as seen from the new Australian front line, looking back to the starting point of the advance. Most of the Australian bodies would remain on the battlefield until after the war.

The Survivors: The only unwounded men left from D Company, 7th Battalion, after the Battle of Krithia. More than 200 men landed with the company on April 25. Now, two weeks later, they were down to twenty-seven.

The Father and Son: The Buckingham family, Victoria, c1905. Private Bill Buckingham (second row, left) would die at Krithia on 8 May 1915. The boy in the front row is his son Jack, who would enlist in 1916 as an eighteen-year-old. He was killed at Ypres a year later.

They had been expecting an Allied landing for weeks. Now here it was, and they seemed unable to respond to it.

As the Anzacs swept forward, the small number of Turkish defenders was gradually pushed back from their exposed forward positions. There were simply too many Anzacs and not enough Turks. And while the Australians were close to the coast, they were well covered by fire from the guns of the Royal Navy. One Turkish platoon leader was desperately trying to organise a new defensive line when a shell burst nearby, blowing his foot off. If things kept going like this, the Turkish retreat was in danger of turning into a rout.

On Keltepe (the future Bolton's Ridge) in the southern sector of the Anzac landing, there was another Turkish platoon, and this one responded to the landing more quickly and with stricter adherence to orders than its comrades further north. Private Adil Sahin was asleep in the reserve position when he was roughly roused by a sentry.

> He shook us and pointed down the slope to the water below. He said he thought he could see shapes out there on the water. We looked out and strained to see in the half-light and then we heard noises and saw shapes of boats with soldiers coming ashore. We were ordered to start firing. Some fell on the beach and I wasn't sure whether we'd hit them or they were taking shelter. They made for the base of the rise and then began climbing. We were outnumbered, so we began to withdraw. It was very confusing. We didn't know anything about this invasion. I was very frightened.[3]

As the Anzac boats closed in on the shore and the Turks on Plugge's Plateau opened fire, platoon leader Ismail Hakki pulled his forward observation posts back and ordered his platoon in the main defensive trench on Bolton's Ridge to fire on the landing troops. He sent runners back to his headquarters with an urgent request for reinforcements and ammunition. They returned without either, but with orders for the platoon to hold out at Bolton's at all costs.

As more Australians landed, Hakki's position came under heavy fire – it was clear that Plugge's had been lost and the Turks on Bolton's were in danger of being cut off. Hakki ordered a fighting retreat and, demonstrating his impressive leadership skills, he led an orderly extraction of his platoon until it had pulled back to Second Ridge without losing a man. On arrival, they were ordered to dig in and wait for reinforcements.

The only other platoon in the area when the Australians first hit the shore was dug in near a small building called Fisherman's Hut, which overlooked North Beach to the north of Anzac Cove. The men in this position started shooting as soon as they saw boats in the water, but they were kidding themselves thinking they could hit anything at such long range. Their platoon commander sensibly ordered them to hold fire and save their ammunition – they would receive much better targets in time. Anzac Cove is not visible from Fisherman's Hut, and so the Turks in this position could only watch helplessly as the Australians landed virtually unopposed, surged inland and swarmed over Plugge's Plateau.

It wasn't long before the defenders at Fisherman's Hut had something to shoot at, however. One group of Australian boats had been tasked with securing the northern flank of the landing and began veering directly toward Fisherman's Hut. The Turkish defenders held their nerve, took a deep breath and then unleashed hell onto the open boats landing on the sand beneath them. This was the only place on the landing beaches where the Australians came under heavy defensive fire, and their casualties were horrific. A Turkish defender described the scene.

We faced them with our few weapons and our faith, and thanks to the devastating fire we rained down upon them, within an hour's time we had felled and destroyed so many invading soldiers that the shores were covered with their bodies.[4]

Exposed in the open boats and under such heavy fire, there was little the Australians could do but curse and pray.

Bullet after bullet went home amongst the men in the crowded boats … In another boat six were hit before reaching the shore, and two more as they clambered from the boat … Here a man scrambled out over the stern of a boat, found the water too deep for him, tried to hang on to the boat, and presently dropped off … Colonel Hawley, second-in-command of the 12th, was getting into the water, when he was hit by a bullet in the spine. In the 3rd Field Ambulance three men had been killed and thirteen wounded before they could reach the bank.[5]

The survivors hit the shingle, leaving their boats full of dead and dying, and raced for the safety of a low bank above the beach. A group of Australians attempted to outflank the Turkish trenches and received a small barrage of hand grenades in reply – probably the first time the weapon was used in the Gallipoli campaign. The Turkish defenders soon realised that they were in danger of being overwhelmed by the masses of Australian troops who had already landed, and so they embarked on a hair-raising withdrawal back to Third Ridge, dodging marauding Australians and trying to stay low in the gullies so they didn't get shot to pieces. They pulled back up Rhododendron Ridge to Chunuk Bair, two sites that would later become infamous as the scenes of New Zealand bravery and sacrifice during the August Offensive. They dug in alongside the scattered remnants of other Turkish platoons and did their best to pick off the Australians as they pushed forward. These encounters were often brief and bloody.

> I went 40 to 50 paces in front of our skirmish line. When I got above the ridge line I could see the Australians advancing among the bushes. A line was also advancing behind them. Without letting the enemy see, I selected a position and had our men moved into it. Suddenly from 200 metres we opened heavy fire. The Australians were shaken by the casualties they suffered. Some heroes appeared amongst them – disregarding death they worked to improve their situation.[6]

Given how much has been written about the Gallipoli landing from the Anzac perspective, and how effectively the attacking troops would eventually be stalled on Second Ridge by Turkish reinforcements, it's extraordinary that the Turkish defence in the opening hours of the campaign was so piecemeal. While the Anzacs were moving battalions around the battlefield, the Turks were moving platoons. The entire Australian covering force, comprising most of the 3rd Brigade – about 4000 men – faced only a single, under-strength Turkish company (about 160 men) during the landing at Anzac Cove. And for the first couple of hours, the entire Turkish reserve consisted of only one other company, about 200-men strong. The Turkish commander was so reluctant to see his reserve wiped out that he initially only committed a single platoon to reinforce the Turkish line. Its lieutenant managed to hoover up a few stragglers as he advanced, but by the time he dug in overlooking Lone Pine, he had fewer than 90 men under his command.

As the bedraggled mob of Turkish survivors dug in on the high ground, they had a startling view of thousands of

Australians advancing relentlessly up the slopes toward them – it seemed as if nothing could stop them. But just when all seemed lost, salvation arrived. The first regiment of a mass of Turkish reinforcements, which had been marching for hours, had reached the battlefield.

— —

At first, Turkish senior commanders didn't know what to make of the flurry of sketchy and slightly panicky messages that came across their desks in the early hours of 25 April 1915. If they were to be believed, there were enemy soldiers landing all over the place – on half a dozen beaches at Cape Helles, at Kum Kale on the Asian side of the Dardanelles, and now at a rocky and precarious cove halfway up the western shore of the peninsula. Of all the messages, the latter was the hardest to believe – the cove was so insignificant it didn't even have a Turkish name. The stream of breathless runners who appeared at headquarters carried hurriedly scribbled reports of a landing 'north of Gaba Tepe' or 'south of Fisherman's Hut'. But this surely couldn't be the case. The ground there was the worst on the peninsula, with high ridgelines cascading toward the sea in a never-ending tangle of gullies and ravines. It was ground tailor-made for defence. The terrain itself was the main obstacle on this stretch of coastline – so much so that the Turks had barely bothered placing any troops there. If the Allies really had landed here, they had a hell of a task on their hands.

General Otto Liman von Sanders, the German commander of the Turkish Fifth Army, wasn't buying it. The obvious place for an Allied landing was at Bulair, where the peninsula narrowed to a lean neck between the Gulf of Saros and the Sea of Marmara. Indeed, there had been scattered reports of enemy activity in this region and von Sanders, fixated on the idea of a landing at Bulair, didn't need more convincing. To the shock of his staff officers, he rushed out of his headquarters, climbed on a horse and galloped off toward Bulair, presumably to witness this 'landing' first-hand. This created a crisis in the Turkish high command. Not only had von Sanders disappeared, effectively without leaving orders, he was now also largely unreachable and therefore unaware of the increasingly urgent reports streaming in from across the peninsula, begging for reinforcements. Von Sanders was so obsessed with Bulair that he stayed there for another two days, obstinately waiting for a landing that never came, while his subordinates begged him to release reserve troops for the very real landings at Helles and Anzac.

Fortunately, von Sanders' subordinate commanders were not quite so spellbound by ephemeral landings. His divisional and regimental commanders were quick to assess the threats unfolding across their battlefronts, particularly at Anzac, where the pathetically outmatched band of defenders was in grave danger of being overwhelmed. One of the most astute Turkish officers was Lieutenant Colonel Mahmed Sefik, a talented but prickly commander who had recently been appointed to command the 27th Regiment during an eleventh-hour reshuffling of Turkish troops. Sefik was as obsessed with the possibility of a landing at Anzac Cove as von Sanders was of one at Bulair, but Sefik's judgement proved far superior to his commander's. Prior to the landing, Sefik had wanted to place all three battalions of his regiment in the area around Anzac Cove but was overruled, ordered to defend the coast with a single battalion thinly spread over a twelve-kilometre stretch of coastline. The two remaining battalions were held in reserve at a camp near Maidos, on the other side of the peninsula, ready to be deployed as required to meet an Allied landing. It was really the only option for the overstretched Turkish defenders, but it was this decision that led to a handful of beleaguered platoons facing the full force of the Anzac landing alone.

On 25 April, Sefik was the right man in the right place and responded quickly to the crisis. When he heard distant fire from the west, he hurriedly assembled his two reserve battalions and harangued his divisional commander for permission to march toward the fight. At first, his commander was unmoved but, after repeated calls from Sefik, the resistance broke and Sefik ordered his regiment to march out at once. His destination was clear. If the enemy had landed at Anzac Cove, their objective would be the high ground of Third Ridge. He had to get there first.

Sefik was a hard taskmaster. His two battalions had been up pretty much all night carrying out field exercises and had only returned to camp at 2 am. Now, after a handful of hours' sleep, his men were on the move again. Sefik pushed them hard to reach the Anzac sector and join the battle that they could hear raging on the distant ridgeline. Before long, the battle came to them.

> Our situation on the march was precarious and dangerous for the sun had risen and was beginning to get high in the sky. Over the whole plain from Boyun we were exposed to attack by naval gunfire and bombing attacks from aircraft. One reason for the battalions being ordered to march along different roads was in order to pass quickly over the dangerous area. Another reason was to reduce the depth of columns, since the enemy was not far away, and to deploy quickly if necessary for battle.[7]

As the battalions doubled-timed across the Maltepe plain, desperately trying to maintain a sense of order as they struggled through scrub patches and across ditches, they came across a bleeding and bruised survivor of the forward outposts who was heading to the field hospital. He told them that the enemy had already reached Third Ridge and that the Turkish defenders were about to be completely overrun.* Sefik was sceptical that the Australians could have advanced so quickly, but the rumour was confirmed when the first men from his regiment to crest the ridge came under fire from a small group of Australian forward scouts. These recklessly brave Aussies had pushed well ahead of the main body of troops and were completely isolated. As soon as they saw an entire regiment of Turkish reinforcements converging from the other side of the ridge, they sensibly withdrew after a brief skirmish. It's difficult to pinpoint exactly who these men were but it was likely a small group commanded by Lieutenant Noel Loutit that had the dubious honour of advancing further than just about any Australian for the entire campaign. Charles Bean later interviewed Loutit about this incident:

> Like all the rest the ridge they were now mounting was covered with scrub, and from its crest they looked over a gully to a similar ridge 400 yards away. On it were Turks in large numbers, who opened heavy fire; and the Australians after passing slightly over the crest of their ridge had to fling themselves down and shoot from behind bushes; the opposing fire was much too hot to allow them to dig.[8]

After chasing off the Australians, Sefik's men began digging in along the crest of Third Ridge. Sefik surveyed the battlefield before him and realised the Turks were in trouble. Two large

---

*   A Turkish report also claims that Sefik's forward elements met a
     detachment of Turks who were escorting Australian prisoners to the
     rear. This is certainly possible – a small number of Australians from
     the initial landing were captured on 25 April – but it's odd that Sefik
     makes no mention of it in his memoirs.

groups of Australians were advancing, and quickly. The Australians had already established a solid position on Second Ridge and were preparing to advance on Third Ridge. One group appeared to be pushing northward, toward the high ground of Chunuk Bair, the key position on the battlefield. Another group was heading straight up the slope toward Sefik's position. He quickly realised that he could not do much about the northern group and that he did not have enough men to drive the Australians off Second Ridge without support. He needed to hold them while he waited for more reinforcements and artillery to arrive.

Artillery was the key to stopping the Anzacs. Rifles and bayonets could only do so much – the Turks desperately needed supporting fire from their artillery batteries. Sefik had pushed his men into action so quickly that he had been forced to leave his slow-moving artillery behind; three Turkish mountain guns that had been positioned on Second Ridge at the time of the landing had been caught completely off-guard by the speed of the Anzac advance and were quickly captured. Without artillery support, any counter-attack Sefik launched would be futile. Just at the right moment, a lone gun trundled onto the ridge, having been manhandled there by its tired crew. One gun wasn't going to turn the tide but it was better than nothing. Sefik ordered it into action as soon as it was in position. It began blasting at the Australians in the southern group, who were digging in at Lone Pine. It did good work and Australians began to drop with entrenching tools in hand. The resplendently named Private Reuben Lucius Hampton, a 23-year-old chemist from South Melbourne, was digging in with the 5th Battalion and was on the receiving end of this fire.

The firing line was well at it, our fellows being simply mowed down by shrapnel to which they could not reply.

Our casualties were enormous. The Turks were getting the better of it by far. We had every available man in the firing line and on the retreat. But as we were between the devil and deep sea, we had no option but to hold out at any cost. Shrapnel fire was something awful raking up and down the valleys and spreading destruction everywhere.[9]

It wasn't long before Hampton received a painful and unnerving demonstration of just how destructive shrapnel fire could be.

Of the shrapnel when one has no cover, it puts the fear of God into one's soul. One dropped on to three of us who were doing picquet and looking for snipers. The mate alongside of me had his enamel mug blown to smithereens and I felt a piece of something about four pound weight hit me in the boot, but when I looked down to see what it was I found a round piece of lead about two-thirds of an inch diameter.[10]

Sefik had nowhere near enough artillery to launch a successful counter-attack, but his keen eye quickly determined that the situation was desperate. With every passing minute, the Anzacs landed more men and captured more ground. Sefik placed a couple of machine guns in position to cover the advance, messaged his headquarters to advise that he was launching a counter-attack, steeled his nerves and then went for it.

At about 9 am, with cheers and bugle calls, the Turks streamed over the skyline and charged straight at the Anzacs digging in on sites that would famously come to be known as Lone Pine and Johnston's Jolly. Small groups of Australians had advanced well beyond their comrades and were clinging precariously to the slopes of Third Ridge. Sefik's men swept over them and killed them all. Four years later, Australian official historian Charles Bean walked this ground and found in small groups across the slope 'the bodies of Australians, their bones rather, still associated with the tatters of their uniforms'.[11]

The Turks continued to charge forward but were met by withering fire from the Australian front line, which was mostly hidden in the thick scrub. Sefik watched the advance through binoculars on Third Ridge:

> All of a sudden among the thickets, a closely packed line of soldiers were seen to rise to their feet. This line moved through the thickets in front of them and rushed upon our riflemen in a bayonets attack. When our riflemen saw this attack of the Australians, they immediately jumped to their feet, all together, and rushed in retaliation at the Australians. Most of the Australians who saw the counter-attack of our men suddenly stopped. While a few of them engaged in a bayonet and rifle duel with our men the others ran away and got lost among the high brushwood. Our men pursued them with rifle fire.[12]

Despite these isolated successes, the Turkish attack soon broke down and the men of the 27th Regiment hit the dirt and began to dig in, facing the Australians on Second Ridge. The attack had halted the Australian advance but, after the pummelling they had received from Australian rifles and machine guns, the Turks weren't going anywhere either.

Sefik's situation was now desperate. He scanned the country behind him in the hope of spotting the battalion of reinforcements he knew was on its way. To his relief, he saw Turkish troops marching steadily forward toward Third Ridge – lots of them. This wasn't just a battalion; it was a whole regiment. Lieutenant Colonel Mustafa Kemal, the man who would make a bigger difference to the outcome of the Gallipoli campaign than just about anyone, had stepped onto the stage and was about to play his defining role.

—-—

Kemal had already been awakened by gunfire when a messenger rushed into his headquarters with news of the Allied landings. Kemal was thirty-four years old and had distinguished himself in several wars. Now, in this new and greater conflict, he had been given charge of the Turkish 19th Division and had done his best to conform to General von Sanders' constricting plans for the defence of the Gallipoli peninsula. The 19th Division was in reserve; Kemal needed specific instructions from von Sanders about where and when he should commit his division to battle. The problem was, von Sanders was nowhere to be found, and his staff officers were of little use – he hadn't left them any orders.

Kemal had a decision to make. He had fought at Gallipoli during the First Balkan War and knew the topography well. If the Allies were able to seize the high ground overlooking Anzac Cove, they would cut the peninsula in two. At 7.30 am, he received reports from despatch riders that a serious assault was taking place in the Anzac sector and that a battalion of reinforcements was urgently required. This was all the encouragement Kemal needed. Instead of sending just a single battalion (and in complete disobedience of his orders), he instructed the entire 57th Regiment – three battalions of infantry, a machine-gun company and a mountain-gun battery – to move to Anzac. It was a decision that would change the course of the Gallipoli campaign.

By 8 am, the regiment was marching, with Kemal out in front of it. Like Sefik, he knew the importance of the high ground of Third Ridge and was determined to get there before the Anzacs. But that was easier said than done. There were no roads between the regiment's camps and the rugged and isolated Anzac sector, and so the battalions were forced into an arduous cross-country slog through thorny scrub that shredded uniforms and sapped spirits. Kemal urged them on, exhorting his men that nothing less than the fate of their country and families was at stake. With such encouragement, the regiment moved fast, despite the ugly terrain. Within a couple of hours, Kemal was standing on the summit of Chunuk Bair.

The 57th Regiment had been encamped north of the Anzac sector, which, in one of the fortuitous coincidences that seemed to define Kemal's career, enabled it to march straight into the path of the Anzac force advancing on Chunuk Bair. But Kemal had raced ahead with only a handful of staff officers and had completely outpaced the regiment. So when he lifted his binoculars and surveyed the tumult unfolding on the slopes below him, he was virtually alone. Directly in front, he witnessed a small mob of Turkish soldiers falling back, hotly pursued by a significantly larger mob of Anzacs.

> Confronting these men myself, I said, 'Why are you running away?' 'Sir, the enemy!' they said, pointing out Battleship Hill. In fact a line of skirmishers of the enemy approached Battleship Hill and was advancing completely unopposed. Then, I still do not know what it was, whether a logical appreciation or an instinctive action, I do not know, I said to the men running away, 'You cannot run away from the enemy!' 'We have no ammunition!' 'If you haven't got any ammunition you have your bayonets!' I said. And shouting to them I made them fix their bayonets and lie down on the ground. When they fixed their bayonets and lay down on the ground the enemy also lay down. The moment of time that we gained was this one.[13]

As the first battalion of the 57th Regiment arrived, Kemal gave it no time to rest and ordered an immediate counter-attack. This was the moment Kemal issued his most famous, and ruthlessly pragmatic, order (although sounding like the stuff of legend, the source of the quote is Kemal himself, as he details in his memoirs):

> Here is the order which I gave verbally to the commanders: 'I don't order you to attack – I order you to die. In the time which passes until we die, other troops and commanders can take our places.'[14]

The furious attack drove the Australians off the high ground and chased them over Battleship Hill. Although the charge had stymied the immediate threat, it broke down as it approached the rough hill known as Baby 700, and the battalion dug in.

Between them and completely on the fly, Sefik and Kemal had instigated an effective and coordinated counter-attack that spelled the end of Anzac hopes of quickly seizing the high ground. Once the Anzacs realised that Turkish reinforcements had arrived, they abandoned plans to charge wildly for their objectives and began digging in on Second Ridge, in most cases on positions that wouldn't move for the rest of the campaign. Both Sefik and Kemal were proud of their early actions and both men lightly jostled in their memoirs for the honour of having launched the first counter-attack of the campaign. Reports are contradictory but, given the timeline, it's likely that Sefik made his attack before Kemal. And even though history has remembered Kemal and lauded his achievements at Gallipoli, in the early hours of the campaign, Sefik did as much as his more famous comrade to prevent the Anzacs from winning the day. His role in the Turkish success should be better known than it is.

Both men were now on Third Ridge and had a firm grasp on the situation. For the time being, the immediate crisis was over. With the Anzacs held up on Second Ridge, it was time to try and push them back into the sea. Kemal established contact with Sefik and took him under his command. He ordered a forceful, coordinated counter-attack, with Sefik concentrating on Lone Pine to the south, while Kemal would focus on the northern sector around Baby 700. The Anzacs were stuck on a scrubby ridge miles short of their objective and the Turks peered down on them from the high ground above. And now they were ready to strike back.

— —

One unintended consequence of the initiative shown by Sefik and Kemal was that Turkish commanders were initially distracted from the real threat of the invasion. The young colonels weren't just doing good work on the battlefield, they were keeping their commanders well informed about it, and so reports to headquarters in the early hours of the campaign were dominated by the events at Anzac. By comparison, the reports coming out of Helles were vague and contradictory, and failed to give an accurate impression of what was actually going on down there – that a huge British and French force was now ashore on several beaches and was advancing up the peninsula. This meant that, for the first few hours at least, a steady stream of reinforcements and equipment was directed to Anzac, giving Kemal all the tools he needed to launch his counter-offensive. He brought up more reserves and artillery, and gave the order for his men to charge.

Kemal's 57th Regiment in the north surged over Battleship Hill and then fanned out. One battalion pressed the attack against a strong but motley Australian force on Baby 700, and another wheeled to the right and charged for the high ground above Fisherman's Hut. It met only token resistance in this rough country and was soon digging in on a strong defensive line that prevented the Anzacs from advancing further north.

Meanwhile, Sefik's 27th Regiment charged at the Anzacs who were digging in on 400 Plateau and its two key features of Lone Pine and Johnston's Jolly. The Turks had already lost heavily in this area and the Anzac positions were much stronger here than in the north so Sefik's men made little progress. But Sefik astutely brought up reinforcements to plug gaps in the Turkish line and positioned two field guns and a couple of machine guns to enfilade the Anzac positions on the plateau. Hemmed in by infantry across their entire front, and now caught in a deadly crossfire of shrapnel and machine guns, the Anzacs on 400 Plateau were going nowhere.

The fighting degenerated into a series of skirmishes. Each junior officer, sergeant or corporal fought his own battle with the handful of men he could gather together in his immediate area. Small groups from both sides clashed in brutal hand-to-hand encounters in the scrub and gullies. Officers who stood up to issue orders were quickly shot down. Private Harry Murray, who would go on to become the most decorated Australian soldier of the First World War, was in the thick of the action in the centre of the Australian line. He described an incident he witnessed involving Percy Black, another future Anzac hero.

Percy Black grabbed his [rifle] and, sighting carefully, dropped a Turkish sniper, who had been crawling along the side of a cliff about 90 yards away. The poor wretch fell down the steep side, caught his legs in a low fork and there he hung for days. We all hoped that the shot had killed him and that he did not have to linger in such a position. Our own casualties began to mount up unpleasantly.

One by one men hurtled down the steep hill, often shot through the head.[15]

In this guerrilla fighting, the more experienced Turks were at a distinct advantage and gradually began to push the Anzacs back. Sefik skilfully employed his artillery and machine guns to support his platoons and the Turks used their most effective close-quarter weapon to deadly effect – the hand grenade (or 'bomb' as they were commonly called). Many Turkish soldiers carried grenades, which they lobbed into Anzac strong points to kill or scatter the demoralised defenders. The Anzacs had not been issued grenades and could do nothing to counter the threat. Sefik's men edged forward but were forced to dig in as they began to outrange their artillery.

Although the Turks were steadily reinforcing their line, the Anzacs were piling reinforcements onto the narrow beach at a startling rate. Soon after 10 am, the first New Zealanders came ashore and, although confusion on the beachhead meant that the landing schedule was perilously delayed, by the end of the day, more than 16,000 Anzacs would be ashore.

Cecil Malthus and his comrades from the Canterbury Battalion were due to hit the beach at noon but it was 4 pm before they scrambled into boats and began the gut-tightening row toward Anzac Cove. The fighting had moved well inland but the new arrivals were plagued by the weapon that would kill more Anzacs on 25 April than any other – shrapnel shells.

Now through the bursting shells we could hear at last the continuous rattle of rifle fire with which we were to become so wearily familiar. As we approached the beach – a narrow rocky one under an almost precipitous rise – we could see people moving in all directions like ants on a log ... Soon we were off for the shore, which was only a couple of hundred yards away, but the boats were so packed as to make painfully slow progress – and we were now under heavy shrapnel fire. Our casualties were mercifully light – I think only half a dozen in the company – and none were fatal, but we heard for the first time that sickening soft thud of shell fragments or bullets meeting human flesh.[16]

Meanwhile, in the north, Kemal called up even more reinforcements and launched another series of counter-attacks. This was war at its ugliest. Waves of advancing troops threw themselves at Anzac rifles and machine guns. The first wave advanced into almost certain death, but the following waves were able to exploit the confusion of the initial attack and break into the Anzac lines. The fighting was up close and brutal. No prisoners were taken by either side.

The Turks pushed the Anzacs off Baby 700 and toward the Nek, the narrow strip of land that would become a killing field later in the campaign. Their casualties had been horrendous but the Anzac position was gradually being choked off. By nightfall, the Anzacs were furiously digging in on Second Ridge, consolidating the positions that would become the front line for the rest of the campaign. Throughout the night, the Turks kept up the pressure, launching localised counter-attacks that failed to drive the Anzacs into the sea but kept them awake and jumpy, as related by Corporal Clarrie Roberts of the 8th Battalion.

During a period of darkness a cry of 'Allah, Allah, Allah' fell upon our ears. It was a new cry to us, but instinctively we knew that the enemy were attacking. It was not possible to see them in the darkness, but without waiting for any command a fairly hot rifle fire commenced. The rifle fire had been heavy, but now it opened out in volume and force until it became almost deafening. From the position of this portion of the line one could look along the trench for several hundred yards, and such a continuous stream of red and orange flame burst from the hundreds of rifles. It was a withering fire and no persons could for long withstand it. The Turks were beating a hasty retreat, leaving many dead and wounded. The cries of the wounded could be heard throughout the night.[17]

The Turks had plenty of problems – particularly with the inexperienced 77th Regiment that came into the line on Sefik's left and quickly disintegrated in the face of withering Anzac fire. But for the most part, the Turkish response to the Anzac landing had been inspired.

Kemal's timely arrival and his decision to commit his entire 57th Regiment could not have worked better if it had been planned on a map table at a military college. By committing his troops early in the south, Sefik had drawn the majority of Anzac reinforcements toward him. Meanwhile, the high ground to the north (the Anzac left), which was the key to securing the whole sector, was only thinly occupied by Anzac troops, who weren't advancing. And it was here that Kemal suddenly appeared and launched his powerful counter-attacks. Against this unanticipated and overwhelming force, the Anzacs had no answer.

Looking back on the day of the landing, the Turks had made a grave strategic error by failing to adequately safeguard the small beach that became known as Anzac Cove. Turkish overconfidence that any landing in the sector would be made at Brighton Beach, to the south of Anzac Cove, almost cost them the campaign – an entire enemy division was able to land before the defenders could rush adequate reinforcements to the sector and halt the Anzac advance. But after this initial blunder, the Turks bounced back decisively and impressively.

The Turkish defenders who had guarded the landing beaches had been ludicrously outnumbered but succeeded in slowing down the landing and buying valuable time for their comrades. The reinforcements who arrived had, by luck and good management, been placed precisely where they were most needed. And the counter-attacks, well coordinated and led by Sefik and Kemal, had driven the Anzac troops back onto a defensive line that they would struggle to hold on to for the next eight months. Thanks to the good work of the Turks, the Anzac campaign was effectively over the day it began.

7.

HELLES: THE FIRST TEN DAYS

As the sun crested the gorse-studded spurs of Cape Helles on 26 April, the mood among Allied troops was dark. Emotions ran high and were decidedly mixed – despondency, exhaustion and anguish were common – but the one feeling that was all-pervading was bewilderment. How had it all gone so horribly wrong? The previous day had stretched on so long, and had been such an unexpected and bloody ordeal, that many men were astonished to realise that the whole shocking saga had only lasted twenty-four hours. Had it really only been *yesterday* that they had clambered into lighters and begun the slow row into shore? Now, as they scratched into the parched earth with their entrenching tools, or wandered back to the cookers near the beach for an unappetising breakfast, they spoke in low murmurs to their mates – at least, the ones who were still alive. All of them had the same nagging concern on their mind: as brutal as it had been, yesterday was just the beginning. They now had to get through today, and tomorrow, and next week, and next month.

Not only was the fighting not going to plan, even the most fundamental elements of a functioning army were also in disarray.

The landing of men, animals and stores had been intended to take sixty hours – in reality, it would be nearly ten days before the final supply boats were unloaded. The situation wasn't helped by a serious manpower shortage. Troops who had been detailed to unload boats found themselves suddenly thrust into the front line to reinforce their hard-pressed comrades, leaving laden lighters bobbing in the shallows as Turkish shells exploded around them. When men could be found to help with the unloading, they were hampered by the soft sand on the beach. Horses and mules had grown doughy and lazy in the holds of the ships and were more trouble than they were worth once brought ashore. In frustration, the beach parties made the back-breaking decision to haul heavy artillery guns from the beach by hand, rather than wasting time with the recalcitrant animals. The campaign was only twenty-four hours old and already the Allies were low on reinforcements, supplies and ideas.

It wasn't just the men who were struggling. In the upper echelons, expectations of triumphant victories had given way to pessimism – a decidedly unmilitary whiff of panic pervaded the halls of British headquarters. Throughout the night of 25 April, reports had filtered back to Major General Hunter-Weston that the Turks were entrenched at Helles in strength and were streaming in thousands of fresh troops by the hour. His assumptions were reinforced by his own ears – from the deck of his flagship, HMS *Euralys*, the din of rifle fire from the newly won British positions was disconcertingly loud and suggested that the Turks were strongly attacking his beleaguered force (he reported to Sir Ian Hamilton that 'attacks during the night were repulsed by rifle fire and gun fire from the ships'[1]). A concerning (and completely false) report that the Turks were advancing on W Beach en masse didn't help. The British generals remained stubbornly deluded that the Turks were occupying Helles in much larger numbers than they actually were.

British commanders were not only confused, they were also indecisive – everyone seemed to have a different priority – and they began to squabble. A contingent of French reinforcements was available to be landed immediately but no-one could agree on where it should go. Hunter-Weston announced that he had captured Hill 141 but then changed his mind – Hill 141, he reported, was still firmly in Turkish hands. The commander at X Beach reported that he had got through the night with only two casualties and that there was no sign of the enemy, but he was reluctant to advance into unfamiliar ground. Given the disaster unfolding all around him, Lieutenant General Hamilton can be forgiven for getting a little flighty.

> What of those men fighting for their lives in the darkness. I put them there. Might they not, all of them, be sailing back to safe England, but for me? And I sleep! To sleep whilst thousands are killing one another close by! Well, why not; I must sleep whilst I may. The legend whereby a Commander-in-Chief works wonders during a battle dies hard. He may still lose the battle in a moment by losing heart. He may still help to win the battle by putting a brave face upon the game when it seems to be up. By his character, he may still stop the rot and inspire his men to advance once more to the assault.[2]

By the morning of 26 April, Hunter-Weston was desperate to get the advance on Krithia and Achi Baba hill rolling again. He turned his attention to the obstacles right under his nose. The survivors of the landing at V Beach held the barest toehold on the sand, and the vitally important Old Fort and village of Sedd el Bahr were still firmly in Turkish hands. Without overcoming these most preliminary of obstacles, the British were going nowhere. The men who had landed the previous day were exhausted and their officers could not rouse them to continue the advance. The only hope was a sprinkling of fresh troops who had landed during the night. After a barrage from the warships that landed on few of the intended targets, the stoic Brits pushed forward. They swiftly overcame the fort but the advance through the village turned into a brutal slog, typified by the sort of house-to-house fighting that their sons would come to recognise and detest during the advance through Normandy twenty-nine years later. The Turks disputed every inch of ground and sold their lives dearly. Two British officers, Captain Garth Walford and Colonel Charles Doughty-Wylie, led the men forward with reckless bravery until shot down. They would both receive the Victoria Cross, as would Corporal William Cosgrave for charging the Turkish wire.[*]

As heroic as the advance was, it was defined by confusion and dithering. Orders for troops to advance from W Beach to support the attack on the village never got through, and it wasn't until the afternoon that anything like a coordinated assault was made from the beaches. By this time, the Turks were abandoning their coastal defences and streaming disorderly back toward Krithia – a concerted push from the British could potentially have broken through. But Hunter-Weston was playing a cautious game; he was jumpy about the risk of attack from a Turkish force that simply didn't exist. Rather than advancing through the flimsy Turkish defences toward Krithia, he ordered his men to dig in and prepare for a Turkish counter-attack. 'There must be no retiring,' he wrote, and added with a completely unwarranted dash of hyperbole, 'Every man will die at his post rather than retire.'[3]

In reality, the Turks had no intention of counter-attacking – they couldn't have even if they wanted to. Despite the

---

[*]   Doughty-Wylie's grave still sits forlornly above the modern village, the only individual Commonwealth burial at Gallipoli.

perception in Allied headquarters, the Turkish troops at Helles were as badly knocked around as the British and were licking their wounds after the exhausting opening day. It was true that reinforcements were trickling into the Turkish lines from other parts of the peninsula, but at a much slower rate than the British estimated. Despite the early reverses, for the first three days of the campaign, the odds were stacked firmly in the Allies' favour. On the day of the landing, a single Turkish battalion guarding the beaches at Helles had effectively held up an entire British division. Recent research reveals that even two days after the landing, there were still only five Turkish battalions in the entire Helles sector, facing thirteen British and French battalions. But while they were short on numbers, the Turks were certainly not idle. On the evening of 26 April, at the precise moment Hunter-Weston was ordering his men to prepare for a counter-attack, the Turks were falling back. They left isolated posts to keep touch with the British line but the main force withdrew to the high ground in front of Krithia. Each battalion had lost an average of 400 men in the chaotic opening days of the campaign, but the British hesitancy gave the survivors the opportunity to gather themselves and dig in. By the close of 26 April, the first traces of what would become a strong defensive line had begun to appear in front of the whitewashed ruins of Krithia.

Meanwhile, the exhausted British troops in the front line were jumping at shadows. They were too bone-weary to patrol, so were completely unaware that the bulk of the Turks in front of them had slunk away. Nerves were stretched taut from days of exertion. The constant rumours from friend and officer alike that a massive Turkish attack was due to fall on them at any moment kept them awake and on edge. Understandably, they were twitchy. When one man thought he saw movement and opened fire, his comrades all joined in, but no-one could say for sure what they were shooting at. One platoon had entrenched in front of an old cemetery and its officer instructed the men to study the location of every headstone and bush lest they be mistaken for advancing enemy soldiers in the gloom. Several hours later, the officer himself was convinced he saw men creeping toward him through the inky night and ordered his men to open fire. It wasn't until morning that he discovered they had been shooting at shrubs.

The British were barely holding on and the arrival of French reinforcements could not come soon enough. They were due to come ashore on the night of 26 April so Hunter-Weston prepared to resume the advance toward Achi Baba on the following day. But as the sun rose over the dishevelled British troops the next morning, it was clear that there were few Frenchmen alongside them. The French had been caught up in the same resupply chaos that was plaguing the British – the bulk of the reinforcements could not be landed until the afternoon. Two French battalions from the 175th Regiment had managed to land in the morning and were hurriedly rushed into the far right of the line to relieve British troops so exhausted that they could barely lift a rifle. The French now held the extreme right of the Allied line, a position they would occupy for most of the campaign. There they would face the toughest ground at Helles, against the strongest Turkish opposition and, with their flank exposed to the Asian shore, the unenviable challenge of waging war while Turkish guns lobbed shells into their lines from behind.

With scant fresh troops available, Hunter-Weston was again paralysed by an overabundance of caution and abandoned thoughts of attacking Krithia and Achi Baba on the 27th. Instead, he ordered the British to simply advance their line to link up all the beaches and to form a good starting position for a big attack the following day. It was a relatively straightforward task but, like everything in the early days of the Gallipoli campaign, it was based on an appalling lack of information. The objective on the left was described as the mouth of a stream, which was marked on British maps as a straight and deceptively inconsequential blue line. In reality, this 'stream' was Gully Ravine, a thirty-metre-deep scar in the landscape whose torturous slopes in the upper reaches would be soaked with British blood by the end of the campaign.

At 4 pm and in dazzling daylight, the weary British and French climbed out their half-dug trenches and edged forward, expecting a torrent of fire from purely imaginary enemy forces to tear into them at any moment. But, of course, no fire greeted them. The Turks had completed their withdrawal while the British were dithering near the beaches. The odd sniper held up the advance in places and two field guns over near Achi Baba half-heartedly lobbed over a couple of shells, but for the most part, the British crossed the uncontested ground without incident. By nightfall, they were on their objective, the first and last time in the Helles campaign that the Allies would accomplish the feat. Even then, there was no respite for the exhausted men; the night of 27 April would be spent digging, not sleeping.

Meanwhile, back at V Beach, the French had finally landed in force. The bulk of the troops had arrived too late to participate in the tentative advance that had taken place during the afternoon but at least the Allies now had some relatively fresh troops at their disposal. V Beach, with the mottled Trojan horse of the *River Clyde* standing like a forlorn mascot on the shore, and won at such cost by the British on the day of the landing, was handed over to the French. For the rest of the campaign, V Beach would bustle with sky-blue uniforms of the *poilu* and would rouse each morning to the strains of 'La Marseillaise'. The main British base of operations shifted northwest to W Beach.

As he prepared to resume the advance on 28 April, Hunter-Weston was faced with some very real and very concerning challenges, none of which had been predicted or planned for. The campaign was only three days old and already his once-proud division was a shadow of its former self. Not only had his brigades suffered appalling casualties, an alarmingly high proportion of the dead and wounded had been officers. Turkish marksmen had been well versed in the art of distinguishing officers from enlisted men, and had put this skill to deadly effect. Twelve battalion commanders had led their men ashore on the morning of the landing; only three of them were still standing by the third day. Losses among junior officers were even more shocking – the 1st Dublins had embarked 1012 men for the landing but since then had lost twenty-one of its twenty-five officers and over 550 men.

The chaos of the opening days meant that those men who were still alive were cold, hungry and low on ammunition. A crippling shortage of pack animals made the job of resupplying the men in the disorderly front line a nightmare. In desperation, the mules of the artillery batteries were pressed into service, diligently plodding to and from the front lines for twenty-four hours straight. Despite how recklessly the troops had blasted through their ammunition in the first few days, there were reasonable reserves of it on the beach. But even if it could be transported to the fighting men, they had nowhere to keep it. Many of them had thrown away their packs during the panic of the landing and now had no way of carrying extra food or ammunition.

Back on the beach, the unloading of supplies was a shambles. It was hard enough to get boxes of biscuits and cans of rifle ammunition ashore; unloading bulky cargo like artillery guns was virtually impossible. If the infantry was going to make any headway at all, support from artillery fire was essential – yet only a fraction of the division's guns had been landed. And with the pack animals of the artillery units busy lugging food and water to the front line, there were precious few available to do the job they were intended for – moving the guns. By the morning of 28 April, only twenty-eight artillery guns were ashore; with no animals to haul them, most of those were stuck on the beach.

With so much going wrong, Hunter-Weston became even more tentative and shelved his plans for taking both Krithia and Achi Baba in one stroke. But setting a pattern he would follow for the rest of the campaign, his revised plans were inconceivably complex and paid scant attention to the realities on the ground, or the likelihood that his exhausted men would be able to carry them out.

Determining that Achi Baba was for the time being out of reach, Hunter-Weston set his sights on Krithia. On the face of it, this was not a bad plan, but he then made the bizarre decision to attack the village at an angle, pivoting the entire line on the far-right flank and requiring his troops to attack diagonally across the peninsula, eventually digging in facing Achi Baba from the west. Even if the attack had gone to plan, which it was almost guaranteed not to, the final Allied line would have formed a decidedly odd (and wholly indefensible) shape like a '7', with the bulk of the troops in a north–south line and the northernmost brigade bent back to the coast at a right angle. God only knows how the unfortunate troops allocated to form the right angle would have defended against enemy troops on three sides, but they would never have to find out. The bizarre attack formation would disintegrate in the opening minutes of the advance and would never amount to anything more than a creative crayon mark on a military map.

The ground here was so uncharted to Allied forces that they hadn't even come up with names for the long spurs that ran along the southern length of the peninsula and defined the

Helles battlefield. It wasn't until after the war that writers trying to make sense of the tangled country suggested giving names to these prominent landmarks, but the ground was so confusing that even the British and Australian official histories can't agree on what they should be called. In the British official history, the four spurs (from north to south) are Gully Spur, Fir Tree Spur, Krithia Spur and Kereves Spur (which faces a gaping ravine called the Kereves Dere). In the Australian official history, they are Ravine Spur, Krithia Spur, Central Spur and Kereves Spur.* If their commanders didn't even have names for the features they were ordering to be attacked, God knows how the troops on the ground made any sense of it.

Not only was Hunter-Weston's plan ridiculously complicated, it was also absurdly inefficient. The Allied line at the start of the advance was about three kilometres long. If the troops were successful in taking all their objectives, the new line would extend to nearly nine kilometres. Just how the survivors of an already battered force were supposed to consolidate a new line three times as long as the one they had started from was not disclosed. The orders also made no mention of enemy dispositions or even artillery support. As the final insult, the entire plan was based on frustratingly woeful intelligence. The British official history is usually exceedingly forgiving of Hunter-Weston's plans and the lack of information he used to compile them, so its account of the intelligence work before this attack is telling:

> The orders were undoubtably meagre, but at the time they were issued the divisional staff had little information to give. They had as yet received no detailed report of the actual line attained by the Allied troops that evening. They were ignorant of the country in front and the extraordinary

---

* For the sake of consistency, this book will use the British terms.

tactical importance of the harmless-looking water-courses marked on their maps. They knew nothing of the enemy's strength or of the position of his defences; they were even uncertain whether any opposition would be encountered within the limits of the day's advance.[4]

It doesn't get much vaguer than that. And just to make sure the demoralised troops were completely dejected before they even set off, the orders stipulated that the men were to make the emergency rations they carried last for two days instead of one, as it was doubtful they would be resupplied. The problem was, as previously mentioned, many of the men had thrown away their packs so weren't carrying any emergency rations. They were already hungry and exhausted, and were now facing the very real prospect of going two days without food.

It wasn't just the men who were worn out; their officers were near the point of collapse. One battalion officer reported that he received orders for the attack with 'horror and surprise', and that when he tried to explain the plan to his company commanders and point out the objective on a map, the 'poor fellows, being dead with lack of sleep and exhaustion, were in no condition to take much interest'.[5]

Under these appalling circumstances, the first large-scale Allied advance at Helles was launched. In later years, it would come to be known as the First Battle of Krithia but that's a generous assessment. The term 'battle' implies that there were two organised forces equally engaged in the conflict; the advance toward Krithia on 28 April consisted predominantly of British and French forces blundering into a storm of fire from an enemy they couldn't see and dying by the thousands.

Preparations for the advance began in the early hours. Artillery gunners, who would be essential to any successful advance, had spent an exhausting night desperately trying to haul guns into position by any means possible. They did sterling work under impossible circumstances, but by dawn only twenty individual guns were in position to support the entire three-kilometre front of the attack.*

For their part, the Turks had regained some of their composure and had been bolstered by fresh reinforcements. Their defensive line was nothing like a continuous series of trenches, but the Turks had made full use of the best asset at their disposal – the ground. The torn and broken landscape of Cape Helles, riven with ravines and gullies, was the Turk's best friend; in every unseen fold in the ground lurked a machine gun or rifle team. Guarding them was a screen of advanced posts, consistent only in their inconsistency. One was in a copse, the next a dry creekbed, another in a hollow. They were well spaced and mutually supportive, and the deep ravines running along the peninsula provided ideal avenues to direct reinforcements where needed. The Turks were tired and depleted, but they were ready.

— —

The opening paragraph in the British official history that details the start of the First Battle of Krithia doesn't fill the reader with confidence that the attack is going to go well. The naval bombardment that kicked the battle off at 8 am is described as 'desultory'. The twenty guns of the supporting artillery provided 'scattered fire'. And the infantry were 'weary' and, after leaving their trenches, 'plodded forward' in the general direction of Krithia.

But despite the appalling lack of artillery support and the exhaustion of the attacking troops, the infantry advance

---

*   By comparison, the Battle of Neuve-Chapelle, which had been launched in France six weeks beforehand, was supported by more than 500 guns on a similar frontage.

began well. The beleaguered Turks in the advance posts, having watched their comrades swamped by repeated Allied advances over the previous three days, were initially reluctant to resist, and at least one Turkish battalion bolted without firing a shot. But those further back, who had been reinforced by fresh troops, had no such compunctions, and found themselves gazing through gunsights down a gentle slope toward thousands of British and French troops advancing slowly in the open. They cocked their machine guns, cycled the bolts on their rifles and opened fire. They couldn't miss against such easy targets.

In short order, the British advance turned from cautious stroll to bloody ordeal as Turkish bullets found their mark. Artillery up on Achi Baba joined in. Soon, the incongruous fairy floss puffs of shrapnel shells were bursting over the heads of the advancing troops and scattering their deadly payload like hail on a lake. Men began to scream and fall, clutching bloodied faces and limbs as they hit the ground. Some writhed; many were still.

Almost immediately, Hunter-Weston's ludicrously complicated plan began to disintegrate. Unsurprisingly (except perhaps to Hunter-Weston), troops who advance into enemy fire coming from directly in front of them are generally loath to turn half-right and cop it from the flank. Accordingly, the attacking troops quickly abandoned any notion of a diagonal advance and pushed steadily forward toward the Turkish lines right in front of them. In the words of the official history, 'the Turkish positions rather than an arbitrary line on a map became the true objective, and by every unit of the brigade all previous instructions were forgotten.'[6] This quickly led to chaos. In the centre of the line, the leading companies of the Hampshire Regiment found themselves 500 metres ahead of the rest of the line and advancing without support on left or right. The advance deteriorated into a series of isolated battles, with every company commander doing his best to contend with the enemy in front of him. After three hours of this, the British troops were bleeding, thoroughly exhausted, desperately short of ammunition and wracked by thirst. Their advance ground to a halt.

On the right, the French (who were to form the pivot of the complicated right turn) either misunderstood their orders to hold fast until the British line advanced and swung right, or were forced by the Turks to ignore them. The gaping chasm of Kereves Dere was by far the most hostile obstacle at Helles. The Turks facing it had wasted little time in reinforcing their already strong positions. As soon as the French tried to manoeuvre through the ravine, they were hit by fire from all sides; their bright blue uniforms and white cork hats made them irresistible targets to Turkish riflemen and gunners. A British battleship blasted the Turkish positions from the straits, but it was never going to be enough to dislodge the defenders. The French advance was over as soon as it began.

In a desperate attempt to get the advance going again, British commanders threw their reserve brigade into the attack, with orders to deliver much-needed ammunition to their beleaguered comrades in the front line and then push on to capture Krithia. The problem was, the reserve brigade was desperately weak, having lost most of its officers and a sizeable chunk of its manpower in the opening days (which is why it had been held in reserve in the first place). Worse still, two of its four battalions had been sucked into the chaos earlier in the morning and sent to reinforce the British right. The two remaining battalions steadfastly advanced as ordered and, through a combination of astute leadership and blind good luck, managed to advance to a straggly wood known as Fir Tree Copse, which stood about two kilometres from Krithia. But such a bedraggled and isolated force was never going to hold on. When confused orders were issued for them to retire, the slim chance of securing Krithia slipped away.

On the extreme left, Lieutenant General Hamilton was watching the British advance from the deck of the *Queen Elizabeth*. But at 1 pm, his grandstand view turned to a horror show. He watched through wide eyes a Turkish bayonet charge break through the British left flank and dozens of British soldiers flee from the battlefield, tumble to safety down the cliff and begin scampering back to their old lines along the beach. In desperation, Hamilton sent his chief of staff, Lieutenant Colonel Cecil Aspinall-Oglander (later the author of the official history), ashore in a small boat to rally them. They were badly shaken but regained their composure and followed Aspinall-Oglander back up the cliff. One wounded Tommy, bleeding from the head and body, had been ordered by Aspinall-Oglander to return to the ships for medical treatment, but then astonishingly appeared at the clifftop, having not only disobeyed Aspinall-Oglander's order but also somehow found the strength to lug a box of ammunition with him. 'I ordered you not to come,' said Aspinall-Oglander. 'I can still pull a trigger, Sir,' the man replied.[7]

As Hamilton watched this drama unfolding through his spy glass, he saw to his horror a large group of Turks surge through the gap where the British had retreated. The gunners on the *Queen Elizabeth* also spotted them and took decisive action:

> One Turkish Company, about a hundred strong, was making an ugly push within rifle shot of our ship. [...] From where we were our guns exactly enfiladed them. Again they rose and at a heavy sling trot came on with their rifles at the slope; their bayonets glittering and their Officer ten yards ahead of them waving his sword. Some one said they were cheering. Crash! and the Q.E. let fly a [15-inch] shrapnel [shell]; range

1,200 yards; a lovely shot; we followed it through the air with our eyes. Range and fuse – perfect. The huge projectile exploded fifty yards from the right of the Turkish line, and vomited its contents of 10,000 bullets [actually 24,000 shrapnel balls] clean across the stretch whereon the Turkish Company was making its last effort. When the smoke and dust cleared away nothing stirred on the whole of that piece of ground. We looked for a long time, nothing stirred.[8]

Just when British morale couldn't get any lower, farce descended on the fight. Several companies from the Royal Naval Division had been ordered into the attack to bolster the numbers of their shattered army comrades, but no-one on the beach appeared to have been informed of their new task. Assuming that their companies had simply been allocated to some other rear-area working party, their commanders ordered them to return to the beach immediately, an instruction that reached them just as they were digging for their lives in the new front line. Unsurprisingly, confusion reigned. Some officers followed the new orders and began withdrawing their men from the front line, giving the impression to other troops that a general retreat had been ordered. It was all the army officers could do to convince their flighty men to hold the line.

In the face of confusion, exhaustion and low ammunition, the British troops did the only thing they could do – they began to dig in. The attack had been a disorderly disaster, with the Allied line barely advancing and Krithia and Achi Baba still as far away as ever. Allied losses were shocking – of the 8000 or so British troops who had gone into the battle, more than 2000 had been killed or wounded. The French had lost another 1000 in their aborted advance through Kereves Dere.

Hamilton saw the bloody results of the battle first-hand but his account of it in his diary bears a touch of the deranged.

On my way back to the *Arcadian* I met a big batch of wounded, knocked out, all of them, in the battle of the 28th. I spoke to as many of them as I could, and although some were terribly mutilated and disfigured, and although a few others were clearly dying, one and all kept a stiff upper lip – one and all were, or managed to appear – more than content – happy![9]

The campaign was only three days old and already the Allied situation was dire. Worse still, Hunter-Weston's timidity had cost them dearly. By midday on 28 April, only five Allied battalions had reinforced the twelve that had come ashore on the first day. But for the Turks, Hunter-Weston's dithering had given them time to reinforce their original two battalions to ten, with more reinforcements arriving by the hour. Had the Allies pushed forward even a day earlier, they might have stood a chance of capturing Krithia and Achi Baba. Now that chance was lost. 'On the 25th,' the official history laments, 'Krithia had lain open to Colonel Matthews at Y Beach. On the 26th, and even on the morning of the 27th, the door to Achi Baba was still ajar. But now it was bolted and barred.'[10]

Whether he realised it or not, in reality, time had probably already run out for Hamilton – and any chance of success had drifted away with it. And the reason was brutally simple: he didn't have enough men. Not only had the Mediterranean Expeditionary Force sailed for Gallipoli with the barest minimum of troops required to get the job done, Hamilton had also then squandered any advantage by splitting his force in the complicated and fragmentary landings at a dozen different points on the peninsula. Had he landed his entire force at Anzac, he would likely have split the peninsula in half within days, completely stranding the small Turkish garrison at Helles and enabling his force to swiftly advance along the peninsula.

Alternatively, had he concentrated solely on Helles, he could have used the Anzac forces as a much-needed reinforcement for the British and French troops who landed on the first day, and pressed the advance from the south with fresh troops. As it was, with his meagre resources scattered across the peninsula and no reinforcements in sight, Hamilton was playing the Gallipoli game like a gambler with too small a billfold in his pocket – by the time he realised he was underfunded, the game had moved on and he was forever playing catch-up. An extra Allied division on the first day might have made all the difference; by the end of the first week, it merely balanced the odds against the surge of Turkish reinforcements.

Hamilton was in a bind of his own making, but it didn't have to be that way. A farcical communications mix-up between London and Cairo in early April had potentially denied Hamilton an entire extra division, a division that could have made the difference between success and failure on the day of the landings. On 6 April, Lord Kitchener was feeling antsy about the relatively small size of the Gallipoli force and had cabled General Sir John Maxwell, commander of British troops in Egypt, asking him to do whatever he could to help bolster Hamilton's force. 'You should supply any troops in Egypt that can be spared, or even selected officers or men that Sir Ian Hamilton may want, for Gallipoli … This telegram should be communicated by you to Sir Ian Hamilton.'

Why Kitchener didn't feel it necessary to communicate this vital piece of information to Hamilton himself is a mystery but this decision was to have far-reaching consequences. For reasons that have never been adequately explained, Hamilton never received a copy of the message. Had he seen it, there is no doubt he would have acted on it and pressured Maxwell for any troops he could spare. The obvious choice would have been the 42nd (East Lancashire) Division, a Territorial unit that had been stuck doing dispiriting garrison duty in Egypt since September 1914. As it was, the division would eventually be sent to Gallipoli but not until Hamilton had specifically requested it on 27 April. (Hamilton's cable to Kitchener was typically timorous: 'May I have a call on 42nd East Lancs. Territorial Division in case I should need them?' he asked like a meek schoolboy talking to the headmaster. 'You may be sure I shall not call up a man unless I really need him.'[11]) By the time the first units of the 42nd Division arrived at Gallipoli on 2 May, it was too late.

On 29 April, the day after the abortive First Battle of Krithia, Hamilton cabled Kitchener that the battle had pushed the British line forward more than a mile. It's impossible to tell whether Hamilton was simply wildly misinformed or was gilding the lily to Kitchener to cover up what a monumental disaster the campaign had become.

But for the men in the front line, there were no such illusions and little good news to lighten their gloom. They began to have the first inklings that this whole Gallipoli show was in danger of turning into a bloody fiasco.

> Back again in their original trenches, it was plain that the day's operation had failed. Units were badly intermixed; casualties had been heavy; all ranks were dead tired: yet there was no chance of being withdrawn from the line to rest and re-fit. Food and ammunition were running out; few of the men had greatcoats; and a cold night with a steady drizzle of rain was adding the last drop to a brimming cup of misery.[12]

The sheer horror of the battlefield alone was enough to sap men's spirits. Captain Albert Mure of the 1/5th Royal Scots was tasked with leading a party to bury corpses, both British and Turkish, from four days of heavy fighting.

The side of the bank of the nullah was quite 10 feet high, and crouched against it were seven Turks. Two were smiling broadly – and all were stone-dead. Three of them were leaning up against three others, and the seventh was keeping them all up, propping and holding them. He had crept in among them, his face to the cliff, and all you could see of him was his back and his heels. Seven Turks as dead as dead could be, and only one of the seven had a mark! His mark was ugly enough for seventy. The top of his head had been blown off exactly as you crack off the top of an egg. Another fifteen yards away was the body of another Turk, disembowelled. He was an appalling sight.[13]

Emptying the pockets of his dead British comrades was the most difficult job Mure would be called on to do in the whole campaign.

The man we had thought the biggest blackguard and the most hardened in the regiment had carried a baby's curl folded away in a tattered bit of silver paper … There were love letters that had come from Scotland, and two that would go there unfinished. An old-fashioned prayer, written out in a cramped, ignorant hand, was signed 'Mother'. A child's first letter to 'Daddy,' printed, crooked, ill-spelt, looked as if it had been carried for years. Scraps of newspapers – one containing a poem, one the report of a prizefight – a knot of blue ribbon, a small magnifying-glass, a pack of cards, a mouth-organ (of course), three exquisite butterflies carefully pressed in an old pocket book, a woman's ring, a snow-white curl, a lace handkerchief, a paper of peppermints – these were some of the mementos I had to sort, and, if possible, send back to the owner's home. Almost every pocket had a photograph; most of them had several.[14]

As exhausted and disillusioned as they were, the men of the British and French divisions would soon be called on to face an even greater test. In the darkness in front of them, more than 15,000 Turkish troops were massing for an offensive of their own. And when the time came, the Allies would need all the resilience they could muster.

8.

ANZAC: THE FIRST TEN DAYS

The Anzac landing had been an unmitigated disaster. By daylight on 26 April, when orders called for the Australians and New Zealanders to be basking in the morning sun on the heights of Maltepe, more than six kilometres from the landing beaches, the Anzacs were hemmed in on Second Ridge, within sight of where they had come ashore. Their line was paper thin, with scattered sections of a short trench barely connected to shallow scrapes and hastily dug pits to give some semblance of a coordinated defensive position. Many men didn't even have that and had spent a cold and sleepless night crouched in gullies and washaways, exchanging rifle shots in the inky darkness with a Turkish foe who was close enough to be heard talking. The Anzacs were exhausted and shaken, and their casualties had been catastrophic.

But in reality, the landing could have been so much worse. The original plan called for the Anzac forces to land mostly at Brighton Beach, the sweeping two-kilometre arch of sand immediately south of Anzac Cove. But as is well known, the landing forces missed their mark and ended up coming ashore in a tangled bunch at Anzac Cove, a result that, since the day of the landing, has been portrayed as a disastrous error that was pivotal in the failure of the campaign. The land behind Brighton Beach rises gently, virtually without impediment, all the way to the crucial high ground of Third Ridge. The land behind Anzac Cove is the opposite – it's steep and scrubby, with gullies and cliffs plunging directly into the sea above the claustrophobic beach. The suggestion has often been made that, had the Anzacs come ashore at Brighton Beach, they would have had a clear march to the high ground and victory, while at Anzac Cove the harsh terrain impeded them so much that they had no chance of securing the high ground before Turkish reinforcements arrived. But this assessment overlooks a fundamental factor – Turkish opposition. Recently uncovered Turkish documents reveal that Turkish commanders had debated where the inevitable landing was most likely to take place. There was some disagreement about the specifics but they all agreed on one thing – if the Allies chose to land on the western shore of the peninsula, they would land at Brighton Beach.

In response, the Turkish defences at Brighton Beach were substantial and intimidating. The beach was covered in thick belts of barbed wire, was much more heavily defended by infantry than Anzac Cove and, crucially, was completely covered by artillery batteries on Gaba Tepe, the huge promontory immediately to the south that overlooked the entire beach. As early as February 1915, the Turks had held fire-planning exercises to practise deluging Brighton Beach with artillery fire. Brighton Beach was such an imposing obstacle that some Anzac officers considered that landing there 'must have been nearly impossible', which even led to speculation that the decision to land at Anzac Cove wasn't as unintentional as has often been thought.[1] Had the Anzacs come ashore at Brighton Beach, they would have faced the same deadly ordeal as their British comrades at V and W beaches at Helles and likely would have been slaughtered on the sand. As it happened, they fortuitously landed at the most protected site on that entire sweep of coastline and got ashore with only a handful of casualties.

The Australians might indeed have been lucky to come ashore at Anzac Cove but by the afternoon of the landing it wouldn't have seemed like it. On the beach, all was chaos. The cramped bay was ludicrously small to serve as the base for an entire army corps, and without proper landing facilities, the job of unloading men, mules and supplies was gruelling. Heavily laden supply craft jostled for space in the surf with lighters loaded with infantry; support troops did their best to find space on the sand for the burgeoning piles of ammunition, food and supplies. Men shouted and cursed, and frightened mules whimpered and brayed, often kicking out in fear at any man foolish enough to wander too close.

To make matters worse, the beach was becoming crowded with wounded men, who were either carried in on stretchers or came limping down the rough valleys from the front lines. Within hours, there were too many wounded and nowhere near enough orderlies to treat them. Medical officers did everything they could for the most serious cases, but no amount of work would be adequate for the hundreds of men who needed attention. With no space for proper aid posts, the medical teams worked in the open on the cold and windy beach. The night of 25 April was an ordeal that few wounded men who were forced to endure it ever forgot. Lieutenant Colonel Percy Fenwick witnessed their suffering at a casualty clearing station on the southern end of the beach.

The beach here was not wider than a cricket pitch and was crowded with wounded, waiting to be evacuated by lighters. Colonel Howse and his officers were working hard, and we joined them. Although we had been told to conserve our water supply, our water-bottles were soon empty. It was impossible to turn a deaf ear to the cry of the badly wounded men for 'A drop of water, mate!' Every minute the numbers of wounded increased; newcomers staggering down the hillside, or being carried there by their mates. Shrapnel burst incessantly over us, but the cliff gave comparative shelter. Many of the wounded, however, were hit a second time as they lay on the beach and one fine Australian whom I was dressing received a bullet through his knee. He said angrily, 'I've been hit once you _____ Turks! Can't you leave a chap alone!'[2]

Throughout this pandemonium, boatloads of new men were arriving every hour. They were shocked by the chaos on the beach and the rows of groaning, writhing men on stretchers. The din from the front line was shockingly close. To the new arrivals, it seemed as if the fighting was taking place mere metres from the beach and that the Turks could break through and be on top of them at any minute. Their officers shouted orders and led them swiftly off the beach and to assembly points at the mouth of Shrapnel Gully. From there, they edged cautiously up the valley toward the maelstrom taking place in the front line on the clifftop just above their heads.

Lieutenant Colonel William Malone was ashore with his Wellingtons and his fastidious mind was struggling with the disorder all around him. He lay the blame for the failure of the landing squarely at the feet of the Australians.

The Australians had carried the heights surrounding the bay but instead of being content with that and then digging in hard and fast had scally wagged for miles, into the interior some three to four miles, got scattered and so became a prey to the Turks, who had been surprised in the first place and had (it is said) only some 500 defending troops at our landing place. Their troops encamped at Bijuk Anafarta and Kojader were brought against the scattered Australians and slaughtered them.[3]

Harry Kelly had landed just after daybreak with the Australian 7th Battalion and was soon in the midst of the confused fighting.

Our order was 'Remove your packs and go forward and give them Hell!' We went forward, but the Turks were retiring and being well hidden in the scrub, they were undoubtedly giving us the Hell that we were told to give them. We with rifles alone were fighting an enemy in the very best of concealed positions with rifles, machine guns and artillery of almost every description. Our men were falling very fast and the enemy snipers in some wonderfully concealed positions were doing some very deadly work.[4]

One of the men who came ashore in this overwhelmed second wave was Private Bill Buckingham, a cooper who had worked for the Carlton Brewery in Melbourne. He had enlisted a few months shy of his fortieth birthday and had left a wife and five kids behind. The oldest boy, Jack, was sixteen. The youngest, William, was one. It's uncertain why Bill felt the need to enlist – the maximum acceptable age in 1914 was thirty-eight, so it's unclear how he even got through the enlistment process. He had done nearly five years in the militia as a younger man so, like many men with military experience, he probably just felt it was his duty to fight. With his confident bearing, piercing eyes and bushy brown moustache, he cut an imposing figure, and became something of a father figure to the younger blokes in his platoon. He landed with B Company of the 6th Battalion and was rushed straight into the line.

Cecil Malthus had landed mid-afternoon and had a clifftop view of the chaos unfolding on the beach. After scaling a precipitous rise, his platoon:

> […] halted and had time to take stock of the situation. It was sufficiently grim. Steady streams of reinforcements were still arriving in boats and barges of every size and description, but those pushing off again were equally loaded with wounded. Even the most badly injured had to be tipped into the boats without their stretchers, which were indispensable ashore and anyhow could have taken the room of six men apiece in the crowded boats. Rows of other wounded were lined along the beach, dumped on a blanket or just on the bare earth or shingle. Those who could move were for the most part cheerfully giving way to more desperate cases, but inevitably there were some who rushed out into the shallows and insisted on clambering aboard the overloaded boats. They were accepted with contemptuous pity.[5]

Getting reinforcements ashore was a vital component of the landing plan. The Anzac commanders knew that the operation was a numbers game and that the only hope for success was to get as many men ashore as quickly as they could. Strict orders had been issued that landing fresh infantry was the absolute priority; wounded men were not to be evacuated in boats that had been designated for fighting men. But the medical officers, who had joined the army to save lives, couldn't stand idly by while men died on the beach all around them. The beachmaster soon took the law into his own hands and ordered that no boat was to leave the beach until it was fully loaded with wounded men. While well intentioned, this order had disastrous results. Transports, now laden with their battered and bleeding cargo, returned to whatever ship they had left from, regardless of whether it was equipped to supply medical care – and most weren't. Some sailors took pity on the wretched souls in the boats and hoisted them aboard, but many ships refused to take them. The wounded men spent indescribable hours crammed in the bottom of rocking transports that ferried from ship to ship in an effort to find one that would take them on board. In all likelihood, they would have suffered less if they had been left on the beach.*

Although the efforts to evacuate the wounded were laudable from a humane point of view, from a tactical standpoint, they were a disaster. Unloading the wounded onto ships was a laborious process and ate up crucial time that could have otherwise been used for landing desperately needed reinforcements. Boats that were intended to complete quick round trips from the transport ships to the beach did not reappear for hours, adding to the already serious delays in landing fresh troops. It was after midnight before the last battalion of the New Zealand Brigade came ashore and it was nearly midday on 26 April by the time the Australian 14th Battalion was finally landed. These wasted hours contributed significantly to the failure of the Anzacs to secure their early objectives.

One of the most important elements to securing the beachhead was also in the shortest supply – artillery. In the cramped confines of Anzac Cove, there was no space to land all the guns and Australian artillery crews were forced to watch helplessly from the ships as the chaos of the landing played out. One particularly astute observer was Sergeant Jim Parker of the 2nd Field Artillery, a thirty-year-old saddler from Richmond in Melbourne. The night after the landing, he and his comrades

---

*   In some cases, the landings were hampered by the enthusiasm of the naval troops who crewed the boats. In the excitement, some sailors rushed forward with the infantry and had to be ordered back to the beach to complete the vital work of landing reinforcements.

loaded their guns and equipment onto pontoons and began the slow and painfully exposed journey toward Anzac Cove.

> At 1 am were towed in by trawler and laid off the landing stage. Several bullets flying about from snipers in the hills facing the beach. It soon made everyone keep their heads down. A couple of our chaps went ashore in their boat for instructions and saw General Bridges. He said we were to return to [our ship]. Reached the ship and went on board again; our CO Major Mills being the only casualty, falling in pontoon and cutting nose and two black eyes.[6]

The aborted landing was an exercise in frustration and Parker was itching to get ashore and contribute to the battle he could see and hear raging on the ridges above the beach. To his great consternation, the ship sailed away from the Anzac sector toward Helles, where there was more room and a greater requirement for artillery.

Given the chaos unfolding all around them on the opening day, Anzac commanders became understandably jumpy. This led to one of the most frequently recounted, but often misunderstood, chapters of the early stages of the Anzac story. At 10 pm on 25 April, General William Birdwood, commander of the ANZAC Corps, came ashore and was promptly informed by his subordinate officers that their men were at the ends of their tethers. It was widely (and reasonably) expected that Turkish forces would launch a strong counter-attack the next day, and the consensus among the Anzac commanders was that there was no chance the line would hold. With the front line so close to the beach, any Turkish breakthrough would spell disaster, so he sent an urgent cable to Hamilton.

Hamilton had been asleep for an hour on his flagship, *Queen Elizabeth*, when he was roughly roused by his chief of staff. He rushed to his conference room, where he found an ashen-faced group of senior staff officers. Hamilton described the sombre scene in his diary:

> A cold hand clutched my heart as I scanned their faces. Carruthers gave me a message from Birdwood written in Godley's writing. I read it aloud:–
> *Both my Divisional Generals and Brigadiers have represented to me that they fear their men are thoroughly demoralised by shrapnel fire to which they have been subjected all day after exhaustion and gallant work in morning. Numbers have dribbled back from firing line and cannot be collected in this difficult country. Even New Zealand Brigade which has been only recently engaged lost heavily and is to some extent demoralised. If troops are subjected to shell fire again to-morrow morning there is likely to be a fiasco as I have no fresh troops with which to replace those in firing line. I know my representation is most serious but if we are to re-embark it must be at once.*

The message was startling, shocking. Up to this point, Birdwood had been reporting the Anzac landing had been going relatively well; now, he was predicting imminent disaster and suggesting an immediate evacuation.

Hamilton was exhausted and completely blindsided. But to his immense credit, he acted decisively and sensibly. After briefly quizzing his staff officers and receiving a consensus that an ill-prepared evacuation under the noses of the Turks would take several days and was likely to result in carnage, he replied to Birdwood stating that no evacuation would take place and that there was nothing for him to do but stick at it. His famous postscript, 'You have got through the difficult business. Now you only have to dig, dig, dig until you are safe,' has endured as one of the most oft-quoted lines associated with the entire Gallipoli campaign – it even spawned the (completely false) suggestion that this is how the term 'Digger' came to be applied to Australian troops. Hamilton's telegram had the desired effect – it bolstered the flagging morale of the Anzac forces, steadied wavering nerves and compellingly spelled out that they were at Anzac for the long haul.

What to make of Birdwood's suggestion that the Anzac sector should be evacuated on the first night? The obvious assumption is that there was a whiff of panic in the air at ANZAC Headquarters and that Birdwood had lost his nerve to carry the fight. But in reality, at least considering an evacuation was a sound military decision. Birdwood wasn't suggesting the Anzacs should pack up and return to Egypt. He was suggesting that, if the Anzac operation wasn't working as intended, his force would be better utilised on another battlefield on the peninsula. And, hypothetically, he was right. Had it been possible to evacuate the Anzac force quickly and with minimal losses, and to redeploy it in support of the British and French at Cape Helles, the sudden influx of such a large force against the already hard-pressed Turks would have proved decisive and the Gallipoli campaign could have been won by the Allies in the opening days. But, realistically, Hamilton made the correct call – the risk of evacuation was too great and, in spite of their meagre achievements up until that point, there was no practical alternative for the Anzacs but to carry on.

In the front line, all was blood and fire. Men fought with bayonets, shovels and fists for scraps of otherwise insignificant land. The Australians were shocked by the violence that had been unleashed on them.

During a brief lull in the onslaught, Harry Kelly ran into his good mate Jack Dixon from the training camp at Broadmeadows. The two men spoke briefly before Harry pushed forward.

Two minutes later, Jack was shot dead. Bert Rowland, who had enlisted with Harry eight months prior, hadn't been heard from all day (he was posted as missing and was eventually classified as killed in action, his body never found). But Harry did get the opportunity to even the score. As his platoon pulled back from an exposed forward position, he saw Turks on the ridge in front of him.

> During our retirement was my first chance of having shot at a good clear, living target but as the range was twelve hundred yards, the six shots that I fired at him were only enough to frighten him into running faster. After this my scoring went on fairly well as far as I could make out.[7]

He was soon back in the main Australian line.

> At last, after retiring for about a mile we arrived at the trenches which were being made for the firing line. Harold Nicholls ['Nick'] and myself picked up a discarded rifle and equipment of which there were hundreds lying about mixed up with hundreds of soldiers who had been killed earlier in the day.[8]

Soon after the new arrivals began to dig in, they were greeted with a terrific bombardment from the Turkish artillery. More men fell but the line held.

On the left of the line, Cecil Malthus and his fellow scouts from the Canterbury Battalion had not received orders after coming ashore so were digging in for a night in reserve. A sudden panicky message abruptly interrupted those plans, as Cecil and his mates were given vague instructions to 'reinforce the left flank'. Cecil and half a dozen scouts rushed back to the beach and began the arduous climb to the front line at

Walker's Ridge. All about them was chaos. The New Zealand troops who were supposed to accompany them never turned up, and scattered parties of Australians (some of them wounded, most not) were making a sharpish withdrawal to the beach. The brief words they shared with the New Zealanders as they passed in the darkness were vague and contradictory. Cecil and his group reached the firing line, where:

> A state of muddle and utter exhaustion existed everywhere and the defence (it was already defence, not attack) was terribly weak. Finally we were seized upon by a harassed Australian lieutenant who begged us to strengthen his handful at the top of the hill. And so, expecting our companies to arrive and reinforce the position, we stayed there and dug in. The whole night was spent improving our trench, while a cold, misty rain reduced us to cowering misery. Such was our inglorious share in the landing.[9]

In the soft morning half-light of 26 April, the Anzacs in the front line anxiously scanned no man's land, with eyes peeled and fingers on triggers, waiting for the Turkish onslaught they knew was coming. But then the sun rose – and no attack came. Turkish artillery continued to probe the front line with sporadic shrapnel shells, but the bombardment was no more ferocious than it had been on the first day. Johnny Turk, it appeared, was as worn out as they were.

Harry Kelly, his good mate Nick and a small group of other privates had spent the night rushing between different sections of the line to face enemy attacks, some real, some purely imaginary.

> That night there was a terrible cry of 'Reinforcements wanted on the right front,' and grabbing a pick and shovel

beside our rifle and equipment we set off as fast as we could to where they were calling for men, but it was only a false alarm for there was no attack. We were beginning to feel the effect of having no sleep yet but as an attack was expected there was no chance of getting any sleep that night. On our arrival here we had to lift a man, who had just been killed, out of the trench and it was a very ghastly sight for the top of his head had been blown away and his brains were scattered all over the trench.[10]

Cecil Malthus and his ragtag platoon of New Zealanders and Australians had had a quieter night in their sector of the front.

We got through the night without interference, though the Turks could have rushed in and overwhelmed us with the utmost ease. Probably their plight was as bad as our own.[11]

We now know from Turkish records that the Ottoman defenders were completely worn out. Sefik's men in particular were barely capable of holding their rifles; between the training manoeuvres on the night of 24 April and their vital role in repelling the Anzac landing the following day, his men had been awake for forty-eight hours. Kemal's men were faring little better and so the Turks contented themselves with spending 26 April resting and reorganising their men and pounding the Anzacs with artillery.

Although the shellfire was deadly, the Anzacs highly prized the ability to turn a blind eye to it, or at least pretend to. Private Reuben Hampton described his response to a heavy bombardment.

Afternoon was hotly bombarded by shrapnel. Shells sweeping over us continually. Whilst digging in we had eight men badly cut up. All manner of guns in action from the big boom of *Queen Lizzy* down to the pom poms. It is marvellous how we get used to these incoming shells. Under good cover one can laugh at them, and they in no way deter us from sleeping.[12]

The Turkish effort to contain the Anzac invasion had been incredibly successful but the cost had been enormous. More than half of the men who had joined the fight on the first day had been lost and casualties among officers and NCOs had been even higher – as many as three-quarters of the men who had led the defence on 25 April were now dead or wounded.

Ironically, the Turks were as apprehensive about an enemy attack as the Anzacs were. They did their best to strengthen their line with the limited reinforcements they had and to more effectively cover no man's land with machine guns and artillery. Kemal also released some troops from the front line to form a local reserve and ordered work parties to begin digging a second line of trenches about a kilometre behind the front line; this would give the Turks somewhere to fall back to if the Anzacs succeeded in breaking through. Kemal also garrisoned this line with cavalry detachments to catch any deserters trying to flee the battlefield. He was brutally determined to maintain discipline in his forces; a group of about two dozen men who had been charged with cowardice or disobedience on the day of the landing were court-martialled and executed in front of their regiments to set an example for other potential troublemakers.[13]

One element that swung the odds in the favour of the Anzacs on 26 April was naval gunfire. Having completed their role covering the landing, the ships of the fleet were now in position to provide supporting gunfire to the infantry and, as the sun crested the ridges of Anzac, the Royal Navy made good use of the clear morning to pummel the Turkish lines and rear area. Although the flat trajectory of the guns meant that men dug into trenches were mostly safe from the barrage, the sight and sound of the thunderous cannonade shattered the nerves of the demoralised Turkish troops holding the line. And while naval fire was relatively ineffective against well dug-in troops, it was devastating to men caught in the open. A large group of Turkish infantry was spotted coming over Battleship Hill (so named because of the pounding from naval gunfire it had already received), and every gun within range was turned on it. In minutes, dozens of Turks had literally been blown to pieces and the survivors scarpered for safety back over the hill. The shocking saga was plainly visible to Turks in other parts of the line and effectively marked an end to Turkish attempts to advance in daylight over ground that was in view of the supporting ships. As the guns of the Royal Navy continued their deadly search for targets, the Turkish batteries were mostly silenced. The Anzacs finally received some respite from the near-constant shelling.

Cecil Malthus was exhausted but relieved the Turks hadn't counter-attacked. As the day brightened, his small party of Australians and New Zealanders could see nothing of the enemy immediately in front of them but spotted small groups of Turks moving through the scrub on a slope about 300 metres away. Cecil got his first taste of killing and was appalled by it.

> We kept up an exchange of shots with them all the morning, and had the satisfaction of seeing several fall, while our casualties were nil. I hit one, and saw him tumbling and sliding down through the scrub. I was quite depressed by this and tried to put it out of my mind. I never mentioned it to anyone for weeks.[14]

Relieved that no attack would fall on them on 26 April, the Anzac commanders spent the day trying to reorganise their tangled units and to link up the isolated sections of trench to form a more robust front line.

Apart from the occasional sniper's bullet, the day was quiet and casualties would have been light, if not for a disastrous misunderstanding on 400 Plateau late in the day. This was a deadly piece of ground. An Australian sergeant who crossed it had to leap from pit to pit under a hail of fire. He arrived safely but discovered that a Turkish machine gun had put three bullets through his cap, one through his boot and one through his coat, and had ripped the bottom out of the bucket in his hand.

In an effort to shore up the line, a small detachment of Australians was ordered to move forward, but for reasons that remain unclear, the 4th Battalion interpreted this as a recommencement of the general advance it had long been anticipating. Without orders or any real understanding of what it was supposed to be doing, the bulk of the battalion climbed out of its trenches, turned half-left and began advancing along no man's land, with the Australian lines on its left and the Turkish lines on its right. At first, all was silent as the Turks struggled to make sense of the bizarre sight of men advancing in the open between the trench lines. But then a torrent of machine-gun and rifle fire came slicing down no man's land. Artillery joined in and, in short order, the 4th Battalion, the only whole and intact Australian battalion on the peninsula, was shattered. Men screamed as bullets found their mark; the survivors turned and raced for the trenches they had just left. By the time the dust settled, the battalion had been decimated. Among the dead was the battalion's commander, Lieutenant Colonel Astley Onslow Thompson. Private Sydney Powell was in the thick of this attack but the lack of clear orders and seemingly suicidal advance made for a surreal experience.

There was something very queer about that order. It was vague to the last degree. I'm not sure if the order was 'advance' or 'attack', but I'm pretty sure that no objective was mentioned. The colonel appeared not to understand it, but his hesitation was summarily cut short by the discovery the troops were leaving their trenches! Seemingly the men had received the order before it reached the colonel. We at once hopped out after them.[15]

Powell did his best to keep up with the advancing troops but struggled even to find them as they veered off toward the enemy trenches.

The air sang with bullets, and in running we crouched as low as we could, and lay on our bellies frequently. I had some strange fancies. The most persistent of them was that this was a field-day; that presently the 'Cease Fire' would sound, and we should march back to camp and the canteen.[16]

Powell was wounded in the head and arm. He limped gallantly back to the Australian lines with bullets bouncing off the ground and his equipment, and was evacuated from the peninsula. He never returned to the war.

By the morning of 27 April, the Anzac line had been strengthened but was still gravely insecure. A few reinforcements had trickled into the Australian positions overnight, though the bulk of the reinforcing had been done by the Turks. Bolstered by new troops, Mustafa Kemal ordered an all-out assault to drive the Anzacs into the sea. This attack was intended to by synchronised all along the Turkish front line, but the new reinforcements were exhausted from marching and the men already in the line were bone-weary from two days' fighting. Instead of a coordinated assault, the Turkish attack turned into a series of small local clashes, which were beaten back with heavy loss from machine guns and naval fire. Kemal ordered the assault to be resumed at night, when the attackers would be safe from the guns of the Royal Navy, and he threw in every man he had. Determined Turkish troops hurled themselves at the Anzac line and in several places broke in. But the fighting was confused and directionless in the dark – Anzac machine guns cut up hundreds of men as they crossed no man's land. As the sun began to rise, the Turks pulled back and daylight revealed a battlefield littered with corpses.

The Turkish assault had been a deadly and dismal failure. Not only were hundreds of lives squandered in uncoordinated and half-hearted assaults, the overall effort had been so ineffective that the Anzacs didn't even realise the sporadic clashes were part of a major attack. The ANZAC Corps war diary makes no mention of an enemy attack, instead describing some limited advances made by the Australians and summarising that the day was 'chiefly devoted to reorganization' and that 'casualties during the day were not excessive'.[17]

After three days of fighting, both sides were exhausted. 28 April was relatively quiet. The Turks had realised that the main Allied effort was taking place at Cape Helles and so the garrison at Anzac received few reinforcements. But it was still a formidable opponent – the eighteen Turkish battalions at Anzac comprised the bulk of the Turkish striking force on the peninsula, though this fact was not realised by Allied commanders until well into the campaign.

Rather than launching attacks, both friend and foe spent the fourth day of the campaign on reorganisation and consolidation. But Anzac was never safe – machine guns and artillery pieces started sweeping every corner of the sector with fire on the first morning and didn't stop for eight months.

The Anzacs were only moderately safe when they were secreted behind hills and deep in gullies. The men in the rear area suffered nearly as much from enemy fire as the troops in the front line. Even the beach was under constant bombardment, with Turkish observers north and south directing heavy artillery fire into the cramped cove day and night. But death came from strange quarters at Gallipoli. In the tight confines of the Anzac sector, where nerves were constantly on edge, accidents were bound to occur. Lieutenant Colonel George Braund, commander of the 2nd Battalion, was returning to the beach after inspecting his battalion's lines one night when he was challenged by a jumpy Australian sentry. Braund was partially deaf and didn't hear the challenge; the sentry shot him dead.

Even when the troops were relatively safe in their trenches, provisioning them while under Turkish observation and fire was at times close to impossible. One forward post of nineteen men clung on tenaciously without water for more than twenty-four hours. In desperation, two men volunteered to take water bottles and attempt the perilous journey back to the beach. Both were soon cut down by snipers. In a ghastly reminder of the fate that could befall any man at any time, one of the dead water carriers 'could be seen for days afterwards upon the skyline, still on his hands and knees, with the bottles slung round him'.[18]

In an effort to help secure the front line, Cecil Malthus and a handful of other scouts from the Canterbury Battalion were ordered to occupy a small hill on the extreme left flank of the Anzac trenches. They didn't know it but it was from this spot that a Turkish platoon had poured fire onto the Australians who had landed near Fisherman's Hut on the first morning. Cecil and his small group crept out to the hill in broad daylight, expecting to be shot by a sniper with every trepidatious crawl forward. Although a few bullets whistled past them, they got to the post without mishap and found a Turkish trench that was empty, except for hundreds of fired Turkish cartridges. Cecil had found the source of the murderous fire that had accounted for so many Australians on the morning of the landing. He and his comrades spent an anxious few hours occupying the position alone, longing for reinforcements and expecting the Turks to come charging at them at any moment. 'It was a ticklish job,' he later recalled, 'and during those hours of waiting our imagination played some weird tricks. We were near enough to blazing away at nothing.'[19] Eventually, New Zealand reinforcements turned up and the position was secured with little trouble. Later in the night, two of Cecil's mates, privates Tom McEvoy and Frank Bird, were scouting forward and lost their way in the dark. In confusion, they ended up firing at each other and McEvoy went down with a bullet in the spine. He lay there for the rest of the night in agony and, when he was finally evacuated in the morning, Cecil knew he was done for. A year later, Cecil heard that 'Mac' had recovered from his wounds and, when the New Zealand Army had rejected his attempts to re-enlist, had joined the Australian forces instead.*

Anzac casualties were mounting at a catastrophic and wholly unsustainable rate. By 28 April, every battalion had lost at least a quarter of its men and the casualties sustained on the ferocious day of the landing had already been nearly doubled. More than 4000 Australians and New Zealanders now lay dead or wounded. The survivors were half mad with exhaustion and from the constant strain of trying to stay alive.

---

* Although Cecil recalled that 'Mac was killed in France near the end of the war', in reality, Tom McEvoy survived his three years of service with the Australian 20th Battalion and returned to Australia in 1919.

Eyes were dull and glazed; some spoke heavily like drunken
men; others with unnatural vivacity ... The strain showed
in a hundred ways, though without a sign of demoralisation.
Men would not run from a shell, though they would turn
savagely and curse it as a dog snarls at his tormentors.[20]

The Anzacs were crying out for reinforcements and their
commanders knew it. In a somewhat desperate move, four
British battalions from the Royal Naval Division were sent to
Anzac to relieve some of the exhausted troops. The original
members of the division had been drawn from the proud and
mighty Royal Marines, so the Anzacs were understandably
relieved to hear that British troops with such a distinguished
pedigree would soon join them at Anzac. The reputation of
the RND was only enhanced by its battalions being named
after the great heroes of British naval history. But the first sight
of the fresh-faced volunteers of the RND in the early evening
light on 28 April brought some of the Anzacs pause. As they
stood awkwardly on the beach in their faded khaki uniforms
and oversized sun helmets, eyes wide at the drama unfolding
around them, they seemed 'strangely young and slender to
represent the old seasoned regular Marines'.[21] The RND, it
appeared, might not be all it was cracked up to be.

Cecil Malthus, a war-hardened veteran after four days on the
peninsula, got a good look at the pink-faced recruits and was
not impressed.

We regarded them with the slightly patronising pity that we
generally felt for the young and inexperienced troops of the
New Army. These seemed to us a fair cross-section, ignorant
and bewildered, with nothing wrong that experience would
not cure, but strangely immature compared with the hard-
bitten, cursing Australians; brave enough normally but

liable to panic, and in such wild surroundings quite out of their element.[22]

After four full days of fighting, with little sleep, the Anzacs presented a fearsome sight to the newcomers. 'Bearded, ragged at knees and elbows, their putties often left in the scrub, dull-eyed, many with blood on cheeks and clothes, and with a dirty field-dressing round arm or wrist, they were far fiercer than Turks to look upon.'[23] Within short order, the Royal Naval men understood why, as they were drawn into the mincing machine that Anzac had quickly become.

The RND battalions were plunged immediately into the firing line, providing blessed relief to Anzac units who had been fighting non-stop for four days. This timely arrival shored up the Anzac line and helped to prevent a disastrous collapse during the first week.

But the RND troops were jumpy and dangerously inexperienced. A day after they arrived, Lieutenant Colonel Walter McNicoll, commander of the Australian 6th Battalion, was handing over a section of trench to his counterpart in the Deal Battalion of the RND, Lieutenant Colonel Richard Bendyshe. Like most of the Australians, McNicoll was unkempt and unshaven. A nervy RND sentry mistook him for a Turk and fired his rifle – the bullet missed McNicoll but killed Bendyshe, the man's own commanding officer. At the sound of the shot, pandemonium broke out and the RND men started firing in all directions, killing one of their sergeants and wounding two other men. McNicoll was wounded fending off bayonet thrusts. Eventually, he was overcome, the marines bound and blindfolded him as a spy and then began marching their prisoner to the beach. 'The first man this party met,' a witness recalled, 'was the 6th Battalion's Adjutant, whose language when he recognised his commanding officer maintained the highest traditions of the A.I.F.'[24] McNicoll spent a couple of days in the field hospital, where Birdwood visited him to congratulate him on his escape from the British.*

In the closing days of April, the Turks were digging hard. By the end of the month, the Anzacs were surrounded by a tangled web of Turkish trenches. Day after day, as the Anzacs continued to absorb the debilitating pressure of an enemy right on top of them, their gaze shifted south, to where they longed to see the promised advance of British troops onto Achi Baba. Little did they realise that the British were more than twenty kilometres away, hemmed in as severely as the Anzacs were and exhausted after their own catastrophes since the landing.

After a week of brutal, close-quarter fighting, the Anzac front line stabilised and would barely move for the next three months. Both sides were intent on crossing no man's land and driving their enemy back but intentions were no match for bullets. Every inch of no man's land faced the muzzles of a nefarious network of well-sited machine guns. The issue for attacking troops wasn't so much the enemy in the trenches directly in front of them – the real problem was the machine guns, which were positioned to fire in enfilade along no man's land. As both sides discovered to their cost during a succession of fruitless assaults, any attack across that narrow strip of land drew a storm of fire from both flanks. For the time being, both the Turks and the Anzacs were going nowhere.

---

* It wasn't all misadventure for the RND men. On the night of 30 April, Lance Corporal Walter Parker of the Royal Marine Light Infantry won the first Victoria Cross at Anzac for crossing 350 metres of bullet-swept ground to reinforce a trench and tend to wounded comrades. The next day, he helped evacuate the wounded, even though he had been shot himself.

Lieutenant Colonel William Malone received an unintended and decidedly deadly piece of grooming, courtesy of a Turkish sniper, on 29 April.

> Last night I had a close call. I was reconnoitring with General Walker and the snipers were trying to get us. At last a bullet just cut my hair on the back of my neck, and goodness knows it is short enough. Still it wanted cutting! So this morning I got one of my orderlies to finish the job.[25]

Since the day of the landing, Sergeant George Greig had been separated from his comrades in the 7th Battalion. He had been fighting in the front lines alongside any Australian or New Zealand troops who needed him, until he was finally able to head back to the beach and search for his battalion. When he found it, he received an unexpectedly warm welcome.

> What a reception I got, being previously reported killed in action. When I enquired I found only three of us sergeants were left out of 13, the others being killed or wounded. We collected spare equipment and rifles and turned in. I had my first night's rest for five nights and days.[26]

The biggest thorn in the side of the Anzacs was Baby 700, a squat hill wedged into the head of Monash Valley like a cork in a bottle. It overlooked the entire upper reaches of the valley and even into the rear of some sectors of the Anzac line. While it was in Turkish hands, the most important route to the Anzac front line was under constant observation and fire. Baby 700's forward slopes were too exposed for the Turks to entrench but the hill offered their snipers an unparalleled firing platform – hundreds of Anzacs were shot down during the first weeks of the campaign. Two of their most famous victims fell on the same day. Brigadier General William Bridges, commander of the AIF, would be hit on 15 May and die on a hospital ship a few days later. Private John Simpson Kirkpatrick, the 'man with the donkey', would be shot and killed the same day.

While Baby 700 was in Turkish hands, the Anzac line was never really secure and its capture became the highest priority in the sector. In the closing days of April, fire from Turkish artillery batteries noticeably slackened. The more optimistic commanders at Anzac leapt to the conclusion that the bulk of the Turkish force had been withdrawn to reinforce its beleaguered comrades at Cape Helles. The truth was much more straightforward and much more deadly – the gunners had reduced their rate of fire simply because they were low on shells. The Turkish trenches were as strongly held as ever.

In light of this appalling miscalculation, the opportunity seemed ripe for an advance against Baby 700. On 2 May, the New Zealand and Australian Division was tasked with the assault. Having witnessed the carnage caused by unsupported daylight advances, the planners called for the attack to take place just as night fell and, for the first time at Anzac, to be supported by a preliminary artillery barrage. At 6.30 pm, the evening air was torn by a torrent of shells from ship and shore – eight ships and five land batteries opened fire simultaneously; it was by far the heaviest bombardment the Anzacs had ever seen. Baby 700 disappeared under a storm of smoke and fire.

Private James Bayne and his mates in the Wellington Battalion provided covering fire to the assaulting troops.

Just before sunset the warships heavily bombarded the ridge that the Turks were entrenched on and as the Turks hopped out of the trenches our machine guns fired on them. When it was dark and the troops were ready to advance we all set up a loud cheering and general noise to make the Turks think there was a lot more of us than reality. The roar of guns and the ceaseless crack of thousands of rifles were so deafening that we couldn't hear the next man to us speak.[27]

At 7.15 pm, the Anzacs surged across no man's land and one of the bloodiest encounters of the Gallipoli campaign began. For the entire night, control of the hill seesawed between the Anzacs and the Turks. As each side gained a new position, the other would counter-attack – the fighting was incessant and bloody in such a confined space. The range was often too short for shooting, so bayonets, grenades and fists were put to deadly use. Corpses littered the shattered trenches and it was difficult to tell friend from foe in the darkness.

Anzac reinforcements who were rushed into the fray lost their way in the tangle of gullies. As the sun rose, fire from Turkish machine guns on the flanks tore into the Anzacs in their newly won positions. Without support they were hopelessly exposed, and the survivors began to withdraw to their old lines. The trickle became a stream when an Australian artillery battery misjudged the range and dropped its shells squarely on the Australian positions. By the afternoon of 3 May, Baby 700 had been abandoned and not a single inch of Turkish ground had been taken. More than a thousand Anzacs had been killed or wounded in less than twenty-four hours of fighting. In spite of several more costly attempts, Baby 700 would never be captured for the entire campaign.

Malone, never one to shy away from an opinion, had watched the New Zealanders attacking and didn't like what he saw.

In my opinion the plan was no good and doomed from the start. They tried to go in where the Turks had been attacked for days. They should have gone in from our left, ie almost other end of Turks. My remaining corporal of machine guns

Copeland was killed. I was within nine feet of him. I had just recommended him for a commission and he deserved it. Poor lad shot through the heart. Not a sound. Another gunner was wounded.[28]

At the same time as the Anzacs were bleeding on Baby 700, small parties of both Australians and New Zealanders were carrying out some of the most daring raids of the campaign. Anzac Cove had been under constant observation since the opening minutes of the landing, from Turkish posts north at Suvla Bay and south at Gaba Tepe promontory. If the Anzacs could destroy the posts, they would hopefully receive some respite from the near-constant barrage that fell on the beach.

On 2 May, fifty men of the Canterbury Battalion were despatched on a destroyer on the harrowing journey northward to Suvla Bay. The raiders landed at the foot of a small hill known as Lala Baba and scaled it quickly as the sun was rising. At the top, they came across a trench full of sleeping Turks. The New Zealanders opened fire, killing several and capturing twelve others. They searched the area, destroyed a telephone line and were back on their ship and returning to Anzac in short order, without having lost a single man.

South of the Anzac sector, an Australian raid on Gaba Tepe was not so lucky. One hundred men from the 11th Battalion, commanded by Captain Ray Leane, embarked before dawn on 4 May and landed just north of the promontory. In a mini re-creation of the landing on 25 April, the party rowed ashore in boats and, at first, the beach was ominously quiet. But as soon as the boats got within thirty metres of the shore, all hell broke loose from machine guns and rifles in trenches that overlooked the beach. A dozen men were hit before the boats reached the sand; the survivors charged up the beach and took cover beneath a sandy cliff. Supporting warships opened fire on the Turkish positions but it was clear to Leane that his mission was hopeless. His focus shifted to getting his men out of there alive. The plan had called for his party to return to Anzac Cove along the beach but there was no hope of carrying the wounded out under the storm of Turkish fire. In desperation, Leane signalled to the ships to send boats in to evacuate the wounded and – unbelievably – the navy responded. Two boats dashed toward the shore and immediately came under a deadly barrage from the Turkish trenches. But in one of the greatest displays of humanity during the entire campaign, as soon as the Turks saw Leane's stretcher-bearers carrying the wounded toward the boats, they stopped firing, allowing the wounded to be taken off unhindered.

The rest of Leane's party would not get off so lightly, however. More boats were sent to evacuate the remainder of the raiders and only the covering fire from the ships prevented a massacre as Leane's men tumbled into the boats in the shallows, and then made the hazardous return journey to the ships under heavy fire. The final extraordinary footnote to the raid occurred just as the ships were preparing to steam back to Anzac. Two Australians had been left behind and could be seen furiously signalling from the beach. Three sailors braved the fury of the Turkish fire to row ashore in a dinghy and rescue them, returning to the ship with frayed nerves but no injuries.

In the face of almost certain catastrophe, Leane's raid had gotten off relatively lightly. Only six men had been killed and eighteen wounded. But the aborted raid demonstrated that Gaba Tepe was a nut too tough to crack. It was never attacked again by the Anzacs for the rest of the campaign. From its heights, the Turks were free to gaze into the backs of the Australian and New Zealand base on Anzac Cove and lob shells on it without interruption.

Life for the men in the trenches settled into a dangerous routine of fighting and labouring. Efforts to improve the tenuous position of their trenches and to discover what the enemy was up to were constant. Private Sam Norris of the 6th Battalion was part of a raiding party that embarked on a risky mission on 3 May.

> On the 3rd May eight of us crawled out in the front of our line and cleared some scrub that obstructed the line of fire. Under a bush we found a dead German officer. Then we explored part of a Turkish trench 20 yards away from ours but found it occupied only by some very dead men. Whilst creeping towards this trench our leading man motioned for us to stop. This we did thinking that he had heard something. However, his reason was so that he could throw a finger at us which he had just found. Finally we put many of the dead that were lying about into the trench and commenced to cover them with earth.[29]

Cecil Malthus and his hardy group of scouts were also busy during this time. In some of the most under-reported acts of heroics of the early days of the campaign, Cecil personally led several small patrols to secure outposts on the left of the Anzac position. It was dangerous work and a few of Cecil's mates were killed during the outings. This tangle of rough country north of the Anzac lines would be the scene of desperate fighting during the August Offensive but, in early May, it was simply a lightly contested outpost of the main line. When an officer asked Cecil if the country was any good for a future advance, his reply was succinct: 'Good rabbit country, but most of it standing on edge.'[30] Cecil certainly covered plenty of that rabbit country – he estimated his furthest patrol ended on the slopes of Green Hill. That's nearly five kilometres into enemy territory from the extreme left flank of the Anzac position, ground that is considered firmly in the Suvla Bay sector of Gallipoli.

And so ended the first ten days of the heroic yet ultimately futile saga of Anzac. Rather than cutting the peninsula in half with a swift advance, the Anzacs had established the barest of toeholds. They had captured just a scrap of Turkish territory and held a perimeter that was barely two kilometres in length. It was less than a kilometre from the trenches to the beach, and that beach was completely exposed to both the weather and the hostile gaze of the Turkish defenders. The whole sector was constantly deluged with bullet and shell. And yet the Anzacs were hanging on, when all the odds suggested they couldn't. The British official history sums up this astonishing achievement with stirring words:

> That the Australian and New Zealand troops never relinquished their grasp; that they made this apparently hopeless position impregnable; that after waiting three months for reinforcements they attacked, and attacked again, and very nearly won, is a story that will live for ever.[31]

9.

THE TURKISH RESPONSE

Down at Helles, the Turkish troops scraping new trench lines into the hard earth in front of Krithia were tired but not disillusioned. Their comrades near the coast had, through sheer guile and guts, held back an Allied force that to rights should have rolled over them. And now that the Turks knew where the Allies were, and where they intended to go, there was a steely determination to their efforts that had been absent only a few days before. They dug short sections of trench, strung barbed wire and cleaned rifles and machine guns. There was nothing like a consolidated line but at least the Turks were in touch with each other and had a somewhat defensible position in front of the village. And with every hour that passed, fresh reinforcements streamed into the line, bolstering both the numbers and the confidence of the defenders.

The rapid surge in troop numbers wasn't happening by accident – having so successfully stalled the Allied advance near the beaches, Turkish commanders were smelling blood and anxious to turn defence into attack before the Allies could recover. On 30 April, General Otto Liman von Sanders, the German commander of the Turkish Fifth Army, received an order from Enver Pasha, Minister of War and de facto Commander-in-Chief of the Turkish Army, to 'drive the defenders into the sea'.[1] Apart from stating the obvious – that was exactly what von Sanders had been attempting to do since the first British boot touched Turkish sand – the instruction was a hollow one. Ironically, by restricting the Allied advance so effectively near the beaches, the Turkish defenders were still plagued by the guns of the Royal Navy, the only distinct advantage the Allies possessed. In daylight hours, any Turkish unit that tried to move received a torrent of naval shells for its troubles. 'The British fleet was sweeping the southern end of the peninsula from three sides,' von Sanders recalled, 'and the Turks had only field guns to oppose this fire.'[2]

The naval fire was more show than substance – the flat trajectory from the ships' guns was not particularly effective at finding Turks burrowed in gullies and ravines – but the effect on men's nerves was debilitating. A German officer, hurriedly sent south to Helles to help bolster the Turkish command, was shocked by the sight of the British warships.

> The closer I approached the battlefield the more powerful was the impression on eye and ear. I recognised the continuous flashes from the fleet which lay in a half circle round the peninsula and bombarded the land with a ceaseless fire, giving an impression of power and might which I can scarcely describe. A frightful thunderstorm which broke with elemental force and with never-ceasing thunder and lightning against the forces concentrated on that small portion of the peninsula. If the English ever give the figures for the ammunition consumed on one of those nights, one will easily be able to reckon how many pounds weight of steel fell per square yard of earth. Even later, in August 1917, in the battles of Flanders, I did not have the same

overwhelming impression of concentrated shelling as during this. Although in Flanders the effect of the individual shell was much more destructive ... the total moral effect was in this case much greater.[3]

If the Turks were going to have any hope of counter-attacking, it had to be done at night, when the ships of the Royal Navy would be blind. They set to the task immediately. By the evening of 30 April, the Turkish garrison had swelled to twenty-one battalions – they had doubled their numbers in less than two days. And although footsore from long marches, the new troops had not yet seen combat and were keen to get to grips with their enemy. Orders for an immediate counter-attack did not mince words, enthusiastically stirring the religious fervour of the Turkish troops to annihilate the infidel invader:

> Soldiers! You must drive the enemy ... into the sea. The enemy is afraid of you; he dare not come out of his trenches and attack you. He can do nothing more than wait for you with his guns and machine guns. You are not afraid of his fire. You must believe that the greatest happiness awaits him who gives up his life in this Holy War. Attack the enemy with the bayonet and utterly destroy him! We shall not retire one step; for if we do our religion, our country, and our nation will perish.[4]

The exhortation to use the bayonet wasn't hyperbole; the attacking troops were ordered to charge with bayonets fixed and rifles unloaded. Their commanders didn't just want a rout – they wanted a bloody, man-by-man massacre. The Turks were so confident of smashing through the Allied lines, and so determined that every British and French soldier would die where he stood, special parties were issued with firebombs to burn Allied boats on the beach.

The orders may have been stirring but a follow-up instruction suggests the German commanders were not confident in the abilities of the Turkish troops to carry them out.

> Let it be clearly understood that those who remain stationary at the moment of attack, or who try to escape, will be shot. For this purpose machine guns will be placed behind the troops to oblige such people to advance and at the same time to fire on the enemy's reserves.[5]

The Turkish force had been strengthened by the timely arrival of a group of thirty-two German marines and their six machine guns, which had been urgently despatched from the cruiser *Breslau* in the Sea of Marmara. A combination of the unfamiliarity of German uniforms and Turkish cluelessness resulted in farce and near disaster when a Turkish patrol apprehended the Germans as English spies, roughed them up and proudly reported the capture of six enemy machine guns to their superiors. The urgent intervention of a Turkish officer, with shouts and kicks, saved the Germans from incarceration and possible execution, and allowed them to join the Turkish attack in time.

At 10 pm on the night of 1 May, the crisp and still night air was shattered by a barrage from fifty-six Turkish field guns, a relatively small complement but still more than twice as many as the Allies had brought to bear in their advance a few days before. Calling on spiritual fortification of frail flesh and blood, the Turks surged from their trenches with wild shrieks of 'Allah!' and charged across the gorse-studded no man's land. This was war at its least sophisticated. The Turkish plan was simply to throw themselves at the Allies and drive them into the sea.

The fury of the attack momentarily caught the Allies off guard, and on the British right, a Turkish assault column smashed into the front line and set the defenders to flight. The exuberant Turks poured through the gap but soon found themselves cut off in the British lines. A swift counter-attack from British reserves overwhelmed them and most of the Turks died where they stood. The assault was less successful against other parts of the British line. The Turks had a lot of ground to cover and their massed formations made easy targets for British rifles and machine guns. As flares arced into the dark sky, the flickering forms of the attackers clearly stood out in British gunsights and men fell in their hundreds. British soldiers, who up to this point had been on the receiving end of Turkish fire, were delighted to see the tables turned and enthusiastically settled the score with bullet and bayonet.

Sergeant Denis Moriarty, of the Royal Munster Fusiliers, recalled the frantic night in his diary:

About 5 p.m. enemy started a heavy shrapnel fire on our trenches … 9 p.m. they started an attack, I am sure I will never forget that night as long as I live. They crept right up to our trenches (they were in thousands) and they made the night hideous with yells and shouting Allah! Allah! We could not help mowing them down … My God, what a sight met us when day broke this morning. The whole ground in front was littered with dead Turks.[6]

On the right of the Allied line, the poor old French were once again copping the heaviest Turkish attention. The Turks launched their strongest attacks in the tangled gullies around Kereves Dere; for several hours, the French line was in danger of breaking. 'The Turks were determined to drive us out of our positions at all costs,' a French officer later wrote in his diary.

'Three times they were successful in breaking through our wire and forcing their way into our trenches, where they were received with the butts of our rifles.'[7]

A desperate French call for reinforcements saw the Howe and Anson battalions of the Royal Naval Division pressed into action and it was only their timely arrival that prevented a catastrophe in the French lines. As dawn broke, the Turks retreated, leaving the battlefield strewn with dead and wounded. The perils of lingering in the open by daylight had been made abundantly and violently clear to them. 'As soon as the light was sufficient to allow the ships to shoot at the Turkish line,' an officer reported, 'an attempt to stay forward was equivalent to suicide.'[8]

As the sun rose, a small party of Turks launched a half-hearted attack against the French lines but they were swiftly shot down and the French rushed forward to occupy the ground. Buoyed by their example, British commanders at Gully Ravine ordered a local counter-attack; British troops swiftly overcame an advanced Turkish trench and captured 123 shellshocked prisoners. Giddy with these limited successes, Allied commanders determined the time was ripe for a general advance across the line; the British and French troops scrambled out of their trenches and across a no man's land that was quickly becoming littered with corpses from both sides. But the advance was poorly coordinated and the supporting artillery had not been adequately briefed about the plans. Joe Murray was in the thick of the action alongside French troops on the right of the line:

At 10 o'clock on this beautiful Sunday morning, whilst the wild birds were singing merrily, we fixed bayonets and marched up the gully to attack, but the Turkish firing squad was waiting. We thought that, after the punishment we had given them during the night, they had moved out – but we were wrong. Machine-gun fire and shrapnel fire soon made us spread out as we continued to advance in short rushes for about four hundred yards. The machine-gun fire made further advance out of the question and we were ordered to dig in to obtain some shelter from the withering fire.[9]

Small groups of men managed to advance and a handful of Turkish prisoners were taken, but each time a British or French unit gained ground, it was cut down by deadly crossfire from invisible machine guns. By 11 am, the whole Allied force was back in its original trenches.

It had been a bloody night and day, for no appreciable gain for either side. The Turks had lost more than 6000 men in their brave but futile advance. Between defending their own line and the ill-conceived daylight counter-attack, the Allies had lost nearly 3000. Such was the ledger of death at Gallipoli – more than 9000 men had been killed or wounded in a single day and the front lines remained completely unchanged.

Both sides spent 2 May licking their wounds and desperately trying to sort out the disorganised rabble of mixed-up units in their front lines. By the next morning, yet another batch of fresh reinforcements had marched into the Turkish lines – their commanders were loath to miss an opportunity to press the attack.* Just before midnight on 3 May, Turkish artillery opened again and the cries of 'Allah!' pierced the night air. A frothing mass of men surged forward and broke into the French lines. Some Turks fought straight through the trenchlines and began advancing toward Morto Bay, but Allied fire had cut the telephone lines connecting them to their headquarters – there was no way of informing their commanders of their success.

---

* By this stage of the campaign, 'fresh' was a decidedly relative term. The Turkish 15th Division arrived at Helles exhausted after a thirty-kilometre march yet was thrust into immediate action.

The attacking troops found themselves cut off and unsupported behind enemy lines. They were swiftly crushed and the survivors retreated. A French artillery lieutenant in the former rear area found himself fighting for his life alongside his fellow gunners:

> Fanatical Turks, good brave soldiers, were killed without mercy by our bayonets in the hand-to-hand struggle. In the course of the night they broke through almost to the Cypress trees not far from our village. We could hear their shouts, their joyful cries in the certain belief that they were close to victory. We retreated, forced back by their savage efforts and faced, above all, by their heavy sacrifice of human lives … The night passed in agonised anxiety as to the likely outcome of a hand-to-hand fight in which the fate of every life was in doubt. The dawn came at last, lighting up a scene of carnage; and the Turks retired to their trenches accompanied by salvos of 75mm shells. We have held the line but the dead and the wounded are legion.[10]

Morning found the battlefield littered with another 4000 Turkish casualties – 40 per cent of the attacking force had been wiped out in ten hours of fighting.

The Turkish counter-attack, over two nights, had been a colossal failure and had cost the Turks over 10,000 troops for no gain. The night attacks of 1 and 3 May demonstrated that the Turks were facing exactly the same problems as the Allies. Even with fresh reinforcements, coordinating a successful attack in the tangled ground of Helles was proving impossible. The Turks made things harder on themselves by inadequate planning and poor communication (there were no telephone lines between the divisions and language difficulties between German and Turkish officers were a constant source of frustration) but, by sunrise on 4 May, it was obvious that they had no chance of driving the Allies into the sea. In the cramped confines of the Gallipoli peninsula, the type of bloody stalemate that would have been instantly and disturbingly recognisable to any veteran of the Western Front was inevitable.

The attacks and counter-attacks had resulted in a debilitating mixing of units in the front lines and both sides spent the next two days desperately attempting to untangle the mess. In the midst of the reorganisation, Field Marshal von Sanders was astounded by the arrival of a telegram from his Turkish superiors announcing that the Gallipoli campaign had been deemed the most important military and political operation confronting the Ottoman Empire and that he was therefore to keep pressing the attack before the Allies had a chance to dig in. Ironically, on the other side of the line, Sir Ian Hamilton was receiving identical instructions from his superiors in Whitehall. Luckily for von Sanders, it was Hamilton who would act first.

10.
RESUMING THE ADVANCE

After ten days of fighting at Gallipoli, the campaign was beginning to be defined by what the Allies lacked, rather than what they had. They lacked information – how many enemy troops they faced, what they were armed with and, most importantly, where exactly they were. They lacked men – Whitehall had made it clear from the earliest days that Gallipoli was to be a limited military operation. After the appalling casualties of the opening days, there was little clue where reinforcements could be sourced to replace them. They lacked ideas – the claustrophobic battlefield on the peninsula gave Allied commanders little opportunity to try anything innovative. Slogging forward seemed the only viable option. But most of all, they lacked the most fundamental requirement of any army – ammunition.

By the end of 1914, the First World War had become an artillery war. The early battles had clearly demonstrated that advancing infantry could get nowhere near trench systems that bristled with machine guns and repeating rifles – unless the trenches were first smashed by artillery fire.

But in 1915, Britain was struggling with a problem that pre-war planners had never imagined – modern, quick-firing artillery guns consumed shells faster than factories could produce them. The huge scale of the battles unfolding on the Western Front quickly demonstrated that this new type of warfare would consume shells at a rate previously thought impossible, and Britain was soon running out of shells.

The situation was bad enough in France. In Gallipoli, it was farcical. Despite constant and urgent requests for more artillery ammunition to be shipped to them, commanders at Gallipoli received only a fraction of the stocks that were being sent to France. The Gallipoli campaign was just over a week old and already gunners were being ordered to ration the number of shells they fired each day.

When examined in detail, the numbers make for disturbing reading. The Battle of Aubers Ridge was launched in France the same week as the Second Battle of Krithia. At Aubers Ridge, the 30,000 attacking troops were supported by 500 guns that chewed through nearly 80,000 shells in the forty-minute opening barrage. Even with that level of firepower, the attack was a disaster – the artillery was unable to subdue the German defenders and more than 11,000 British troops were killed or wounded without gaining an inch of ground. This appalling loss of life was decried in British newspapers, blame squarely laid on the shoulders of a War Department that was accused of failing to adequately supply its army with artillery shells. The 'shell crisis' eventually felled the government – the Liberal Party was forced to form a coalition with the Conservatives on 25 May to hold on to power.

If Fleet Street was driven to apoplexy by the situation in France, it was a good thing it didn't have the full picture of what was unfolding at Gallipoli. As Lieutenant General Hamilton planned the next stage of his dogged advance, which he hoped would eventually bring him to Constantinople and glory, artillery support was the thorn in his side. This was understandable – he effectively had no shells.

At the beginning of May, the entire supply of British artillery ammunition at Gallipoli was a paltry 49,800 shells[1], an amount that the guns would have chewed through in twenty minutes at Aubers Ridge. Worse still, these were nearly all shrapnel shells, which burst in the air and sprayed a cloud of metal balls toward the ground – a deadly effective weapon against men in the open but practically useless for destroying trenches. And even those pitiful numbers were not fully available for Hamilton to use in an attack – 10,000 shells needed to be held in reserve for use in emergencies.

Even the British trump card, the one they placed their faith in to bring them victory in the campaign – the warships of the Royal Navy – was causing Hamilton headaches. Naval commanders still clung to the fanciful dream of eventually steaming into Constantinople and bombarding the Turks out of the war, so they were reluctant to part with ammunition that would be needed for that epic future battle. Hamilton was told the navy could spare fewer than 2000 heavy rounds to support the entire Cape Helles operation, an amount so negligible it barely rated including. Even when the ships did fire, they found it so difficult to spot shore targets from the sea that their fire was essentially at random. Hamilton was in a bind.

He did, however, have one major advantage over his better-ammunitioned comrades in France. At Gallipoli, the British were not facing strong, fixed trenchlines. In only ten days of fighting, the Turks at Gallipoli had not had time to construct anything resembling a cohesive line and were staging their spirited defence from mostly improvised positions – short sections of unconnected trench, ditches, and the natural defensive features that abounded at Helles such as gullies and dry riverbeds. Unlike the trenches in France, almost none of these strongpoints were protected by barbed wire. If the Allies could get close enough to the Turks, they stood a good chance of breaking through.

But here was the rub – improvised positions were harder for the Turks to defend than a strong trench system but much easier to hide. Any attack on them was going to struggle unless each defensive position could be identified and accurately plotted on a map. Until the British knew exactly where the Turks were, all the shells in the Empire weren't going to help them – their guns would have nothing to shoot at.

Unlike the Turks, the Allies had no high ground from which to observe the build-up and deployment of enemy forces. For the entire Gallipoli campaign, the Allies were looking uphill. This meant that attacking troops were forced to 'advance to contact', a deceptively innocuous term to describe the terrifying proposition of advancing in the open until the enemy opened fire. In the early days at Helles, every Allied attack was on the receiving end of an ambush.[*]

But were Allied commanders as blind as this situation would indicate? In reality, they had a lethal asset at their disposal, one that they spectacularly under-utilised during the battles at Cape Helles – airpower.

From well before the landing, the Allies had a small but exceedingly useful air fleet stationed at Gallipoli. This included a Royal Naval Air Service base on the island of Tenedos that could have its BE2 or Nieuport 10 aircraft over the front lines in just twenty minutes. (Interestingly, two of the observers who

---

[*] This stage of the campaign was also defined by the surreal circumstance that the Allies held the upper hand during the day, when Turkish movements were hampered by the guns of the Royal Navy. But the Turks held the upper hand at night, when they were free to reinforce and strengthen their positions without interference. Control of the battlefield effectively shifted between the two sides every twelve hours.

flew with the British pilots were Australian: Major Charles Miles and Captain Arthur Jopp.) Seaplanes launched from ships or hastily improvised harbour ports played a valuable role in observation and enemy suppression, and even dropped the occasional bomb. Aircraft also joined the propaganda war, dropping stirringly composed (yet hugely ineffective) leaflets over enemy positions that promised warm beds and ample rations to any soldier who surrendered.

Probably the most intimidating air asset available to the Allies was an observation balloon that could ascend to heights of over 1000 metres while tethered via winch to the deck of the balloon ship *Manica*. The courageous daredevils who clambered into the baskets of the observation balloon had to contend with wind, weather and the ever-present threat of enemy aircraft – their exploits in the skies over Gallipoli were some of the most electrifying of the campaign. On one occasion, they spotted a Turkish steamer unloading supplies in the port town of Maidos, on the opposite side of the peninsula. With the use of binoculars and a field telephone, they brought its attention to the mighty warship *Queen Elizabeth*, which responded by firing one of its 15-inch guns and lobbing car-sized shells across the peninsula and into the waters of the Dardanelles from a range of over fifteen kilometres. The first shot burst dramatically but harmlessly in the water 100 metres behind the ship. After correcting the range, the balloon observers watched the second shot land short and demolish a shed beside the dock. Having successfully bracketed the ship, the observers called in another minor adjustment and the third shot landed dead on. The steamer disappeared in a shower of twisted steel and charred wood.[2] It was such a spectacular demonstration of the potentially deadly relationship between aircraft and heavy guns that General Birdwood trumpeted the news to his beleaguered Anzac garrison in a Special Order the next day.

The French also established a base at Tenedos but it came into action too late to provide assistance during the Second Battle of Krithia. The life of a pilot in a flimsy cloth-and-timber aircraft on a battlefield was fraught with danger, as Sergeant Henri Dumas attested in a letter home.

> I have just installed a camera on my new biplane. I say 'my new biplane' because the Turks destroyed my old machine five days ago when I was landing at Cape Helles. Two shells fell right on the machine. A few stones and clods of earth in the face, that was my lot, but the machine was mincemeat.[3]

Dumas might have been fortunate on this occasion, but his luck ran out on 25 August when his aircraft was caught in a squall while returning to Tenedos and crashed into the sea. Both he and his observer were killed.

Aircraft were not just vital for spotting and calling guns onto enemy positions. They also carried out a highly valued, if somewhat improvised, support role for advancing infantry. Early battles at Anzac demonstrated that Turkish gunners were loath to reveal the locations of their carefully concealed batteries when an Allied aircraft buzzed overhead, even if it meant missing the opportunity to fire on prime targets like infantry caught in the open. This meant that aircraft became the infantryman's best friend, effectively silencing Turkish guns that would otherwise be free to rain fire on them. In short order, planes were being sent aloft specifically to carry out this task. In spite of this tactic being widely known among Allied forces, inexplicably, it was not employed at Helles. Although several observation flights were conducted every day, they were not timed to coincide with infantry advances. And so, not only were the advancing infantry denied eyes in the sky to help direct them and their artillery onto enemy targets, the

Turkish batteries were also free to fire on the advancing troops unimpeded.

It seems that commanders at Helles made poor use of airpower not just because of limited access to the assets but also because of a frustrating series of impediments that they seemed strangely reluctant to remedy. When flying missions to correct fire for artillery batteries at Helles, pilots discovered once they were airborne that ground-based units could not pick up their morse code signals. The army sets did not have the correct bandwidth and only ships could receive the transmissions. This rendered the aerial observation practically useless. On more than one occasion, a frustrated pilot resorted to landing his aircraft near an artillery battery, climbing out of his plane, storming up to the battery commander and pointing out the correct targets by jabbing an oil-stained finger at a map. Pilots were forced to identify enemy batteries by dropping flares on them, which alerted the gun crews that they had been spotted, giving them the chance to cease firing or drag their guns to safety.

In an effort to improve communications between commanders and aircraft, in the first week of May, a flat site immediately adjacent to Major General Hunter-Weston's headquarters at Hill 138 was cleared by engineers. Fuel, spare parts and ground crew were flown in to create a makeshift forward base. Two aircraft were stationed there from 5 May, which allowed observers to report directly to army officers or for written reports to be dropped on the base from aircraft passing overhead. Although this went some way toward improving communications issues that had thus far stymied the full utilisation of airpower, it came too late to provide intelligence for the upcoming battle at Krithia.

The upshot of all this was that Hamilton had a difficult choice to make. By delaying the assault on Krithia, he had more time to build up his forces and to make sure they were well supplied and rested. He would also learn more about where his enemy had dug in, with the result that his limited artillery would be better able to destroy Turkish targets and support the attack. On the other hand, the longer he waited, the more time he gave the Turks to improve their defences, and the larger the challenge the attacking troops would face. 'If we wait one week the Turks will have become twice as strong in their numbers,' Hamilton wrote in his diary, 'and twice as deep in their trenches, as they are to-day.' It was a precarious situation and there were no easy answers. With his limited resources, every decision Hamilton made was a gamble – and from the outset, he was playing with a compromised hand. There was a constant tug-of-war between Whitehall and Hamilton about what the Gallipoli campaign was and what resources were needed to fight it. Kitchener had been clear: Gallipoli was to be a limited military exercise, so that the bulk of British resources could be deployed to the Western Front (and the French certainly embraced this notion – their contribution to Gallipoli was puny compared to their efforts to fight the Germans on their home soil). But the realities of the campaign were at extreme odds to this position and had been from the day of the landing. To be successful at Gallipoli, Hamilton needed more of everything: ships, ammunition, guns and men. And the longer he waited for them to arrive, the harder his task would be. He had to act.

If he had any chance of pushing forward, Hamilton needed more men. But he was bizarrely diffident to ask for them. The French had already alerted Kitchener to the potential need for more men on 26 April but it wasn't until the Royal Navy sent an alarming report about the dire state of the land battle to Whitehall on 27 April that Kitchener realised just how much trouble the campaign was in. In response, he urgently cabled Hamilton, offering to send him more troops, and also alerted

General John Maxwell in Egypt to prepare to embark every spare man he had available. By the time Hamilton timidly requested more troops, they were already on their way. The 42nd (East Lancashire) Division had been immediately despatched from Egypt but only one brigade arrived in time to participate in the upcoming battle.

The reinforcements were nervous but enthusiastic to be joining the fight. But a swift and disconcerting dose of reality was dumped on them from an old hand as they were preparing to sail. Second Lieutenant George Horridge recalled:

> As we left Mudros, there were a lot of transport ships in the harbour. Some of the transport ships had wounded people that had already come off the peninsula. As we were leaving Mudros harbour, somebody shouted 'Are we downhearted?!', to which of course everybody yelled out 'No!'. Then a voice from another ship said 'No? Well you bloody soon will be!'[4]

The 29th Indian Brigade arrived at about the same time as the Lancs, although British commanders were concerned about how the brigade would perform in battle and elected to hold it in reserve for the near future.

Now that Hamilton had a smattering of fresh troops, the question was what to do with them. His options were limited, to say the least. The advances at both Anzac and Helles had failed spectacularly. In both sectors, the front line hadn't even reached the objectives set for the covering forces on the first morning, let alone the main objectives that would determine control of the peninsula. Hamilton only had enough reinforcements to resume the offensive in one sector. Should it be Anzac or Helles?

It didn't take long for him to decide. Helles had always been viewed as the main battlefront on the peninsula. The ground was far easier to cross than at Anzac and any advance there could be made under the protective blanket of the guns of the Royal Navy. His decision was reinforced when Kitchener cabled to inform him of plans to transfer the Anzac mounted regiments (minus their horses) from Egypt to Gallipoli, and giving him the presumptive, and completely misguided, advice that the Anzacs 'could spare you a good many men for the advance'.[5] This was all Hamilton needed to form a plan that would effectively define the rest of the Gallipoli campaign. Despite the Anzacs hanging on to their front line by their fingernails, they would release two brigades to reinforce the British and French troops at Helles and, for the time being at least, the Anzac sector would become a backwater. The troops who remained there would be tasked with simply holding on and tying up as many Turkish battalions as they could. The main thrust for control of the peninsula would be made at Cape Helles.

Time was of the essence. While the Turks had undoubtably lost tens of thousands of men in defending the peninsula, consistent reports from aerial observers and prisoner interrogations revealed that streams of Turkish reinforcements were arriving at Gallipoli every day and heading straight for the front lines. The opportunity to overwhelm the Turks by shock and awe had already passed. Now the narrow window to take the key high ground before the Turks could dig in was rapidly closing as well. There was a genuine concern that if the Turks continued to build up their troops, they would squeeze the British beachhead so tightly that there would be no room for further Allied reinforcements, even if they could be found.

The pressure on Hamilton to renew the advance went up a notch when he received a cable at 9.45 pm on 4 May from Kitchener, expressing his 'hope the 5th will see you sufficiently reinforced to push on to Achi Baba at least, as time will enable Turks to bring reinforcements and make unpleasant preparations for you'.[6] Apart from stating the obvious, this cable reveals the yawning gap between the perception of the campaign in London and the reality of the situation on the ground. The suggestion that a full-scale attack on a well-prepared enemy could be launched with a few hours' notice might have seemed feasible from a map spread on a desk in Whitehall, but the realities of exhausted troops, tough terrain and Turkish machine guns appear to not have featured prominently in Kitchener's thoughts.

British commanders at Gallipoli had a knack for taking an already complicated situation and making it nearly unworkable – the build-up of forces at Helles for Hamilton's advance on Krithia was a perfect example. The British 29th Division had suffered so many casualties since the landing that it had to be patched up with whatever troops were available. The newly arrived 125th Brigade and 29th Indian Brigade were therefore simply tacked on to it, despite those units never having worked with the 29th Division before and lacking the staff officers and lines of communication that would be essential in battle. The situation for the Anzac brigades was even worse – they were carved out of the divisions they had trained and fought with since their formation, and were forced to relocate to an unfamiliar battlefield and fight alongside troops who came from a different nation's army. In order to give them some sort of structure, Hamilton hoovered them up with a couple of spare battalions from the Royal Naval Division into a 'Composite Division' under the command of Major General Archibald Paris. If these arrangements sound messy, they were – the newly arrived units were now under the instructions of officers they didn't know, fighting alongside troops they had never met, on a battleground they had never seen. On arriving in the trenches, one of the new British officers reported that his men were 'as ignorant of their position as if they had been dropped from a balloon'.[7]

All in all, Hamilton had about 25,000 troops at his disposal, but how such a disorganised force would fare in battle was anyone's guess. Facing them were about 10,000 Turkish troops who were probably even more disorganised than the Allies – desperate for reinforcements, their commanders had simply slotted men into the line wherever they were needed.[*] The Turks had a couple of distinct advantages, however – in the tangled landscape of Helles, it was much easier to defend than to attack and the Allies still had absolutely no idea where the Turks were.

Hamilton's orders for the advance are as confusing as the landscape, with objectives defined by a succession of complicated map references and vague descriptions of landscape features ('the valley of the stream running through square 176.V.8., W.4., W.3., S.5.'[8]).

Hamilton was a relentless wishful thinker and, throughout the campaign, demonstrated that he was not a man to let common sense get in the way of a bold plan. But at Second Krithia, he was about to outdo himself. Faced with an unknown enemy, a difficult landscape, a stretched and battered attack force, and a debilitating shortage of ammunition, he devised a plan for the attack that was unnecessarily complicated, overly ambitious and completely unrealistic. After several conferences with Hunter-Weston and General Albert d'Amade, commander of the French forces, orders for what would become the Second Battle of Krithia were issued at 1.45 pm on 5 May. By the time the 29th Division had digested them and drafted orders for its

---

[*]   Official records compiled immediately after the war, including in the British official history, state that the Turks had about 20,000 men in the line at the time of the attack. But recent research in the Turkish archives by historians, including Harvey Broadbent and Edward J. Erickson, reveals that the actual number was about half that.

brigades, it was well after 4 am – only seven hours before the men were due to go over the top.

The plan called for two advances, one on each end of the Allied line, to be made in three stages. In the first phase, British troops would attack on the left, along the two northernmost spurs, Gully and Fir Tree spurs. They would capture the forward Turkish positions and pause about two kilometres in front of the village of Krithia, facing what Hamilton and Hunter-Weston assumed would be the main Turkish defences safeguarding the village. In the second phase, they would pierce these defences and capture the village, with their line then pivoting to face inland on the lower slopes of Achi Baba, a manoeuvre that would be difficult to coordinate on a training ground, let alone in unfamiliar country while under fire. In the final phase, the British main line would sweep forward and capture the summit of Achi Baba. No precise timeframe was given for each stage of the advance but it was assumed that Achi Baba would be in British hands by nightfall.

Meanwhile, the French would advance on the right of the line, covering less ground but in much tougher country and facing much stiffer resistance than their British comrades. They would take their first objective and dig in, providing covering fire for the British advance on Achi Baba. The key to the success of the whole operation was the pivot point (the 'point d'appui' as Hamilton flamboyantly referred to it in his orders) – if the French could not successfully gain ground on Kereves Spur, the whole British line would be exposed, even if they managed to successfully capture their objectives. The job of reinforcing the vital pivot point was given to the Royal Naval Division, who would have the unenviable task of trying to keep in contact with both the British on their left and the French on their right while crossing some of the most inhospitable terrain on the battlefield. It was a big ask.

Joe Murray had entered the line next to the French the previous day and was bemused by what he found.

The line at this point consisted of a series of funk-holes, each about two feet deep. The French had stuck bayonets into the ground and stretched a wire across the road up the nullah. To this wire they had tied a number of old jam tins with stones inside them; not by any standards effective but the idea was there … The sector was quiet and we sat under the stunted trees and among the bushes and brewed tea. The Turks were miles away – or so it seemed – but snipers were active. A strange feeling to be sitting at ease in the front line, without a care.[9]

It's important to note that the plan called for no attack in the centre of the line. Krithia Spur was lower than the two spurs on either side of it, so any troops who tried to advance along it would be exposed to murderous fire from the higher flanks unless both Fir Tree and Kereves spurs had been captured. The Composite Division, which included the two Anzac brigades, would be positioned as a reserve force on Krithia Spur; elements from it would advance to link up the British and French troops once they had successfully captured their objectives.

Given the difficulty of the task, General Hamilton wisely suggested the attack should take place at night and that the Allies should rush upon the Turkish lines in the 'grey dawn'. This was especially important considering the lack of cover on the battlefield – the attack force would be clearly visible to Turkish observers on Achi Baba from the moment it left the rear area to advance to the front line. But, once again, the decidedly odd and unmilitary relationship between commander and subordinate reared its head – Hunter-Weston was adamant that a night attack was impossible. The battalions had lost too many officers to successfully navigate in the dark, he said. It was a tenuous argument – the obvious advantage of advancing with darkness shielding the troops from artillery and machine-gun fire surely outweighed the risks – but Hamilton abandoned military common sense in the face of obstinance and acceded. The Second Battle of Krithia would be launched at the decidedly gentlemanly hour of 11 am.

Even with the difficulties of launching an attack against an unknown enemy in bright daylight over difficult terrain, one factor could have turned the odds in the Allies' favour – artillery. With a heavy enough bombardment, the Turkish machine guns could have been silenced, the defending soldiers killed or driven away. But, of course, there simply weren't enough guns or shells to fire from them. Once the diaphanous opening barrage was over, the infantry would be on their own.

The supporting artillery barrage was due to open at 10.30 am but it was not until 7.15 am that orders were issued detailing the role of the guns. As meagre as his artillery assets were, Hamilton was determined to make full use of them. He now had about eighty field guns and six howitzers at his disposal, a trifling number to support 25,000 troops. The real issue was shells – the Allies didn't have anywhere near enough of them and they were almost entirely shrapnel. Added to the fact that the gunners were uncertain about where the Turks actually were, the chances of this barrage doing any meaningful damage were slim. The ships of the Royal Navy would also play their part, with five battleships contributing to the initial bombardment and another battleship and four cruisers operating on the flanks of the attack to bombard any Turkish targets that presented themselves during the advance. It wasn't much but it would have to do. Ready or not, the Allies were on the move.

11.

THE ANZAC MOVE TO HELLES

Now that Hamilton had planned his next gamble, he needed to get his chips on the table. British reinforcements were already steaming toward the peninsula from Alexandria and now it was the turn of the Anzacs to join the ragtag army that was hastily assembling at Helles.

On the morning of 3 May, Birdwood was summoned to General Headquarters (GHQ) on board *Arcadian*, where Hamilton spelled out his new plans and then dropped a bombshell: Birdwood was to transfer as much of the Anzac contingent to Helles as he could spare. Birdwood recorded the meeting in his diary without revealing his personal thoughts about this dramatic change of direction but it must have been shocking. For eight days, he had been desperately trying to shore up the slender slice of enemy territory his corps had managed to snag on the day of the landing and had been consistently begging Hamilton to send him more men. Hamilton had also issued a stinging rebuke when Birdwood raised the possibility of evacuating Anzac on the day after the landing – now, a week later, Hamilton was proposing to eviscerate the already overstretched Anzac garrison to support his flailing efforts at Helles.

Later in the morning, Hamilton cabled to confirm the details of their discussion:

> Please detail two brigades and two bearer sections of a Field Ambulance to embark tonight for Cape Helles, where they are required to take part in the attack on the Achi Baba position tomorrow.[1]

It's important to spell out how potentially catastrophic this order was (even ignoring the absurdly short twelve hours of notice). The Anzacs were barely holding on. Having advanced only about a kilometre inland, they were holding a precarious line that was hemmed in by Turkish trenches on three sides. For the time being, they had successfully resisted Turkish attempts to drive them into the sea but they also had little hope of advancing. If the Turks continued to build up reinforcements, the situation could quickly turn to disaster. A stark look at the numbers makes this decision even more alarming. There were only five Anzac infantry brigades at Gallipoli. Hamilton was asking Birdwood to release *40 per cent of his total forces*. Little wonder that Birdwood felt it necessary to communicate to Hamilton that he 'never contemplated sending either of these for present operation' and that he was 'a little anxious' about holding his line with a much-depleted force.[2] But Birdie was nothing if not a team player. He set about making plans to move his two best brigades – the Australian 2nd Brigade and the New Zealand Brigade – south to Helles.

Needless to say, the transfer of more than 5000 troops and their associated equipment was a complicated operation that couldn't be rushed. These weren't reserve troops sitting idly behind the lines. They were combat troops in the trenches, fighting tooth and nail in some of the toughest parts of the line to stop the Turks breaking through and overwhelming the entire

Anzac force. In order to free them up, Birdwood needed to sneak them out of the line and find someone to replace them, all under the attentive and suspicious gaze of the Turks. And, of course, to transfer the brigades to Helles, he needed ships to load them onto and a practical plan for embarking them without attracting a storm of enemy artillery fire. Sorting all of this out in the space of a day was clearly impossible, so Birdwood was relieved to receive a cable from GHQ at 1.15 pm advising that the operation had been postponed, and that he would receive twelve hours' notice before his troops needed to be on the move. Hamilton wasn't being magnanimous with this change of heart – the other reinforcements he was waiting for had been delayed, so he elected to push back the whole enterprise by several days.

Birdwood might have considered these two brigades his 'best', but the Anzac brigades had been gutted by casualties. When they had first sailed, each brigade was about 4000-men strong. But after the carnage of the opening days and the high cost in lives to hold the meagre gains at Anzac, the brigades were shadows of their former selves. Birdwood reported on 4 May that the New Zealand Brigade was down to 2500 men. The Australian 2nd Brigade was in even worse shape and could only pull together 2300 men. A somewhat deflated Birdwood told Hamilton that he wished the brigades were stronger and promised to 'send every available man I can get'.[3] The two brigades had been deprived of about 700 reinforcements each due to a mix-up with the despatch of a ship from Lemnos but Birdwood still considered them his strongest brigades.

Most accounts of the Gallipoli campaign gloss over the details of the transfer of the Anzac contingent to Helles in a curiously cursory fashion, but like most things at Gallipoli, the simplest manoeuvre could turn into an ordeal. The campaign had been born with such haste that the whole endeavour was permeated with a strong whiff of disorganisation. The Allies were in a mess from the start and struggled to regain their footing throughout the campaign. This embarkation was no exception. The night sailing down to Helles was to become an exercise in frustration and exhaustion.

The uplift of 5000 troops, at night and under the nose of the enemy, was a complicated military manoeuvre that required meticulous planning and coordination between the navy and army. The orders for the move were relatively comprehensive but the plans unravelled pretty much as soon as the operation began. What should have been a fairly straightforward process of loading battalions onto boats quickly deteriorated into farce – and, as was so often the case, it was the men who bore the brunt.

The orders issued from Birdwood's headquarters were thorough and called for fourteen ships to arrive off Anzac Cove at 8.45 pm – seven destroyers to transport the New Zealand Brigade and seven fleet sweepers (a type of fast sloop) to transport the Australian 2nd Brigade. The timing was crucial – the troops needed to be loaded and underway after the sun had set but before the moon had risen, while allowing enough time for the small armada to complete the 25-kilometre journey to Cape Helles before dawn. It was anticipated that both brigades would be embarked and on their way by midnight.

At first, the plan went well. The troops were able to leave their trenches without difficulty, partly thanks to a ruse concocted by the Royal Naval Division, which was holding the trenches beside the Anzacs. On the night of 4 May, the men of the RND let loose a long burst from a machine gun and then began shouting and waving their bayonets, as if they were about to launch an attack. In response, the Turks opened fire and hunkered down to face an onslaught that never came. The same ruse was conducted by the 4th Australian Brigade the following night and the pandemonium enabled the two Australian and New Zealand brigades earmarked for Helles to steal away from the front line without being detected. The men left the trenches and formed up in assembly areas for an orderly march to the beach.

The leading units of the New Zealand Brigade were the first to arrive at Anzac Cove, which had been cleared of animals and stores to make the going easier.

Cecil Malthus had been alarmed to hear that the New Zealanders were being pulled out of the line – surely they weren't evacuating the peninsula? But the scenes of dedicated industry on Anzac Cove swept his misgivings away.

> We were completely reassured on marching round to Anzac Cove, now a busy port with thousands of twinkling lights and a constant hurry and bustle of traffic on both sea and shore. There was no suggestion of demoralisation here. Everything stood for solid permanency and progress.[4]

Once on the sand, the advanced New Zealand units marched gingerly along flimsy piers and boarded lighters (which would be towed to the destroyers by steamboats) 'rapidly and without confusion'.[5] As the men sat shivering in the small boats, word was passed that the destroyers were late and were nowhere to be seen. Inconceivably, no-one on the beach had thought to confirm that the ships they were supposed to be ferrying the men to were actually there before loading the lighters – from that point onward, the embarkation plan completely disintegrated. Officers were told they could either leave their men in the lighters or unload them 'as they preferred', resulting in chaos as hundreds of men clambered back out of the boats and returned to the beach, where they milled around like a crowd before a football match. Before long, the Australian brigade arrived and, instead of finding an empty beach and an orderly queue of small boats waiting to ferry them to the sweepers, they were greeted by chaos, as thousands of men congregated aimlessly on the beach. Others, by this stage frozen to the bone and green from seasickness, bobbed around in lighters still tethered to the piers.

Just as it seemed the situation couldn't get worse, a naval officer at the southernmost pier decided he was sick of waiting and towed off his string of lighters even though they were only two-thirds full. He puttered around for several hours, vainly searching for destroyers that weren't there, before giving up and depositing his thoroughly dejected human cargo on the nearest fleet sweeper (intended to carry the Australian troops), thereby completely destroying the plans that sensibly called for the two brigades to travel to Cape Helles separately. By the time the mistake was discovered, it was too late to unload the men and they ended up making the voyage to Cape Helles as part of an untidy jumble of New Zealand and Australian troops.

The soldiers on the beach settled in for a long night. It was too risky to light fires on the exposed shore, so they huddled in small groups and did their best to keep warm, as an icy wind chilled them to the bone and whipped the coarse sand into their faces. Periodically, a Turkish shell would lob overhead and burst in the water, providing a visceral and unwelcome reminder of just how dangerous this operation really was. Occasionally, a man would cry out and grab an arm or leg in pain – spent bullets fired by the Turks on the front line high in the hills above would sometimes thud onto the beach and, with so many men packed into the small space, woundings were inevitable.

It was after midnight by the time the destroyers eventually arrived and it was hours before the New Zealanders were safely loaded aboard. Lieutenant Colonel William Malone and his men had spent four excruciating hours crammed into lighters, pinnaces and other tiny craft, without untying from the pier. 'A long, cold job'[6] was how he described it, with customary understatement. Cecil Malthus shared the sentiment. 'With incredible difficulty,' he wrote in his diary, 'we were crammed aboard lighters – the man in full marching order, once he is sitting or lying, is hopelessly helpless.'[7]

The Australians fared even worse – their fleet sweepers didn't turn up until 2.30 am, by which time the troops had been huddled on the freezing beach, without sleep but with a surfeit of griping, for more than five hours. Their officers had long since given up hope of organising the men onto boats in cohesive units and were now simply desperate to get them away before the sun came up. As dawn broke the, last gaggle of Australians finally embarked for the long and uncomfortable sea journey to Helles on whatever boat they could find to carry them.*

It had been a long night and, far from being well rested and ready to take part in a battle, the men were 'more disorganised than they had ever been since the commencement of operations'.

A report into the debacle ended with an ominous statement: 'It is not yet known whether [the night on the beach] had any ill effect on the readiness of the two brigades for action on arrival at Cape Helles, but the above facts are placed on record in case it had.'[8] It had been cold and chaotic but the Anzac brigades were finally on their way to Helles.

---

* It's interesting to note how tenuous the Anzac commanders felt their position was in these opening weeks of the campaign. ANZAC Headquarters notes in its unit diary that, although the embarkation had not gone smoothly, it 'proved a useful rehearsal for the operation of reembarking the whole force should that prove necessary'. The thought that the Anzac position might have to be hastily abandoned was always front of mind.

12.

6 MAY

The morning air was crisp and clear as the small armada carrying the Anzac brigades arrived off Cape Helles. The troops were exhausted but excited. Since the day of the landing, they had received regular updates from their commanders about the sterling work being done by the British and French on the southern toe of the peninsula. Their own rumour mill had worked overtime to furnish them with gripping, yet often contradictory, tales of British advances and French triumphs in the fields of Helles.

The destroyers and sweepers weaved through the fleet of warships stationed off the famous British landing sites from the opening day; the Anzacs crowded the rails, eager for their first glimpse of the battlefront they had heard so much about. On the shore, they could make out distant figures on W Beach, which thrummed with activity as men and mules ferried supplies from makeshift piers, up bare slopes scored with rough tracks to the distant and as-yet-unseen front line.

At 5 am, the troopships veered toward shore and their landing spot at V Beach. As they neared the beach, the battered bastions of the Sedd el Bahr Fort loomed above them and the patchwork hull of the mighty SS *River Clyde*, the Trojan horse that had starred in stirring accounts of the British landings, stood as an oddly dignified sentinel on the waterfront.

The Australians and New Zealanders transferred into the cramped and hated lighters and were towed to a pier that had been fashioned from barges lashed to the hull of the *Clyde*. As they neared the hulk of the great ship, they noted the ugly rash of bullet scars along her flanks, a sobering reminder of the hail of fire the British troops had come under as they landed. The British had filed out of the *Clyde* through sally ports cut into her sides – the Anzacs noted with dark humour that some wag had scrawled in chalk above each port a reminder to 'Duck your nut'.[1] Given the barrage of fire the British had faced during the landing, a bump on the head from a low doorway was surely the least of their worries. The Anzacs clambered out of the lighters and, weighed down by their gear and rations, struggled to stay upright as they filed along the unstable pier before stepping onto the sand of V Beach, the scene of so much death just over a week before.

This was nothing like the beach they had left behind at Anzac. No sheer cliffs towered over them and the beach rose sedately to a grassy plateau. To the south, the troops could clearly make out the Asian shore of the Dardanelles, a thin line of grey hills on the edge of a choppy sea, with snow-capped peaks crowding behind. It was difficult to believe that whole far horizon was occupied by the enemy but the point was made abundantly clear when a large shell came screaming over from the southern shore with the noise of a freight train, bursting in the water beside the *Clyde* and sending up a geyser like a spouting whale. In response, a battleship steamed past the beach and began blasting the southern shore with a deafening fusillade. A shrapnel shell detonated off the beach and sprayed its deadly pellets in the water like a thunder shower.

Another enemy shell came tearing in and exploded dangerously close to one of the fleet sweepers that was unloading Australian troops. The Aussies simply pulled their hats a little tighter onto their heads and continued disembarking.

There was one thing V Beach had in common with Anzac Cove – it was busy. Porters shouted and swore as they unloaded lighters weighed down to the gunnels with crates of stores, French drivers in khaki tunics and bright red trousers cracked reins as they steered heavily laden carts led by recalcitrant mules up the slope away from the beach and teams of British gun horses jingled along the roadway toward distant batteries.

Cecil Malthus was struck by the distinction between Helles and Anzac.

> The country at Helles was in marked contrast to the savage ravines of Anzac. It was quite pretty and open, with fruit trees, olive and mulberry, elms, crops, streams, fields of poppies, lupines and daisies, old towers, cottages and wells. The roads were alive with traffic, including numbers of picturesque French and African troops, strapping Senegalese and colonial Zouaves with their broad red baggy trousers.[2]

Sam Norris, a young private in the 6th Battalion, referred to the upcoming assault on Achi Baba as 'another Spion Kop', which didn't bode well for the success of the operation. The comparison between Anzac and Helles was stark.

> When I saw this place I felt thankful that it had not been our task to land here instead of at Anzac. Here at Helles there was a narrow beach flanked on one side by high cliffs and on the other by the fort Seddul Bahr [sic]. The top of the beach was defended by acres of barbed wire; wire about a quarter inch diameter with a two-inch barb every

quarter of an inch along it. Barbed wire had also been fixed under the sea near the beach. Two graves in the sand, one containing officers and the other men, held more than 700 bodies and testified to the difficulties overcome in gaining a foothold.[3]

The Anzacs assembled on the beach, divided into companies and began marching inland on a dusty, white cart track. The pace was relaxed. Harry Kelly said that the Anzacs were 'strolling along as if at a picnic'.[4] A cliff hemmed in the beach on the western end; above it stood another battered fort that had been pummelled by naval shellfire before the landing. Two large Turkish guns had been smashed and blown from their mountings and lay askew in their emplacements (as they still do today). Shell craters, large and small, pockmarked the slope above the beach, giving the whole place the appearance of a dusty Australian mining settlement. As the marching troops reached the top of the slope, the entire Helles battlefield unfolded before them. It was like nothing they had seen at Anzac and reminded more than a few of them of the great Napoleonic battlefields they had read about as boys. Before them, the road wound down a gentle hillside, through undulating fields of green unharvested wheat and low grass. Olive trees and elms were scattered across the field; off to the right, the Anzacs caught their first glimpse of the river-like waters of the Dardanelles, the glittering prize that had brought them to this godforsaken peninsula in the first place.

The scene was so idyllic, so unexpected, that the British official history briefly abandons its normal clumsy prose and launches into a flight of whimsy:

The grassy slopes that crown the cliffs are carpeted with flowers. The azure sky is cloudless; the air is fragrant with the scent of wild thyme. In front, beyond a smiling valley studded with cypress and olive and patches of young corn, the ground rises gently … to a frowning ridge beyond, its highest point like the hump of a camel's back. Away to the right, edged with a ribbon of silvery sand, lie the sapphire arc of Morto Bay, the glistening Dardanelles, and the golden fields of Troy.[5]

'This country is beautiful, sweet-smelling and thickly cultivated with fruit trees of all descriptions and other flowers,' an Australian remarked in his diary. 'The poppies are beautiful.' His reverie didn't last long, however, and he soon learned that Helles was shrouded in the same sensory unpleasantness as Anzac. 'This perfume is at times marred by the stench of some dead Turk.'[6]

Directly in front, about nine kilometres distant, was the rough hump of Achi Baba, the hill that could just be spotted from the southern slopes of Anzac and which the Australians and New Zealanders had watched intently through field glasses in the days after the landing, desperately hoping to see British troops cresting the summit. In the shadow of Achi Baba was a small settlement of white buildings beside a row of windmills – the village of Krithia.

In a clump of low trees to the left of the road, a French field gun roared and sent its deadly payload arcing toward the distant Turkish lines. It wasn't just the noise that startled the troops – it was the gun's proximity, only a couple of hundred metres above the beach. The rumour mill had led the Anzacs to believe the fighting at Helles had advanced to the slopes of Achi Baba. The sight of a gun battery in action so close to the beach was completely unexpected, and alarming. 'Great Scott!' said an Australian officer. 'I can't understand this. Here's a French battery in position. Surely they can't be firing from here.' As if in response, the gun roared again. 'Seems to me they've got very little further than we have,' someone muttered. 'Just a foothold – no more.'[7]

As the Anzacs continued inland, they passed more gun batteries, British and French, which had been dug in behind hedges and the smashed remains of stone cottages. Occasionally, a gun roared and the men could see its shell bursting in a fleecy puff about halfway to Achi Baba, evidently over the position of the Turkish front line. Although the line was a good few kilometres away, it seemed disturbingly close.

The two brigades marched a few hundred metres into the valley and were ordered to dig in in a green field fringed by elms and watered by a muddy stream. 'They can see you from Achi Baba,' said Colonel James McCay, commander of the Australian 2nd Brigade, 'so get dug in just as fast as you can. They'll have their shrapnel on to you in a few minutes.'[8] The men didn't have to be told twice and began tearing into the soil with their entrenching tools. They had dug about half a metre when water began pooling in the shallow trenches. Realising the water table was far too high for trench digging, they did the only thing they could – they piled the muddy earth up to form breastworks and then crouched down behind them. The breastworks wouldn't provide much protection from a heavy bombardment, but they were better than nothing. Within a couple of hours, the Anzacs had transformed the grassy meadow into a veritable village of low mud walls and were taking advantage of the surfeit of water to bathe and shave. William Malone was conscious that his battalion could be called on to fight at any moment but also relaxed by his surroundings.

My bivouac is in a sort of bank and stone wall just above the creek ... in green fields with elms and walnuts on the boundaries, a running stream of clayey water or two – wildflowers, dog roses, poppies and others strange to me.[9]

Malone was so proud of his neat bivouac that, when his commanding officer arrived to discuss the upcoming action, Malone made him clean his boots before coming inside. Malone was relieved to be away from the chaos of Anzac and to have some space from the slovenly Australians he had been forced to serve beside.

> It is a relief to get in where war is being waged scientifically and where we are clear of the Australians. They seem to swarm about our lines like flies. I keep getting them sent out. They are like masterless men, going their own ways. I found one just now crawling like a big brown fly over my bivouac. I straightened him up, not a bad lad either I believe, but a ten-foot road was not good enough for him, he wanted to walk or climb on a six-inch ledge – strange!

Cecil Malthus and his comrades in the Canterbury Battalion were settling into their new muddy bivouac and were preparing an unappealing dinner, with whatever they could scrounge from their ration packs, when shouts suddenly rang out. A terrified hare burst from the scrub and made a panicked dash for freedom in front of the Canterbury line. 'Nobody had time for a shot at it, but several men tried to grab it as it passed right by them, and finally when it reached our platoon Harry Pike knocked it out by throwing himself flat on top of it.'[10] Cecil and half a dozen of his mates ate well that evening.

The Anzacs settled in for a long and chilly night. Never keen to let a little trans-Tasman rivalry slip by without comment, the New Zealand official history reported that the New Zealanders were aggrieved to have received a poorer standard of rations than the Australians but that the mood was lifted when a Kiwi began a stirring sing-along of 'There's Something in the Seaside Air'. Always quick with a whimsy, and no doubt recalling the stench of the battlefield, author of the history, Captain Fred Waite, added that this was 'unfortunately true'.[11]

The following morning, the Anzacs were startled to see a huge batch of fresh-faced troops in crisp, clean uniforms march into the camp. Due to an administration mix-up, more than 1000 Anzac reinforcements had been languishing in Mudros Harbour without orders for the past three days. Eventually, they were rushed to Anzac Cove but arrived just in time to discover that their brigades were no longer there. They were quickly bustled back onto their ship and steamed immediately to join them in Helles.

Although on paper the Allies were barely strong enough to keep the campaign going, to Harry Kelly it appeared that Helles offered an abundance of men and resources.

> They had a good supply of horses so we did not have to work for the artillery, of which they had a good supply, and when a bombardment was taking place the noise was almost deafening. At Anzac we had Tommies and Indians but here they also had thousands of French and now they had Australians and New Zealanders, but I could never find out the idea of our being sent there for they seem to have plenty of men.[12]

As the Anzacs finished digging in, word was passed along the line that the battle they had been sent here for was about to begin. At 10.30 am, the field guns began blasting in unison. At 11 am, there was a swelling chorus of yells as the British and French infantry left their trenches – and then a disturbingly fierce reply from Turkish machine guns and rifles. The Second Battle of Krithia had begun.

––

The British and French troops who were ordered to advance on Krithia on the morning of 6 May 1915 must have felt like they were trapped in a never-ending nightmare. They had been in almost constant combat since the morning of the landing, eleven days before, and had watched helplessly as the proud divisions they had sailed with had been cut in half on beach, in fort, in village and now on open plain. Even by the torturous standards of the First World War, this was a gruelling ordeal and the strain showed on the face of every man. They were sleepless, unshaven, hungry and disillusioned. Torn and filthy uniforms hung from gaunt frames; eyes that had seen too much stared from sunken sockets.

Even the British official history – a source that goes above and beyond to convince the reader that the Gallipoli campaign was a near-run thing and that, with just a bit more luck and a stiff upper lip, the plucky Brits could have given Johnny Turk a jolly good thrashing – struggles to paint the Second Battle of Krithia as anything other than a disaster in waiting. 'Even the Great War,' it declares, 'furnishes few examples of a series of offensive operations being entered upon with troops so worn out by continuous fighting and lack of sleep as those who took part in the Second Battle of Krithia.'[13]

The Allied units tasked with capturing Krithia and Achi Baba were a mixed and mottled bag. The 88th Brigade, which would attack roughly in the centre of the British line, had lost half its men and had only one battalion commander left standing after the hellish advance from the beaches. The majority of its company, platoon and section leaders were dead or wounded, and not a man in the brigade had had a decent night's sleep in a fortnight. It was a 'skeleton of its former self'[14] and yet was facing an advance more perilous than anything it had ever been asked to do. On its right, the Composite Division, with its multinational lucky dip of brigades from Britain, Australia and

New Zealand, was both combat-weary and disorganised. Only the 125th Brigade on the extreme left of the line was fresh but it had only arrived from Egypt the day before. Not only did it have no clue of the battlefield it was about to advance across, it also wasn't even attached to its own division, having been sliced off from the 42nd Division and attached to the left of the 29th.

The new arrivals were already anxious about what they would face on the battlefield but their anxiety went through the roof when they talked to men who had lived through the bloody ordeal of the first weeks.

> Most of C Company had gathered round two weary-looking privates of the Munster Fusiliers who were unwittingly spreading alarm and despondency. They said they had lost their battalion and were the only survivors of their platoon, that all officers and NCOs were marked men, that the Turks had been committing atrocities, and that we must be on our guard against the devilish German officers who seemed to know the name of every British regimental officer and who during the night crept up to our trenches and shouted false orders … With their soft Irish brogue these two Munsters made an extraordinary picture of disaster as they stood there in the hot sunlight, their short rifles slung heavily over their mud-stained shoulders and their soft field-service caps, each with its big green shamrock badge, on the back of their heads.[15]

The French 1st Division, which would advance on the British right through the perilous Kereves Dere, was arguably in even worse condition than the British, having borne the brunt of the Turkish night counter-attacks for the past week. On 4 May, Hamilton had received a disturbing report from General d'Amade that basically declared that the French were at the end of their tether. He had used up all of his reserves, his men had had no sleep for several nights, the Turks were pounding his lines incessantly with artillery fire and nearly all his officers were lying in hospital beds or freshly dug graves. The highly regarded Zouaves and Foreign Legion had reached breaking point, and his Senegalese units were so unsteady that he considered it unsafe to leave them in the line. Never a man to let bad news dissuade him from a plan, Hamilton effectively disregarded d'Amade's concerns, reaching the perverse conclusion that if the French were suffering this badly, the Turks opposite them must be in an even worse way. To add insult to very real injury, Hamilton tasked the French with the toughest advance of the battle, through the tangle of gullies facing the Dardanelles and exposed to flanking fire from the Asian shore. At least the French could rely on their artillery – unlike their British comrades, the Corps Expeditionnaire d'Orient had embarked for the peninsula with an adequate complement of guns and enough shells to do the job.

With insufficient guns, a critical shortage of ammunition, an attack force that was leaderless, disorganised and exhausted, an ally that was stretched to breaking point and absolutely no idea how many enemy soldiers he was facing or where they even were, Hamilton was ready to resume his advance to Krithia and glory.

— —

The Second Battle of Krithia opened with a whimper, not a bang. The artillery did all it could to provide a preliminary barrage before the infantry advanced, but given the shortage of guns, their meagre supply of ammunition and the complete lack of knowledge about the enemy location, this initial bombardment was always going to be painfully inadequate.

Quite how inadequate it was, however, took everyone by surprise. The British official history refers to it (in one of its few moderately colourful phrases) as a 'slight sprinkling' of artillery fire. The Turkish defenders were so unmolested by this feeble fire that one observer, in a later report about the battle, wrote that the British appeared to have advanced without any artillery support at all.[16]

Sergeant Jim Parker was one of the gunners tasked with contributing to the opening barrage. Although his diary for 6 May describes lots of action on the battlefield, disturbingly little of it is devoted to his battery actually firing its guns.

> Saw the Field Artillery and infantry on our right advancing and capturing trenches. Lancashire Fusiliers from Egypt landed and passed us on our right. Sikhs and Gurkhas and British troops coming and going to trenches alongside us. Pack horses and mules taking ammunition up day and night. Fired 390 shells.[17]

The guns of the Royal Navy chipped in and, although their fire created a large amount of noise, dust and smoke, their aim was based mostly on guesswork rather than observation, so the Turks escaped the onslaught relatively unscathed. Even if it had found Turkish targets to knock out, the naval fire soon slackened, as the ships did not want to risk hitting Allied troops as they advanced.

All in all, the combined barrage from land and sea lasted less than thirty minutes. Compared to the preliminary barrage before the Battle of the Somme, staged one year later and lasting a full seven days (and even then failing to subdue the enemy), the barrage before the Second Battle of Krithia was pitiful. Turkish accounts make no mention of any meaningful damage being inflicted by it and, although a small number of Turkish troops were undoubtedly killed or wounded, it's likely that not a single trench was destroyed or a solitary machine gun put out of action. All it effectively did was alert the Turks that an attack was about to take place and give them time to load their weapons and wait patiently for the Allied troops to advance into their gunsights.

The first British troops to climb over the parapet were the men of the 88th Brigade, who would advance along Fir Tree Spur directly toward Krithia. A screen of scouts left the trenches at 11 am, as soon as their patchy supporting barrage had died down, and edged forward, with three battalions of infantry spread out behind them. This was war at its most cautious – the scouts advanced slowly and methodically, crouching behind low shrubs and any other cover they could find, scanning the landscape for signs of the enemy, dashing to the next piece of safe ground and repeating the process. The scouts knew that, in an advance to contact, they were the tripwire for the whole attack and they moved forward in hunched postures, expecting machine-gun fire to tear into them at any moment. For the first few hundred metres, all was deathly quiet. Then the scouts came upon the advanced Turkish outposts, themselves a screen for the larger mass of men behind them. A few rifle shots cracked and then grew in volume. Then the machine guns joined in. Men began to fall.

The men of the 88th pushed on, their numbers thinning as the Turkish fire found its mark. As the fusillade grew from a spattering to a tempest, they realised that the bulk of the fire was not coming from directly in front of them, in the direction of Krithia, but from the left and right flanks. It was clear the British and French troops on both sides of them were not attacking and that the 88th Brigade was advancing at the point of a deadly arrowhead. The men did the only sensible thing – they hit the ground. Most of the fire from their right seemed to be coming from a couple of machine guns in a small wood of fir trees surrounding a small daisy meadow. A group of the 88th charged the wood and made it to the near side, before the fire became too heavy and they were forced to withdraw. Exhausted and shattered by losses, the brigade dug in.

On the left, the 125th Brigade was tasked with what was essentially an elaborate flanking manoeuvre. It would advance along the coastline at Gully Spur and overcome the right of the Turkish main line, providing protection for the British and French troops advancing up the spurs on its right. But from the outset, the advance was a disaster. It was poorly planned and the issued orders were even worse. The officer in charge of the leading company received a flurry of late orders, which included an objective he could not locate on his map. A private who would advance on the left flank was told he would be carrying a large blue-and-white flag during the attack, so that a supporting British warship could easily track his progress (as could every Turkish marksman within half a mile). No-one could even agree what time the attack was due to begin. The commanding officer received a phone call at 9.30 am giving him a range of vague and contradictory instructions. He was told (incorrectly) that the 88th Brigade would advance at 10.30 am, and so he should attack at 11 am, and that if the 88th was held up, he should definitely be on the move to support them by 11.30 am. Thoroughly confused and having no idea how the 88th was progressing – he couldn't see them from his position – he finally ordered his men to leave their trenches at 11.30 am, a full thirty minutes after the supporting artillery had stopped firing and the 88th had begun to advance. Unsurprisingly, the preceding hour of activity along the British line had fully alerted the Turks that an attack was coming. They opened up with a hail of machine-gun and rifle fire as soon as the leading men of the 125th left their trenches.

The 1/6th Lancashire Fusiliers led this assault and men started dropping within the first few metres. The leading companies went to ground and tried to inch forward, but every time a man rose to crawl or run forward, he was met by a stream of Turkish bullets. This was the first taste of battle for the battalion and the men were shocked by the violence unfolding around them.

> The heavy staccato of enemy machine-gun fire didn't sound a bit like the more ladylike cracks of the blank cartridges we had fired with such enthusiasm in our mock skirmishing in Egypt. But worst of all was the low raking fire of the shrapnel which tore holes in our ranks. There was consequently indescribable confusion, quite a lot of panic, and after the first shock we did what we should have done in the first place – what we should have been told to do before landing – dodged for whatever shelter we could find in the lee of the low cliffs and crouching behind every stone and blade of grass.[18]

By sheer force of will, the battalion managed to get near the plateau above the old Y Beach (ground that the British had held and abandoned on the day of the landing) but machine guns on the far side of a gully cut down every man who tried to advance further. The Lancs could do no more than to dig in where they were and pray that nightfall would bring them some reprieve from the hellish fire. They had lost more than 350 men to gain a pitifully small amount of ground.

On the right flank, the French faced the toughest obstacles and fiercest opposition on the battlefield – anyone who expected their beleaguered troops to somehow rise up and overcome them was swiftly disappointed. Like their British comrades, the French were due to begin the advance at 11 am, but thanks to another round of shoddy communication and unclear orders, the French didn't leave their trenches until 11.40 am (spare a thought again for the poor old 88th, who by this time had been advancing unsupported for forty minutes). At first, the troops on the French right made good progress. The Metropolitan Brigade was able to advance to high ground overlooking the mouth of the Kereves Dere virtually without being shot at. But as soon as the brigade tried to push forward, a storm of machine-gun and rifle fire greeted it from the far side of the gully.

Lieutenant Henri Feuille from the 30th Artillery Regiment was serving as a forward observer and had a disturbingly clear view of the French advance.

> They advanced as on exercise, no gaps in the ranks, punctuated by flashes of bayonets and the blue glint of the rifles reflecting the rays of the mid-day sun. You would think they were on a training ground. But what is there to say? This wall of steel stops, hurls itself at an obstacle that it can't breach, hesitates, immobile for an instant. Then, all the geometric lines fall apart. Groups running right, left, thrown into confusion. All the while Turkish machine guns, rattling away, tearing at the air, ceaselessly firing into a wall of palpitating flesh.[19]

To move into the gully was clearly suicidal, so the Metropolitans dug in where they were and began exchanging shots with the Turkish defenders. This advance didn't amount to much but it was actually quite an achievement compared to the progress of French brigades on the left and in the centre. They faced a series of Turkish redoubts and emplacements that were far stronger than in other parts of the line – here, the Turks had managed to construct something that resembled a main line, and the French were met by the sort of concentrated machine-gun, rifle and artillery fire that their comrades on the Western Front would have recognised and dreaded.

The advancing French made for quite a sight: although they would soon adopt a khaki uniform at Gallipoli, early in the campaign, the more exotic units brought a flair and chicness to the battlefield that was typically French. The Senegalese went into the fight in dark blue uniforms, the Zouaves wore baggy red trousers and the Foreign Legion sported a sky-blue ensemble that was enhanced with a range of colourful additions. This might have made for an impressive sight on the parade ground, but on the battleground the French stood out like beacons. The Turkish defences in this sector were bolstered by a detachment of German machine-gunners from the warships *Goeben* and *Breslau*, and one of its officers described the peril of the French advance.

> In thick columns, always fifty to sixty men all bunched-up, they were death-defying in their advance, offering the Turkish artillery and our machine guns an easy target. In rows they were mowed down, but more and more columns were detailed to storm forward. When our machine guns had completely expended all their ammunition, the crews took rifles from dead Turkish soldiers and continued to fire at them ... The red trousers and red caps of the French offered excellent targets.[20]

Within minutes of the battle opening, grotesque, colourful bundles littered the battlefield. No French troops got further than 350 metres in the day.

The key feature of the entire plan was the pivot point, which would enable the British line to swing toward Achi Baba once Krithia had been captured. But with both the British and French attacks stalled within sight of their own front line, the

Royal Naval Division, which was supposed to form the pivot force, found itself with the unenviable task of trying to link up the besieged British and French forces. With the French pinned down, a dangerous gap had formed on the left of their line, and so the Hood and Anson battalions (plus a small party from the Howe Battalion) were rushed forward to join the advance. The RND attacked with exceptional bravery but, as in all parts of the line, they were met by a deluge of fire every time they moved and paid a high price for their courageous advance.

Joe Murray was in the thick of this action.

> The Turkish fire was murderous and we lost a lot of men. There were no trenches to be seen but the Turks must have had their machine-guns perfectly sighted. It was terrifying; fewer men rose after each rush but we still charged forward blindly, repeatedly changing direction, but it did not appear to make the slightest difference. The fire was coming from all directions yet we could not see a single Turk or any sign of a trench.[21]

The marines were ordered to charge through an open gate next to a farmhouse. The Turks had a machine gun trained on the opening and dozens of men were hit as they rushed through. Only Joe and three mates named Townshend, Horton and Yates survived the dash – they had to climb over the dead and dying to get through the gate.

> We crawled up more or less line abreast but the bullets were hitting the sand, spraying us, hitting our packs. 'How about another dash?' Off we went. Another fifteen yards, one drops, everybody drops. We got down again! We decided to go a little bit further. We'd got to keep bearing to our right slightly, because we seemed to be dodging the line of fire.

But it was still winging overhead and flying about, hitting the ground … We decided to go a little bit further and all four got up together. Yates was in front and all of a sudden he bent down. He'd been shot in the stomach, maybe the testicles, but he was dancing around like a cat on hot bricks, fell down on the ground. As soon as we got somewhere near him he got up and rushed like hell at the Turks and 'Bang!' Down altogether, out for the count … Young Horton, he was the first to get to Yates and he got a hold of him and sort of pushed him to see what was wrong when a bullet struck him dead centre of the brow, went right through his head and took a bit out of my knuckle. Poor old Horton. He kept crying for his mother. I can see him now. Hear him at this very moment. He said he was eighteen, but I don't think he was sixteen, never mind eighteen. He was such a frail young laddie.[22]

The Hood Battalion's commanding officer was Lieutenant Colonel John Quilter, an affable forty-year-old from Suffolk who had spent several years in Australia before the war, on secondment from the British Army. Throughout the advance, he urged his men forward, waving an oversized walking stick in an effort to keep them on course. Late in the advance, he rose from behind cover and was peering through his field glasses, trying to spot the Turkish line, when he was shot dead. The men of the RND were going nowhere – they began to dig in.

— · —

While the British and French were bleeding, the Anzacs were spectating. Once they had constructed their breastworks and conducted their usual drills and fatigues, the Aussies and Kiwis were pretty much free to explore. The weather was warm and clear – the opportunity to stroll through sun-dappled meadows of knee-deep grass and wildflowers was surreal after the chaotic and claustrophobic confines of Anzac. A nearby knoll offered a grandstand view of the battle as it unfolded – and the sight was astonishing. 'To those who had grown accustomed to surprise attacks at dawn or dusk on narrow crests where fighting was from one steep gully to another,' Charles Bean relates in the Australian official history, 'the setting of this battle was as unreal as that of a drama upon the stage.'[23]

William Malone had a good wash and a shave, and then spent the rest of the day watching the battle from the top of the knoll.

> It is ideal fighting country, open undulating country. I could see our troops and the French advancing but not one of the Turks, yet an incessant roll of rifle fire goes all day. Next to us is an Australian Brigade, then there are Indian troops. We all take things as a matter of course, after our experience at [Anzac] this is a sham fight. Yet now and again we get shrapnel fired at us and an odd man gets hit.[24]

As the battle waned, the Anzacs returned to their muddy bivouacs and began to prepare an unappealing early dinner of bully beef and biscuits. They huddled in small groups around smoky campfires and spoke in low voices about the extraordinary and disconcerting sights they had witnessed during the day. A few half-hearted jokes brought a disproportionately lusty response. The men welcomed the distraction; it helped push away the nagging thought that they might be a part of it all tomorrow.

Out on the battlefield of Krithia, after a long day of dashed hopes, missed opportunities and painful sacrifice, finally the sun began to sink low in the sky. The attackers dug their shallow new trenches a little deeper and stared silently into the distance.

The defenders, deprived of good targets for the first time all day, settled down to take stock and let their weapons cool. In no man's land, the lonely bundles of khaki and blue lay still.

By any measure, the Allied advance on 6 May had been a colossal, disorganised, bloody failure. Casualties had been appalling and the advancing troops had gotten nowhere near their first objective, let alone the other two that were supposed to follow. But once again, a lack of clear information and communication was going to have deadly consequences for the troops in the front line. Instructions for the attack had been so vague, and positions so hard to determine on maps, that officers struggled to work out where they actually were on the battlefield and how much ground they had crossed in their aborted advance. And as men are wont to do when under pressure and riding a wave of adrenaline, they grossly overestimated their achievements. Almost without fail along the entire British and French line, commanders were reporting they had captured hundreds of metres of ground that was, in reality, still firmly in Turkish hands. The 88th Brigade, which had been cut down from both flanks and had advanced barely 250 metres, reported that it was within striking distance of Krithia. French commanders stated that they had captured ground that was later discovered to be nearly a full kilometre beyond the point where they had dug in. The British reluctance to utilise air assets was also rearing its head again – an observation flight would surely have given Hamilton a more accurate picture of how far his troops were from their objectives. With misinformation flooding into his headquarters, Hamilton now made a crucial decision – he was going to resume the advance the next day. (In his diary, Hamilton admitted that the line had only advanced a few hundred yards but added the galling remark 'so far so good', as if that had been his plan all along. He also took a petulant swipe at Hunter-Weston: 'I still think we might have done as well at much less cost by creeping up those 200 or 300 yards by night.'[25] It is revealing that he didn't feel capable of conveying this opinion to his subordinate.)

The British official history, as always keen to fall in on Hamilton's side, paints an optimistic portrait of the situation. 'Though the smallness of the Allied achievement was in vivid contrast to the wide objectives allotted to the troops,' it states with laughable understatement, 'a perusal of the Turkish official account … suffices to show that the Turkish position was far from impregnable.' It then wanders off into fantasy, speculating that if only Hamilton had received an extra division of reinforcements and a large resupply of high explosive shells, he 'might well have secured success,'[26] conveniently overlooking the fact that it was completely impossible for him to receive either.

By the time the guns fell silent on the night of 6 May, the battered battalions had dug in on their new line and were exhausted and demoralised. In spite of their best efforts, and the appalling number of corpses now scattered across the battlefield, it was painfully clear to the troops in the front line that the Allied assault had only encountered the most advanced Turkish positions. The main Turkish line, wherever it was, had not been touched.

At the very least, the advance to contact should have revealed where the enemy was so that future attacks would have a clearer picture of what they were facing. It wouldn't be much to show for a couple of thousand casualties but at least it would be *something*. But even that scenario was a cruel dream. The advancing troops had been cut down by an unseen foe and the whereabouts of the Turks remained as much a mystery as it had in the preceding days. (A note of desperation was creeping into Allied planning by this stage. Hunter-Weston's orders issued at 10 pm included the plaintive request for his brigadiers to 'report as soon as possible the position of any entrenchments etc. of the enemy which have checked their advance today. These positions must be indicated as clearly as possible in order that Artillery Fire may be brought down on them tomorrow before the advance commences.'[27] If the divisional commander was still completely in the dark about the location of his enemy after a full day's fighting, what chance did the men on the ground have?)

The opportunity to paint a clearer picture of enemy positions from the air had also been lost. Air units had flown a dozen sorties during the day but only a couple of those were tasked with observing Turkish targets. Crucially, the flights hadn't been coordinated with the infantry advance, the time at which the Turkish defenders would be most active and therefore easiest to spot. Time and time again, the misuse of air assets at Helles represents a frustrating missed opportunity.

Although the Allies were still completely in the dark about the composition and location of their enemy, the story was not the same for the Turks. They knew exactly where the Allies were and where they wanted to go.

From their commanding vantage point on Achi Baba, the Turks peered fiercely through field glasses at the entire Helles sector, as if in a dress circle looking down on a stage. Any Allied troops who moved to join the attack would be under their gaze and in their gunsights from the moment they left their support positions – long before they even reached their own front line. Forewarned and decidedly forearmed, the Turks were waiting, fingers poised on triggers.

13.
7 MAY

As dawn broke on the morning of 7 May, the Allies were preparing to resume the advance that had failed so spectacularly the day before. Nothing had changed in their favour – even the most meagre advantages they had enjoyed before the battle had evaporated. They had fewer men, fewer shells and absolutely no element of surprise. All the advantages now lay with the Turkish defenders.

A good demonstration of how quickly things were getting away from the Allied commanders was the total confusion in the day's orders. After meeting with Hamilton and d'Amade on the afternoon of 6 May, at 10 pm on the same day, Hunter-Weston issued orders for the resumption of the British advance the following morning. The problem was that the orders bore no relation to what was happening on the ground. A combination of inaccurate reports from commanders on the ground and wishful thinking led Hunter-Weston to order his troops to advance to the objectives spelled out in phase two of the attack plan, in spite of them being well short of the objectives for phase one. Far from having Allied troops closing in on Achi Baba, the hill was 'almost as far away as ever',[1] according to the British official history. This effectively made the orders redundant from the moment they were issued – all the troops could do in practice was leave the safety of their trenches and push on as far as they could.

The Allies had a major problem on 7 May that they hadn't had to contend with during their advance the day before. Having captured a small amount of ground, their troops had dug in on a new front line at the furthest point of their advance. They were exhausted and demoralised, and couldn't be expected to advance again, so the attack had to be taken up by fresh troops. But these men were in support areas, hundreds of metres behind the new front line, and would have to cross the same killing field as their comrades had the previous day – and this simply to reach the new front line. Had there been more time, pioneers would have dug communication trenches that linked the old front line with the new one and troops destined to attack could have moved forward, protected from enemy fire. This was the system that was followed on the Western Front, where stages of an advance were separated by days or weeks. But at Krithia, the troops barely had time to dig a new frontline trench, let alone communication trenches to link it to the rear. To reach the new front line, the attacking troops would be exposed to fire from the moment they began to advance. The solution was obvious – the attacking troops should move forward after dark. But, inexplicably, the suggestion of a night advance is not mentioned in any of the official documents. Having been discounted the previous day, it appears not to feature in considerations again. (The British official history states that a night attack was considered 'impracticable', without offering any explanation as to why.[2]) Once again, the timetable at Gallipoli was set to bankers' hours – the attack would begin at 10 am.

Cecil Aspinall-Oglander, as always endeavouring to portray the commanders at Gallipoli in a favourable light, had a challenging task in front of him in the official history – to paint the advance at Krithia on 7 May as anything other than a murderous cock-up. He makes a valiant effort, even resorting to quoting verbatim the stirring 'message of encouragement and exhortation' that Hunter-Weston sent to the 125th Brigade before the attack:

> To the 125th Brigade is allotted the glorious task of seizing Hill 472 and the slopes west and south of it, safeguarding the British left. The eyes of Lancashire and the world are on you, and the honour of your country and the welfare of your own folk at home depend on your deeds to-day. The Major-General knows that no fire and no losses will stop you, and that you will win through to a glorious victory.[3]

Sadly, even the most inspiring words from the commanding general were going to provide scant protection from machine-gun bullets. The task of sticking up for Hunter-Weston proves too much even for Aspinall-Oglander, who gives up the fight in short order. 'The story of 7th May,' he announces with a palpable sigh, 'can be told in a few words.'[4] His 'few words' proceed to describe one of the most pointless and bloody advances of the entire Gallipoli campaign.

The first troop movements of the day did not involve the British or the French, but the New Zealanders. Although the Anzacs had observed the previous day's fighting from their reserve positions, it had been difficult from their distant perspective to tell how the battle was unfolding. An indication that all might not have been going to plan came in the form of an overnight order advising the New Zealanders that they had been removed from the Composite Division and were now under command of the 29th Division, and that they were to immediately separate from the Australians and move into reserve behind the British left flank. Extra ammunition and entrenching tools were distributed to the men, a clear and unnerving sign that they might soon be thrust into the fight. At 4 am, the New Zealanders farewelled their Australian comrades and began quietly filing into the dark fields. Bonds that had been forged in the fire and dust of Anzac were suddenly broken. For many, it was the last time they would ever see their antipodean chums.

For hours, the New Zealanders marched cross-country, encountering British units that were hurrying forward to get to the front line before the start time for the attack. No-one seemed sure where the New Zealanders were supposed to be going. 'We made our way slowly in artillery formation,' said Cecil Malthus, '– each platoon as a close unit but widely spaced from its neighbours – along towards the left flank, with frequent halts and signs of indecision.'[5] After a long march, they came to Gully Beach, where they rested at the wide mouth of Gully Ravine.

As they sheltered there, the battle kicked off again. At least the advance of 6 May had benefitted from a small amount of time being put into its planning. The attack on 7 May was thrown together in a matter of hours, and the results of this lack of planning showed. The artillery was once again called on to provide whatever support it could before the advance began, but if it had been short on shells on 6 May, on 7 May, the cupboard was effectively bare. All it could manage was a feeble fifteen minute display and, given that it still had no clue what it was actually shooting at, it was forced to probe likely targets across the entire battlefield – an area of more than twenty-five square kilometres. Unsurprisingly, the barrage did little but rearrange some topsoil and alert the Turks that the advance was about to resume. Demonstrating how woefully short of ammunition the artillery truly was, an Australian gunner recorded in his diary that 'our Battery opened fire at 11 am but was shortly after ordered to cease and never fired again during the day'.[6]

On the left flank, Hunter-Weston was well aware of the hidden machine guns that had cut the 125th Brigade to ribbons. What his solution lacked in subtlety it made up for in cordite. He ordered the battleship *Swiftsure* and the cruiser *Talbot* to take up a position off Y Beach and, with observation provided by the balloon ship *Manica*, to obliterate the Turkish defenders by literally blowing off the top of the cliff. After a thorough hammering from the ships' guns, large sections of the clifftop were indeed removed, but the balloon observers reported they could spot no trace of an enemy trench, leaving the Turkish defenders with pounding heads but no significant impediments.

The advance against them was allocated to the 1/5th Lancashire Fusiliers, who came under their fire as soon as they left the old British line. Their advance was effectively a repeat performance of the one made by their sister battalion the previous day, although now the Turks were thoroughly primed and waiting for them. Despite the noise and smoke from the naval bombardment, the fire from Turkish machine guns appeared even heavier than it had been twenty-four hours earlier – it's likely that the Turks had brought up at least one extra machine gun overnight. The Lancs were cut down crossing the same ground their comrades had the previous day. Their bodies crumpled and joined the corpses that already littered the battlefield. Second Lieutenant George Horridge was in the thick of it, leading his platoon on the far right of the advance.

> There were a few hisses of bullets, and the further we went on these got more and more. We came to a trench which we got into, and then we got out of the trench and advanced still further, and the amount of rifle fire we were under seemed to get bigger still. I began to lose control of my platoon

because I simply couldn't see them in the scrub. All I could do was blow my whistle and we would advance, along with the line in front. I hoped their NCOs were doing their job.[7]

After a murderous advance, his platoon reached a trench just behind the new British front line. In the frantic dash forward, the entire company had become mixed up, so all Horridge could do was call on his platoon to keep advancing and hope that enough of his men were within earshot to follow him. The Turkish machine-gunners could see them clearly now and their bullets seemed to fill the air. Horridge climbed out of the trench alongside Private Fred Collinson, a 41-year-old who had served with the battalion for years.

> I got out of the trench and Collinson got out of the trench. We had to go at the double because the fire was very heavy then. Bullets were hissing around: *Swish! Swish! Swish! Swish!* We ran halfway to the trench and there was a mound. We got behind this and then, after a minute's rest, I said to Collinson, 'Look, we've got to go on,' and so we set off again. I wasn't too bad a runner and I outstripped Collinson and eventually leapt into the front line trench. I'm sorry to say that Collinson got hit in the last ten yards, through either the chest or the stomach. We got him in but he died later.[8]

The Lancs toppled into the trench alongside the survivors of 6 May, sucking in air in large gasps and painfully aware that their task had just begun – this trench was their allocated start point for the day's attack. 'We got mixed up with the rest of the brigade who were already in these trenches,' Horridge said, 'so they were fairly crowded.'[9]

In a desperate effort to provide some support to the beleaguered attackers, Hunter-Weston ordered reinforcements to try to outflank the Turks by advancing under the clifftop and another group to sneak up the gully to the right. When both groups made no headway, he ordered *Queen Elizabeth*, the biggest ship in the British fleet, to bombard the clifftop with her 15-inch guns. The world seemed to disappear under a storm of fire – surely nothing could survive such a bombardment. But as soon as the Lancs climbed out of their trench to advance, they were greeted by the familiar rattling of Turkish machine guns. Once again, Horridge was leading the charge.

> The order was given to advance, so we got out of the frontline trench. The fellows were firing from the parapet of this trench at presumably the Turks, who I hadn't seen. I couldn't tell where they were, but their fire was very heavy. The Turkish bullets were hitting our trench like you might imagine on a rifle range. We didn't get more than about ten or fifteen yards before it became quite obvious that if we didn't lie down we were going to be hit. So we lay down, and you could see the bullets cutting the grass.[10]

Realising that to continue was suicidal, Horridge ordered his men to veer left and take cover under the cliff edge. Several men were hit during the dash to safety, but the survivors tumbled down the slope until they reached the shoreline, where they took shelter and waited for orders. The attack was over.

On their right, the reserve units of the 88th Brigade were also attacking – and were also meeting the same fate as their comrades had on the previous day. It seems inevitable that troops asked to attack in broad daylight over the same ground as a failed attack from the previous day would achieve the same results but this logic appears to have been lost to the commanders at Gallipoli. After two hours of dogged determination and appalling casualties, the 88th had managed to enter Fir Tree Copse again and, once again, was forced to retreat by heavy fire. Given that the 125th had not managed to advance a single yard on its left, the 88th was sliced apart by flanking fire from the left – it's miraculous that the brigade made any progress at all. Most men retreated back to their starting trench after suffering heavy losses but a few isolated outposts managed to push forward a couple of hundred metres.

With the attack stalled along the entire front line, Hunter-Weston called on his reserve brigade, the 87th, to attack at 4.30 pm over the same ground where the 88th had failed. The artillery fired the handful of shells it had left; then the 87th went in, facing exactly the same machine-gun and artillery fire its fellow brigade had faced over the previous two days. Unsurprisingly, it lost heavily and advanced little. As the sun set, and with nearly 1000 casualties added to the ledger of death, the British attack faded away.

On the right of the Allied line, the French were understandably gun-shy from the shellacking they had received the day before and showed a good deal more common sense in limiting their exposure to danger. They made a few half-hearted attempts to seize ground from the Turks but were quick to call it off when it became clear the advance was futile. D'Amade summed up French activities for the day in typical Gallic style, when he reported succinctly to Hamilton: 'Quiet day, but impossible to leave trenches owing to intensity of enemy's fire.'[11] It was pretty clear the French were going nowhere unless they received some support from the British on their left.

Joe Murray and his fellow marines in the RND had advanced a short distance on the left of the French but were being cautious, having been mauled the previous day.

Just before five in the evening we set off to make contact with the main Turkish army; we just had to defeat it and then walk at ease to Constantinople. Well, that's just what they told us … We went forward a few hundred yards. It was slow and heavy going up a slight slope. At about sunset were ordered to dig in. We were a long way ahead of the flanks, both of which had been held up yet again. The French on the right, however, had made some progress up the Kereves Dere ridge.[12]

During the day, the New Zealanders had not been idle. Mid-morning, they had been ordered to move forward along Gully Ravine, and to occupy the positions recently vacated by the 87th Brigade when it had joined the attack.

As the Kiwis moved forward, the din of battle assaulted them from all directions. They were mostly protected by the high walls of the valley but an occasional shrapnel shell burst overhead and threw up the dust with its deadly payload. As they advanced, they passed men from the Lancashire battalions who had been wounded in the futile advance along Gully Spur, and who were now limping in disconcertingly large numbers away from the front line and back to the beach. Even more disconcerting was the amount of British gear that was strewn all over the gully. This bore more of the hallmarks of a rout than an advance; the New Zealanders wondered uneasily what they were being led into. The only consolation was that many of the Kiwis were able to secure a highly prized British pith helmet, which offered far better sun protection than the standard-issue cap and later made the survivors the 'envy of Anzac'.[13] Having spent the entire day on the move, the New Zealanders were exhausted and looking forward to digging in for the night, but at 9 pm, they received fresh orders to move further up the gully and into reserve trenches behind the front line. The men dragged themselves onward. It was 1 am before they were ordered to halt. 'On both sides of the road were some

old Turkish trenches, in a filthy condition,' the New Zealand
official history recorded. 'Sticking up in the parapet was a dead
man's hand, like a stop sign, seeming to indicate "this far and no
further".'[14] The New Zealanders didn't realise it, but they were
now in the former front line and digging into the same trenches
that the disastrous advance had commenced from two days
before. It took several hours for the men to find comfortable
resting places in the cramped line and they spent the rest of
the night shivering in the dank trenches, with British troops
moving past them in both directions. They hadn't slept in more
than twenty-four hours.

As 7 May drew to a close, the British line was effectively in the
same position it had been on 6 May. Turkish fire faded away –
as the British official history rather ominously notes, 'there was
little or no firing during the night of the 7th/8th May – the enemy
was busy digging.'[15] The advance had been so abysmal that the
Royal Naval Division units that were responsible for linking
the British and French forces did not need to move from the
trench they had dug the previous day. But once again, officers
on the ground drastically over-estimated how much ground
they had captured, and reported to headquarters that they were
much closer to Krithia than they actually were. A sketch map
compiled by 29th Division Headquarters to summarise the day's
advance shows the British left having taken a significant chunk
of ground, and the line now lying tantalisingly close to Krithia,
in spite of all evidence to the contrary. At a later time, probably
after the campaign, possibly even after the end of the war, an
unknown hand has taken to the map to correct the historical
record. 'Map inaccurate. Squares wrong,' it has scrawled in
angry red ink. 'These positions are as reported. They should be
further back. The map is inaccurate.'[16]

The final insult of this whole sorry saga is that the Allied
advance was so ineffective that not only did the Turkish

defenders not have to call up any reserve troops to defend against it, they also didn't even realise they were being attacked. The British official history somewhat forlornly sums up the Turkish accounts.

> There is mention of an unsuccessful attack on the (Turkish) right flank, and of heavy fire near Y Beach from naval guns, but no serious engagement is mentioned, and the Turkish high command does not appear to have realized that anything in the nature of a general attack was attempted this day by the Allies.[17]

So what to make of the decision to advance on 7 May? The British official history, in its attempts to vindicate Hamilton and Hunter-Weston, falls back on the flimsy defence that there was no way of knowing the Turks were as strong as they were and that it's only with the benefit of hindsight that the true dangers of the advance are clear. That's quite a flight of fancy, even by the lenient standards of Aspinall-Oglander. A field of battle strewn with corpses and a failed advance that could be measured in metres rather than kilometres should have been all the evidence required to demonstrate the Turks were a formidable foe who wasn't close to breaking. Which makes the next decision from Hamilton almost impossible to fathom. After two identical days of failure, after thousands of men had been killed or wounded in pointless advances, after an unseen enemy had demonstrated he was growing stronger by the day, after the artillery had completely exhausted its already pitiful supply of ammunition, after the hell on earth that the Helles battlefield had become – the advance on Krithia would resume the next day, on 8 May. Hamilton was going to roll the dice one more time, and this time, the Anzac troops would take their place at the table.

14.
8 MAY

Sir Ian Hamilton could have been accused of many things but an inability to look on the bright side was certainly not one of them. Given two days of pitiful advances, the exhaustion of his already meagre supplies of ammunition and the pile of corpses littering the battlefield, his communication to Kitchener on the night of 7 May is a study in wishful thinking. Whether this was due to Hamilton's natural inclination toward optimism or an attempt to cover up how quickly the campaign was unravelling is impossible to say. At 10.48 pm on 7 May, he cabled Whitehall:

> During a long day's fighting failed to get the Turks properly on the run or to make good Achi Baba. But we have improved our position on the right where the French have captured trenches and on the left where just before sunset General Marshall with 87 Brigade relieved the Lancs Territorial Brigade and pressed the enemy back nearly up to Krithia. Attacking again tomorrow.[1]

Hamilton's obfuscation is startling. The Turks certainly weren't 'properly on the run'. Their main line had not even been approached during the previous two days – the only running they had been doing was to swiftly reinforce their trenches with fresh troops. The vague assertion that the French had 'captured trenches' is misleading – the tiny number of French gains had been made on 6 May. On 7 May, they had advanced no further. But the boldest assertion is that the 87th Brigade had pressed the enemy 'nearly up to Krithia'. In reality, the 87th had been cut to pieces trying to advance along Fir Tree Spur and had dug in on a line that was effectively in the same spot its sister brigade had ended the previous day.

As a final absurdity, and demonstrating that Hamilton really had no clue of the gravity of the situation, he concluded his cable with a bit of gratuitous arse-kissing. 'Please tell Prime Minister his son is progressing well,' he wrote, 'and doctor hopes will not have a stiff joint.'

Despite his optimism, Hamilton had effectively run out of ideas and his sparse orders for the day reflect this. Force Order 5, which had detailed the advance for 6 May, stretched to three full pages and included instructions for everyone from the artillery to the quartermaster. Force Order 6, for the resumption of the advance on 8 May, comprises five paragraphs and barely covers a single page. Apart from detailing the swapping around of a couple of regiments, it is effectively just an exhortation to bend backs and carry on. The important consideration here is intent. The first day's detailed (albeit complicated) plans for advancing to specific points and manoeuvring in specific ways have been replaced with vague notions of the attack on Krithia and Achi Baba being 'pressed with the utmost possible vigour'.[2] The battle was only forty-eight hours old and yet the nefarious scourge of 'objective creep' was already permeating Allied thinking: as the disappointments piled up in front of Achi Baba, the importance of the squat little hill began to swell in Hamilton's mind. By 7 May, Achi Baba was swiftly ceasing to be seen as merely an early stepping stone on the long road to Constantinople and instead became the key objective in and of itself.

Worse still, Hamilton's headquarters was still plagued with the same misinformation that had clouded the previous day's decision-making. His orders for 8 May call for the French to 'continue to consolidate' their position on the vital pivot point, despite not having gotten anywhere near it during the previous forty-eight hours. They were also instructed to resume their aborted and costly advance across Kereves Dere. Once again, there was to be an embarrassingly insignificant opening barrage. Once again, the attack would occur in the bright light of morning. In order to see his vision through, Hamilton finally decided to come ashore. His orders stated that he would establish his headquarters at Hill 114 at 10 am on 8 May.

As vague as they were, at least Hamilton's orders stressed the importance of the whole line advancing together. By the time they had passed through Hunter-Weston's hands, these plans had been dramatically watered down and it was left to the New Zealanders to face the consequences, and the guns.

Just before midnight on 7 May, Hunter-Weston had sent a warning order to his division, announcing that the advance would resume at 10.30 am the following day. The Composite Naval Brigade would remain where it was, the 87th Brigade would hold its position on the left and the New Zealand Brigade would pass through the 88th Brigade position to continue the advance. The Australian and Indian brigades would take up a position close behind, ready to charge at Achi Baba once Krithia was taken by the New Zealanders.

At 8.55 am on 8 May, Hunter-Weston's formal orders reached the brigades, confirming that the main thrust would be made by the Kiwis straight up Fir Tree Spur, with their objective nothing less than the village of Krithia and the network of trenches that defended it. Small parties from the 87th Brigade would advance in support up the gullies on either side of the spur but, apart from that and the commotion the French would be making on the far right-hand side of the peninsula, the New Zealanders would be on their own. It is impossible to reach any sensible understanding as to Hunter-Weston's intentions with this ludicrous order so long after the fact. Two brigades had failed to take this ground over the previous two days – now Hunter-Weston was expecting half that number of men to achieve twice as much. The British official history, uncharacteristically heralding an inevitable catastrophe, summed up the task in ominous tones: 'Four weak battalions of New Zealanders were to attack, in full daylight, a position held by at least nine battalions of Turks.'[3]

Given that Hunter-Weston's orders had only reached the New Zealanders ninety-five minutes before they were due to advance, there was a mad scramble among the battalions to issue instructions to the attacking troops. The overnight warning had given them some advance notice, but it was 10.10 am before the New Zealand Brigade issued formal orders to its men – only twenty minutes before they were due to launch the attack. The orders issued to the New Zealand battalions were vague, contradictory and easy to misinterpret. The New Zealanders were ordered to spread out in the reserve line, with the Canterburys on the right, the Aucklands in the middle and the Wellingtons on the left. The Otago Battalion, which had been mauled on the slopes of Baby 700 back at Anzac and was the weakest of the four, was in reserve.

In the Wellington Battalion, William Malone, like always, was up early, doing everything. Noting how long it had been since his weary men had had a decent meal, Malone set out in search of rations and was delighted to encounter a carrying party that was bringing up supplies for one of the Lancashire battalions that had already joined the advance. The opportunity to organise the unexpected booty was too much for Malone's fastidious mind to ignore and he 'revelled in straightening up the cases of stores and taking stock. Bacon, corned beef (tinned), biscuits, iron rations, tea, sugar, salt, jam, some dried vegetables. It was a veritable godsend.'[4] An hour or so later, with full bellies but still little idea where they were expected to go or what they were expected to do, the Wellingtons waited for the order to attack.

Cecil Malthus and his fellow Canterburys were on the right – the appalling state of the battlefield did not fill them with optimism about their chances of success in the upcoming attack.

> At early dawn a weary mass of humanity disentangled itself from that hateful trench and plodded about a mile up a creek bed which at one spot was full of monstrous swollen corpses … We shuddered to think that we had just filled up with a drink from the stream below them.[5]

The Canterburys advanced until they reached a trench occupied by the bedraggled remnants of the Munster and Dublin fusiliers. The two regiments had been so badly mauled in the previous day's advance that the survivors had been amalgamated into a composite unit christened the 'Dubsters'. 'Hardly encouraging for us,' Cecil grimly noted.

At 10.15 am, the artillery let loose. If the barrage had been thin on the previous two days, today it was positively emaciated. Artillery commanders were forced to raid their emergency supplies for enough shells to even join in the shooting – their focus was squarely on firing off enough rounds to provide a contribution to the barrage, rather than chewing through shells in the task of eliminating Turkish defences. Sergeant Jim Parker's battery in the Australian 2nd Field Artillery was running perilously low on shells and 'only fired a few'.[6]

The navy also joined in, sending over a fusillade of high-explosive shells but, again, compared to the previous days, their fire was noticeably lacklustre. An analysis of the numbers bears this out: in the three days of the battle, HMS *Swiftsure*, one of the key British naval assets in the theatre, fired only *sixteen* rounds of 10-inch ammunition, which was representative of the work of most of the Royal Navy vessels. Worse still, the Turks were beginning to realise the limitations of naval gunfire. Its psychological effect, which had virtually paralysed them in the opening days of the campaign, was waning. Although naval fire created a huge amount of noise and smoke, the Turks realised that the shells from the ships flew in a flat trajectory and therefore couldn't find them if they hid low in the gullies. As naval shells screamed overhead and burst relatively harmlessly behind them, Turkish machine-gunners crouched in their trenches and redoubts, ready to pounce on the infantry advance they knew was coming.

As guns from land and sea continued to roar, the New Zealanders were also crouched in their trenches, waiting for the barrage to end. In front of them lay 450 metres of unbroken open ground that led to the new British front line. This was ground that the New Zealanders should have crossed the previous night, the darkness shielding them from Turkish observation and bullets. To cross it in daylight meant that not only would they be exposed to murderous fire, but their advance to the front line would also give the Turks ample warning that the attack was resuming.

It's difficult to tell exactly where the New Zealand advance started to go wrong, but once it did, it went wrong quickly. It appears that Colonel Francis Johnston, the brigade commander, intended for the New Zealanders to advance to the British front line while the barrage was falling, in the hope that it would offer a measure of protection and enable the New Zealanders to attack from the front line at 10.30 am, as soon as the barrage lifted. This was certainly the understanding of the Canterburys, whose officers ordered them forward as soon as the shells started falling. But on the left, the Aucklands and Wellingtons remained resolutely in their reserve trenches throughout the opening barrage – either they misunderstood Johnston's order or didn't have time to comply with it. It wasn't until 10.30 am, the exact moment the supporting artillery fire died away, that the two battalions climbed out of their trenches and began to advance across the open ground toward the front line, and the waiting Turks.

At first, the Canterbury Battalion made good ground – Johnston's plan had worked to a degree, and the Turkish defenders were pinned down by the barrage and slow to react. Cecil Malthus was in this first wave.

> We sprinted the distance all abreast, in fine style, and thanks to our smartness it was only in the last few yards that the enemy woke up and loosed his fire. The tragedy of it was that from that moment he remained awake, and we were left with the certainty, in our next advance, of having to face a living stream of lead.[7]

To their left rear, the Wellingtons and Aucklands were just beginning to advance and this 'living stream of lead' was exactly what greeted them. The results were bloody and instantaneous. Even the commanding officer was not safe. Malone was advancing with a fellow colonel when 'a bullet passed between our heads and went right through the lobe of his ear'.[8]

The Wellingtons and Aucklands doggedly pushed forward, their numbers thinning as Turkish bullets found their mark. As the troops crossed the bare, open plain, Turkish artillery joined in and shrapnel shells burst overhead as rifle and machine-gun fire ripped through the low scrub. Assaulted from both high and low, the Kiwis were caught in a deathtrap. Men fell all around.

Captain Kenneth Gresson of the Canterburys gave an impressively nonchalant account of this harrowing ordeal.

I'd covered about 75 yards at my top speed when my legs suddenly went from under me, as if struck by a hammer and I fell over and lay still among the daisies. After a few seconds, perceiving that I was not dead but had merely been shot through both legs, I raised my head cautiously and looked about me. The ground all round me was plentifully dotted with khaki-clad figures, for the most part ominously still, though here and there, there was to be seen one endeavouring to crawl to the trenches in front. Just in front lay the [British] trench and as I looked one of the men in it beckoned to me with his finger. I made ready to act on it by unfastening my equipment and allowing it to fall off. As I was unable to get up I had no alternative but to shuffle along as best I could. By using this mode of progression I reached the trench and lay there in great pain, but sheltered from the constant stream of bullets.[9]

The Canterbury Battalion had now lost both its early momentum and the advantage of surprise; forced to wait for the other two battalions to catch up to it, it could do little but crouch behind the frontline trench as the storm of steel swelled around it. 'This front line was held by men of the Worcester Regiment,' Cecil Malthus recalled. 'They were even more dirty and woebegone than the Irishmen. They assured us it was madness to think of advancing, which certainly seemed to be dead right.'[10]

Eventually, the survivors of the Auckland and Wellington battalions succeeded in crossing the deadly ground leading to the British front line and flopped down in the dust beside their

Canterbury comrades. They were exhausted, having crossed nearly a kilometre of ground since they had left Gully Ravine, and were fatally behind schedule.

With nothing to shoot at, the Turkish fire slackened and for a moment the battlefield was ominously quiet. No other British troops were advancing anywhere along the line, so Turkish gunners were free to charge their magazines and machine-gun belts and to train every muzzle onto the narrow strip of trench where they had seen the New Zealanders go to ground. Surely it was only a matter of time before they re-emerged. 'It was about 800 yards to the enemy main line trench,' the New Zealand official history gravely notes, 'but scattered in front of his line, in every depression and behind every clump of bush, were machine guns and hosts of enemy snipers.'[11]

The New Zealanders had gone to ground in front of the Daisy Patch and Fir Tree Copse that had proved such a deadly obstacle to British troops in the previous two days. This strange stretch of ground had probably been planted with crops before the war; now it was overgrown with long grass and dotted with poppies and daisies. It was only about 100 metres across but was completely devoid of cover. A dry creekbed hemmed in the right-hand side, affording excellent cover to Turkish snipers and the dense clump of fir trees, home to several enemy machine guns, dominated it with interlocking fields of fire. As word was passed along the New Zealand line from mouth to adjacent ear that the advance was to begin again, the British troops in the trench just in front of them were stunned. A thickly accented British voice sung out: 'You're not going to charge across the daisy patch, are you?' 'Of course we are,' an Aucklander answered. 'God help you,' came the reply, and nothing more was said.

With a roar, the New Zealanders flung themselves over the top of the British trench and charged for the Daisy Patch. Perhaps the Turks were caught off-guard by the suddenness of the attack but, for several seconds, no fire greeted the Kiwis. But it didn't take long for the Turks to regain their composure; the New Zealand battalions were only about a quarter of the way across the Daisy Patch when all hell broke loose. Machine-gun fire swept the ground like a hose and the Kiwis were cut down. Cecil Malthus recalled the excitement and terror of the advance.

> That first dash – I believe I was the first man out of all our line – not only gave me a thrill of self-importance but probably saved my life, for we had covered fifty yards or more before the hail of fire began. At any rate, the scouts had no casualties, but the other unfortunates, rising to follow our example, were met by the wall of fire and were cruelly slaughtered.[12]

Cecil rushed forward about 200 metres then hit the dirt in a small depression. As bullets sliced through the air inches above his head, he was perversely struck by the beauty of the poppies and daisies blooming in the torn earth. But the sheer horror unfolding all around him soon brought him back to earth.

> Now the storm was let loose, and increased every moment in fury, until a splashing, spurting shower of lead was falling like rain on a pond. Hugging the ground in frantic terror we began to dig blindly with our puny entrenching tools, but soon the four men nearest me were lying, one dead, two with broken legs, and the other badly wounded in the shoulder. A sledgehammer blow on the foot made me turn with positive relief that I had met my fate, but it was a mere graze and hardly bled. Another bullet passed through my coat, and a third ripped along two feet of my rifle sling. Then the wounded man on my right got a bullet through the head

that ended his troubles. And still without remission the air was full of hissing bullets and screaming shells.[13]

Cecil and his mates who were still alive dug in as best they could. A small group had made it to the creekbed, which afforded them some protection from the fury of fire, but most of the Canterbury Battalion retreated to the safety of the British trench. The Aucklands had also attempted to advance across the Daisy Patch and had met a withering fire, not just from in front but also from the left flank, from the same machine guns above Y Beach that had cut down the Lancashire battalions over the previous two days. The attacking troops were caught in a deadly domino effect: because the Turkish machine guns on the far left were not being attacked, they were free to direct enfilade fire across no man's land and into the left of the New Zealanders. This fire prevented the New Zealanders from attacking the Turks in front of them, who were then free to fire in enfilade on the New Zealand centre. And so it continued along the line. This created an interlocking belt of fire from dozens of machine guns that was impossible to penetrate. The attacking troops were facing a wall of lead. The New Zealanders lacked nothing in bravery but it was a futile endeavour. The Australian official history recalled the horrific scene:

> Parties constantly tried to cross the field, but every time, when they were half-way over, they were seen to stumble and fall. Some men rose again and staggered on; but almost always the dust raised by machine-gun bullets sprang from the ground near by, followed, and caught them.[14]

On the left, the Wellingtons had been held up by the murderous fire – no-one had advanced more than a couple of hundred metres. Two companies from the already depleted

Otago Battalion were sent forward to help shore up its shaken sister battalions, but by midday, the advance was effectively over. For several hours, the Turks fired relentlessly at anything that moved. Wounded men who lay in the open were hit again and again; for many, like the man on Cecil's right, a bullet through the head or heart finally spelled the end of their suffering.

While the New Zealanders had been pitting flesh against lead on the left of the Allied line, the French had been resolutely refusing to do the same on the right. Their artillery had pounded Turkish positions above Kereves Dere but as soon as a *poilu* head appeared over the parapet it was met by a storm of machine-gun fire. 'On the right, not an infantryman had stirred in the French sector,'[15] Aspinall-Oglander derisively declared, but his attitude softened somewhat when he realised just how big an obstacle the French were facing. While the French advance had been stalled, the Turks had been furiously digging and their positions on Kereves Spur were now stronger than ever. In effect, the only Allied troops who were up against the main Turkish defensive line on 8 May were the French. D'Amade reported to Hamilton that, once again, his men could not advance until the British had captured Krithia and outflanked the Turkish line.

By 3 pm, the shattered New Zealanders were doing their best just to stay alive. Isolated outposts dug in as best they could in no man's land, stretcher-bearers tried to creep forward to retrieve the wounded and reinforcements came into the reserve lines with the hope of supporting their comrades once the sun had set. Hundreds of men lay dead on the battlefield. Cecil Malthus was still lying where he had gone to ground hours before.

We now began to do a little shooting, but seldom had a visible target except a vague and distant line of trench, where we could see the dust of our bullets rising. There were snipers at quite short range in vantage points up Krithia Nullah, but we could not get at them. Our helplessness was perhaps the most heartbreaking feature of the day.[16]

The entire New Zealand force was exhausted and shaken. And then, shockingly, an order arrived from Hunter-Weston at 3 pm that caused outrage and disbelief in equal measure. The New Zealanders were to attack again at 5.30 pm. The plans had not changed – the New Zealanders would advance alone. There would be a brief preliminary bombardment and the line would push forward. Colonel Johnston, the New Zealand commander, was apoplectic. He called Hunter-Weston and told him in no uncertain terms that to continue the advance meant the destruction of the entire New Zealand Brigade. Hunter-Weston wouldn't hear it – the attack on Krithia would resume at 5.30 pm.

While this drama was unfolding, Hamilton was wrestling with his own demons. Clearly the attack had been a dismal failure, for the third day in a row, but to call it off now would be admitting that the entire Mediterranean Expeditionary Force was incapable of capturing even the preliminary objectives it had set itself for the first day. And if the Allies weren't advancing, what *were* they doing? The only option left would be evacuation. It was a pill too bitter for Hamilton to swallow. Bean makes a valiant effort to summarise this farcical situation with minimal disdain in the official history:

It was true that the shell-supply, always small, was rapidly approaching the point beyond which it could not be reduced, and that in two and a half days' fighting the Turkish line had not yet been reached or even seen by most of the troops. But the opinion was still held that, if once it were reached and pierced, the whole Turkish front line would collapse.[17]

What Bean doesn't mention is that this 'opinion' was based on desperation rather than considered thought. The result was that, once more, military common sense was abandoned in the face of wishful thinking. Hamilton was determined to have one large, final, decisive wager at Krithia. And this time, he was going all in.

— —

If you were standing on one of the small hills that dotted the Allied sector at Cape Helles in the early evening of 8 May 1915, the scene before you would have been eerily familiar from the actions that had taken place over the two days beforehand. Along the line, you would see gun teams scurrying around their batteries, as an overstretched and under-supplied artillery contingent prepared to fire its paltry supply of shells. To the right, you would see the bright jackets and trousers of the weary French brigades preparing to throw themselves at the ferociously strong enemy positions on Kereves Spur. On the left, you would see the shaken and depleted brigades from Britain and New Zealand steeling themselves for a final push along the heights of Gully and Fir Tree spurs. The sacrifice of the previous days would be plainly apparent on the battlefield, as the pathetic little bundles of khaki and sky blue lay still in the evening air. But there would be one noticeable and alarming difference from the preparations that had taken place before the previous days' attacks. Directly in front on you, on the open and gently rising plain that extends all the way to Krithia, there would be movement. On this exposed ground, which had been deemed too deadly to cross even by the lethal standards of 6 and 7 May, the troops who had held this dangerous ground in reserve prepared to move forward and join the advance. This time, the Australians would no longer be spectators. This time, they would be in the thick of the action.

On 6 and 7 May, the officers of the Australian 2nd Brigade had spent much of their time watching the battle unfold from a small knoll near their bivouac. From this position, roughly in the centre of the line, they had a disturbingly panoramic view of the aborted French assaults against the trenches and redoubts above Kereves Dere, and the carnage of the British attacks along the high ground on the left. They had seen lines of men cut down by machine-gun fire, the wounded dragging themselves into whatever shelter they could find and the disheartening spectacle of their Allied comrades streaming back to their own lines after facing a wall of lead in front of the Turkish trenches. They had seen the New Zealanders detaching from their Composite Division and heading off to reinforce the British brigades on their left. On the morning of 8 May, when they heard the yells of the renewed attack, the reply of machine guns and the screams of the dying, they had no idea that it was their comrades from New Zealand whose bodies were now littering the battlefield. Even though they knew little of the grand strategy of the battle, it was clear the attacks had failed. They suspected that any potential role they might have played in the advance was now over.

At 11.15 am, as the battle was raging all across the line, 2nd Brigade commander Colonel James McCay had received a cable from the Composite Division commander, Major General Archibald Paris, ordering the brigade to leave its bivouac and move into reserve positions in Krithia Nullah to support the 29th Division if required. For the first time since the AIF had left Egypt, an Australian brigade moved out in artillery formation, with the battalions and men spread out so that they would suffer a minimum of casualties if they came under enemy artillery fire. They entered the lower reaches of the nullah and edged forward along a dry creekbed. Within a few hours, they had reached the reserve position but, noting it was in full view of Turkish observers on Achi Baba, McCay led the brigade about 800 metres further along the creekbed and ordered it to dig in where a depression screened the battalions from the prying eyes of the Turks. By 3.45 pm, the brigade was digging in and had sent out a liaison officer to make contact with the New Zealanders on the spur to its left.

The reserve trenches in this area were held by the Indian Brigade and the remnants of the 88th Brigade; the Australians squeezed into the cramped gully as best they could, digging into the shallow remains of abandoned trenches on the right bank. The British troops in the reserve line appeared on edge and were manning their trenches with rifles at the ready – the Australians realised that the battlefront must be disturbingly close. This was confirmed when a salvo of Turkish shrapnel shells burst overhead, killing a sergeant from the 6th Battalion. Once dug in, the Australians opened their ration packs and lit fires to cook a warm dinner. The battle raged ahead of them but appeared to be dying down – the fury of fire had given way to the intermittent *pop-pop-pop* of scattered rifle shots. The Australians settled in for an uncomfortable night in the trenches.

Their meal was nearly ready when an orderly rushed into brigade headquarters with a fresh order, issued by General Paris in response to instructions from Hunter-Weston. Brigade Major Walter Cass accepted it with no great alarm, assuming it was probably the standard instructions for manning the support trenches and bringing up supplies. It was 4.55 pm when Cass read the order and he was stunned by it:

You will be required to attack at 5.30pm precisely between
the valley you are now in and the valley just south-east of

the Krithia-Sedd el Bahr Road. Move forward at once until you are in line with New Zealand Brigade on your left and your right on the valley south-east of the Krithia Road. This will be in advance of the Composite Brigade. [The Composite Brigade] under Colonel Casson will support you. Your objective is the ridge beyond Krithia with your right somewhat thrown back to join hands with the French or 2nd Naval Brigade who are at present on the French left.[18]*

Cass alerted his fellow officers to the new orders and no-one could quite believe it. The Australians were to attack, along the deadly Krithia Spur ... in just thirty-five minutes' time!

Not only was this order completely unexpected, it was also delivered at such short notice that few of the Australian officers believed it was humanly possible to comply with it. At no other time during the First World War would an Australian brigade be ordered to attack at such short notice.

It's worth pausing to note how slapdash this order really was. It reflected the desperation leaching out of every headquarters from Hamilton's down. The start point for the advance was so vague as to be practically useless: 'move forward until you are in line with the New Zealand Brigade' – where were the New Zealanders, and how would the Australians know when they had reached that point? The Australian objective was given as the elusive 'ridge beyond Krithia' – where exactly was that? In a landscape riven with ridges and gullies, how would everyone agree on where to stop? How would the Australians even know they were advancing toward the correct ridge? And what does the instruction 'right somewhat thrown back' mean

---

* A follow-up message, not marked with a receipt time but clearly sent immediately after the first one, states: 'GOC in C [General Hamilton] expects every use to be made of the bayonet in this general attack.'

in practice? Does it mean that the left part of the Australian line has to advance further than the right? If so, how would the Australians deal with the enemy in between them? How would this procedure be coordinated, especially with less than forty minutes' notice? But the ultimate nod to disorganisation must be the vague reference to the 'French or 2nd Naval Brigade' – the order was issued in such haste that Paris didn't even know which unit was on the Australian right.*

Regardless of the absurdly short timeline and the paucity of information they had been given, the Australian commanders sprang into action. Messengers were despatched to warn the battalions to be ready to move at one minute's notice. It took ten minutes to assemble the brigade staff to write formal orders for the battalions – there were now only twenty-five minutes until the attack would begin.

At that moment, the situation turned from chaotic to downright farcical. The telephone rang. It was Paris with an urgent request for McCay. Hamilton wanted the Australians to advance with as much display as possible, to give encouragement to the French on their right. 'Have you any bands with you?' Paris enquired. Records don't indicate McCay's immediate thoughts when his commanding officer requested his men march into machine-gun fire with bands playing and flags waving, but his reply was curt.

---

* For comparison, the orders for the brigade's attack on the French village of Pozières just over a year later stretched to three full pages of tightly packed typed text and included details as specific as the identification of British troops on the flanks, the composition of enemy forces, the designation of three distinct objective lines marked to within metres, the colour of signal flares to be used and the precise locations where defensive strongpoints should be built. Crucially, an accompanying map detailed where the supporting artillery barrage would fall and clearly pointed out the final objectives. These orders were issued two full days before the attack was launched, giving ample time for every man in the brigade to work out where he was supposed to be and what he was supposed to be doing.

'We have none,' he said. He then took the opportunity to tell Paris that he doubted the order to attack could be carried out in time. 'It has got to be done,' Paris replied, then hung up. And so began a flurry of activity in the Australian line.

The warning to be ready to move had reached the battalion commanders at 5 pm. Their formal orders were delivered between 5.10 pm and 5.20 pm, giving them just ten to twenty minutes to read them, form a plan, issue instructions to their company commanders and get the men in position. McCay had had no choice but to be concise with his orders – the 6th and 7th battalions would form the firing line of the advance, with the 8th and 5th behind them. McCay did his best to translate Paris's vague instructions into something practicable for the battalion commanders, but in the end, he effectively gave up. He simply instructed the battalions to move forward to link up with the New Zealanders, stretch out across the spur until they reach the valley on the right, and then move forward to capture Krithia. Almost as an afterthought, he instructs the men that 'every opportunity is to be taken to use the bayonet,'[19] as if they would forget to use the weapon if not specifically reminded.

The battalion commanders rushed to issue instructions to their company leaders, who then raced off to inform their platoons. As the orders permeated to the smaller units, the time remaining fell and heart rates rose. The men in the trenches only found out they were about to attack when their sergeants shouted at them to drop their mess tins, don their packs, grab their rifles and move forward. 'You are about to attack the enemy,' they were told, no doubt causing their last spoonful of bully beef to stick in their throats.

George Greig was one of the sergeants doing the rushing and yelling. During the melee, he ran into Sergeant Hector Bastin, an old chum he had known since training in Broadmeadows. They chatted briefly and Greig 'held out his hand and said quite cheerfully to me, "Well Hec, shake. I'm going to go out in this action."[20] Bastin tried to buck Greig up but he was having none of it. They parted ways and went back to the urgent business of getting their men ready to attack.

Given how rushed the whole process was, the Australians fell into line with impressive skill. The battalions moved forward quickly and spread out by platoons across the scrubby plateau. The 6th Battalion on the left began moving as soon as its men were in line, leaving the 7th Battalion to dash behind them to fall into position on their right. As a consequence, the 6th advanced slightly in front of the 7th (and inadvertently complied with Paris's obscure order for the left to advance ahead of the right). It was 5.30 pm – the Australians were bang on time. But as soon as they began to move forward, they got into trouble. They had no idea where the Turkish trenches were, or even which direction they were supposed to be advancing. With no-one else to guide them, several of the brigade's senior officers – including Major Walter Cass, Lieutenant Colonel Robert Gartside (from the 8th Battalion but temporarily in command of the 7th Battalion) and even Colonel McCay himself – rushed forward to lead the men from the front, an unusual and highly dangerous development.

The depression where the brigade had originally camped extended across the plateau, so as the advance began, the Australians were screened from Turkish view by the dead ground and a scattered row of straggly olive trees immediately in front of them. Suddenly, the covering artillery barrage let loose and the air behind the Australians was filled with the detonations of the British heavy guns. The Turkish positions remained ominously silent.

Australian gunners did their best to support their infantry comrades but their hands were tied by the chronic shortage of ammunition. Despite this, the shelling seemed to be having an effect, as recounted by Sergeant Jim Parker of the 2nd Field Artillery.

> From 5.30 to 7pm we joined in at a great rate, firing 174 [shells] in 1 1/2 hours; total for day 224. Din was incessant, 10 pounders, 60 pounders, 6-inch, 18 pounders, and French 75's, also ships' guns all on the job. Could see hundreds bursting in Krithia village and along the enemy's position.[21]

Staff Sergeant Les Goldring of the 12th Field Artillery confirmed that the gunfire appeared to be taking a heavy toll on the Turks, noting in his diary: 'It was a most ungodly sight to witness the township and the Turks being blown sky high.'[22]

Private Frank Brent of the 6th Battalion was also awed by the apparent ferocity of the barrage.

> It was indescribable. The noise, the dust. You just couldn't hear each other speak. And that went on for about a quarter of an hour and then everything was as silent as the blessed grave. And that was the time when we had to hop out. And the barrage had been so heavy that we thought, 'Well, this is going to be a cake walk, there's nothing to stop us.'[23]

It's important to note that this was the first time most of these men had experienced a concerted artillery barrage up close. Although it appeared fearsome, a year later on the Western Front, this level of artillery fire would be considered insignificant. As for the men on the receiving end of it, the Turkish defenders were well hidden and most of them came through the bombardment unscathed.

The Australian infantry continued to cautiously advance until they reached a trench full of Indian troops who were acting as the reserve for the attack. The Aussies didn't know it but this had been the British start line for the opening day of the attack on 6 May – where they had seen the advancing British troops cut down two days before. As far as the Australians knew, this was the British front line and they were now entering no man's land. The trench had been hurriedly dug and was narrow – the Australians stepped across it, knocking dirt down onto the irritated Indian troops as they advanced. As they crossed the trench, the brigade spread out in artillery formation, extending until the right platoons reached the gully on the right side of the plateau. It made for an impressive sight and the Australians performed it effectively on instinct. They began to move forward.

On the slopes of Achi Baba, just over four kilometres away, Turkish observers scanned the British lines with binoculars and spy glasses and were startled to see a fresh wave of troops emerging from the scrub and advancing toward them. They grabbed field telephones and wasted little time in alerting their artillery crews to the new targets. Turkish machine-gunners cocked their weapons and took aim. The Australians pushed forward. The Turks began to fire.

> Bullets, coming from a long distance, were now whistling thickly overhead and through the lines. Between the dry grass-blades and low tufts of dingy herbage the dust began to rise in spurts like the sea at the commencement of a thunder-shower.[24]

Now the Turkish artillery batteries opened up. The white puffs of shrapnel shells began to burst above the Australian battalions, an all-too-familiar reminder of the early days at Anzac.

> The expected result came presently in salvo after salvo of shrapnel, bursting in fleecy little clouds over the

7th Battalion and whipping up other clouds of tawny dust close below, where the hissing pellets struck the dry plain, sometimes obscuring with haze the hurrying platoons ... It was, I thought, like walking against a dust storm in Sydney. The bang of the guns at this stage relieved us from the tension caused by the whiz of passing bullets.[25]

The shellfire and steadily increasing rate of rifle and machine-gun fire created a terrifying spectacle, but the effects at this long range were negligible in the early stages of the advance. Charles Bean reported that 'one signaller ... received a shrapnel burst full in the face; but for the most part the companies escaped almost without loss'.[26]

Bean was well placed to report on the advance as it unfolded – he was in the middle of it. Hearing that the 2nd Brigade was joining the attack on Krithia, he had rushed forward and, rather than stay in the rear and observe at a distance, as his official orders and good sense dictated, he couldn't help but advance with the men.

As Bean moved forward, just behind the attacking battalions, Turkish fire increased and Australians began to drop, some with a groan, most with a sigh. Private Ed Lakeman of the 6th Battalion was advancing beside his chum Private Bill Buckingham, the cooper from Melbourne who had become a father figure to the younger blokes in the battalion. A shrapnel shell detonated overhead and Bill went down. Ed couldn't tell how badly Bill had been hit, but he had no choice but to push on and leave him for the stretcher-bearers. He briefly huddled over Bill, trying to make him as comfortable as possible, and then said a quick farewell. It was the last time he would ever see him.

Corporal Clarrie Roberts in the 8th Battalion understood immediately that the Turks could observe every move the

Australians made and bring down fire directly onto them.

> Immediately the attack commenced the Turks brought
> artillery fire to bear upon us, and their shooting was very
> accurate, for the shells were bursting along the creek where
> the troops were advancing, under cover of the bank. It
> was not a pleasant thing to contemplate, working our way
> through that curtain of fire, seeing the men ahead falling
> at every shell. Someone must go down, and it appeared
> that few could pass. The alternative from passing through
> this shell fire was to cross the creek, and work in the open,
> but which was the more disastrous, the shell fire or the
> rifle and machine gun fire which swept the plateau ahead.
> There was little to choose between; death followed every
> man, at each step.[27]

The men pushed on, laden with the weight of their full battle
kit and their heads down as if walking into a strong wind.
They expected to come across the Turkish front line at any
moment and were itching to get stuck in with the bayonets they
had so frequently been reminded to use. After what seemed
like an age, they suddenly and unexpectedly came to a trench
stretching across their whole front. Any move to use the bayonet
was quickly stifled; the trench wasn't occupied by Turks but by
British soldiers who had dug in after the advance on 6 May.
The Australians were stunned. Dozens of their comrades had
already been shot down and it was only now that they had even
reached the British front line.

Worn out and fearful, the Aussies either flopped down
behind the trench or crammed into it alongside the British
troops. They had reached the line marked on British maps as
Composite Brigade's Trench, which was packed with survivors
from the advance of the Lancashire Fusiliers. From then on, it

would be known to the Australians as Tommies' Trench. Some men wondered if their job was in fact to reinforce the trench but their hopes were soon dashed when McCay, never a man to shy away from a good fight, stood up on the parapet of the trench and called out, 'Now then Australians! Which of you men are Australians? Come on, Australians!'[28]

The men started to rise from the trench, and one of the bravest Australian advances of the First World War began. The Turks were now fully alerted that a fresh assault was taking place and their fire was heavy and accurate. Bullets smacked into the parapet of the trench, showering dirt onto the faces of the men below; puffs of dust from rifle and machine-gun bullets rose thickly across the plain. Shrapnel shells burst overhead, adding to the chorus of death.

Private Sam Norris responded instantly to the call.

The ground we passed over was strewn with daisies and big shell cases. It was a lovely sunny day. One of those days when you wish to be at peace with all men. The hill before us appeared to bristle with guns and the flat surface of the ground afforded us no shelter. Breaking into a run we reached our first line trench in a very fagged condition due to our packs. We expected a spell here but no it was 'Forward, Australians!' On we went again at a run, flopping down occasionally (not every 25 yards as the textbooks direct) for a few seconds' rest.[29]

Harry Kelly had done well to stay alive up until this point but, given what the Australians were facing, he didn't expect his luck to last long. 'Now the casualties began in dozens,' he wrote, 'and men could be seen falling everywhere and I do not think that there were many among us who expected to come out of this <u>Hell</u> alive.'[30]

Charles Bean was in Tommies' Trench alongside the Australians, spellbound by what he saw.

I had watched from the Tommies' Trench line after line of men scramble to the parapet, stand there for a moment astride of the trench, with rifle and bayonet clutched across their chests, glaring to the front with eyes puckered to pick up any trace of where the tempest of bullets came from. I noted in my diary: 'Their faces were set, their eyebrows bent, they looked into it for a moment as men would into a dazzling flame. I never saw so many determined faces at once.'[31]

He reached for his camera to capture what he thought would be 'the finest photograph of the war', and discovered that, in his haste to join the advance, he had left it back at the starting line.

As Bean looked up, he saw a man advancing into the storm of fire and holding a shovel in front of his face 'like an umbrella'. Bean was overwhelmed with admiration for the brave Australians and this emotive image stayed with him for the rest of his life. He repeated the anecdote often – in his diary, in *Gallipoli Mission* and in the official history. But fascinatingly, the same story was told in a letter to *The Bulletin* in November 1915, from a different perspective and an unexpected source – one of the men involved in the shovel incident. Bean had come under some stick in the magazine for being a dull reporter and, as part of a movement to defend him, a soldier who identified himself only with the initials 'FJS' wrote to the magazine from his dugout at Gallipoli. He stated that his first sight of Bean had been 'under rather sensational circumstances' and that he wanted to convey 'what sort of a fellow he is'. His description is so absorbing it deserves quoting in full:

On May 8 we advanced up the creek towards Krithia. At the trenches of the Lancs. our men came out to open country and deployed. Then the advance was made in short rushes of about 50 yards. It was after the third rush, and we were about 1000 yards from the Turks. My left-hand neighbour (we were in support about 100 yards behind the firing line) had a shovel arranged as an armor-plate before his head. We were both pancaked out as flat as possible, breathing only long ways and side ways, so as not to rise any, noses buried in the earth, packs drawn right up over our heads, discussing the probable effect if a bullet struck the shovel. I held that it would ric[ochet] and enter the ribs of the platoon commander, who was lying next door. My companion said the bullet would certainly rise. While we were endeavouring to convince each other a tall, gaunt figure stalked over our line and strode away ahead towards the firing line. We were so astonished that we leaned up to watch. Only once his head suddenly swung aside – probably a bullet had droned past rather close. Then we remembered the dangerous posture we were in, and, cursing ourselves for our carelessness, we flattened out again, and saw no more of the gaunt officer till we spotted him sitting under a tree at the rear, writing up his notes after the show was over.[32]

Bean certainly could never be faulted by his bravery – it says a lot that he was still walking forward, armed only with a pencil, when the soldiers who were supposed to be attacking were lying flat out in the dirt.

As described by 'FJS' above, the Australians advanced in short rushes, desperately trying to cover as much ground as they could before the fire overwhelmed them and forced them to ground. Although they were moving forward at impressive speed, they were neglecting a crucial aspect of a contested advance – covering fire. Each platoon should have been firing in support of its neighbours as they surged forward, but the men were so anxious to charge the Turkish lines that practically no-one was using their rifle. Even if they had remembered the covering fire drill they had practised so many times, they were faced with the very real issue that no-one knew where the Turks were or where the fire was coming from. A report from an officer after the battle summed up the situation with an understandable touch of despondency. 'There was no shooting from the Australian line,' it said. 'There was nothing to shoot at.'[33] The Aussies were advancing into a hurricane of fire with little to defend them.

Harry Kelly was charging forward when:

> I got a violent smack in the left shoulder which knocked me over. I knew what had happened for the blood was running freely so, taking hold of a turf of grass, I pulled myself out of my equipment with my wounded arm following but it was sticking out behind me and becoming suddenly weak. I fell back onto it, unable to hold myself up, and the pain was intense until another lad, slightly wounded on the side of the face, saw the cause of the pain and rolled me over.[34]

Harry lay in the dust, as bullets continued to rip the air and smack into the dirt, when he saw an old chum.

> Imagine my surprise on seeing, only five paces away from me, my old pal Nick who was wounded in the muscle of the right arm. He rolled over to where I was lying and my other comrade who had rolled me over said that he would try and dress my wound. Borrowing Nick's knife, he began

cutting the sleeve off my tunic, and while doing so he was shot right in the forehead, killing him instantly in the act of doing myself a good turn.

Harry was bleeding heavily and wanted to make a run for it back to the Australian lines, but Nick talked some sense into him. They lay pressed into the dry earth until dark and then began the painful five-kilometre journey back to the beach. After a couple of kilometres, they reached a dressing station, where Harry's vicious shoulder wound was attended to. Nick wouldn't let the orderlies touch his, noting that there were far more seriously wounded men who needed attention. Harry and Nick hobbled back to the beach, where Harry was taken into a field hospital and then put onto a hospital ship.

Back on the battlefield, the survivors of the 2nd Brigade continued to press forward but their numbers were thinning with each rush. Their officers were doing as much as they could to lead and inspire them from the front, but this made them prime targets for Turkish marksmen. One by one, the Australian officers fell, half of them wounded, half of them dead (and of course, for every officer who was hit, dozens of their men fell alongside them).

In the 7th, advancing precisely as they had been trained to do, Lieutenants Wale and Carmichael were killed, and Lieutenant J. A. K. Johnston mortally wounded, in the first or second rush. Lieutenant Scanlan was hit through the chest and Lieutenant Fraser through the head within 200 yards of the Tommies' Trench. Captain Hunter – a famous Victorian athlete – was wounded and then hit again and killed. In the 6th, both the leading company commanders – Wells (the same who had charge of part of the line on [Lone Pine] on April 25th) and Keiran, a born leader of men – were mortally wounded … [Major Cass] was standing correcting the men's aim when he was struck down by a bullet which pierced his breast. Lying beside the road he sent word by a wounded man to Captain Henderson, instructing him to take over the advancing line. After two further rushes Henderson, rising to his knees to look through his glasses, was himself shot through the head … Colonel McNicoll, after being knocked down by a bullet as he rose from the Tommies' Trench, was seriously wounded 250 yards farther on. Captain Borwick was hit, and hit again as he lay on the ground. After 400 yards Colonel Gartside of the 7th was mortally wounded. Lieutenants Pozzi and Dangerfield of Borwick's company were killed and Captain Lowe wounded.[35]

Gartside, a much-loved officer who was commander of the 8th Battalion but temporarily leading the 7th at Krithia, had been rising to lead a charge with a cry of 'Come on boys, I know it's deadly but we must get on,'[36] when he was hit in the stomach by machine-gun bullets.

This was turning from an attack to a slaughter but there was nothing for the men to do but push on, either until they came to grips with the Turks or were killed in the effort. Finally, they got close enough to see Turkish helmets bobbing behind a parapet about 500 metres ahead, but to their horror, they discovered that most of the fire was not coming from this main trench but from a screen of rifle pits about 150 metres in front of it. Just as it had during the vicious attacks of the previous days, the Allied advance was being smashed by Turkish outposts, without ever getting close to the main trench line.

Sergeant Sam Wilson of the 6th Battalion had to this point escaped injury and, as his mates fell all around him, thought he was leading a 'charmed life'.

This was not so, for when about 300 yards from the Turk's trenches, I got a bullet through the right ear. It just felt like the prick of a penknife. I called them a good Australian name and was going on further, when I got two more in the shoulder … I was smothered in blood, even my eyes were full and I could not see, and while I was trying to get it out of my eyes, I got knocked on the right shoulder with shrapnel.[37]

Wilson began crawling to the rear and came across a wounded British soldier. He dressed the Tommy's wounds and the two men began a painful journey to the aid post, supporting each other as best they could. The British soldier gave Wilson his watch in appreciation. 'I was putting him down behind a bit of cover, when a shell fell between us. It blew one of his legs off, and left his lifeless body in my arms. This was the end of the poor chap.'

On the left of the Australians, the New Zealanders were copping the same brutal treatment. The navy blasted away at the Turkish positions and the Kiwis managed to creep forward another couple of hundred metres, until they stalled in the face of withering fire. The Turks were forced to pull back their advanced posts, and the hated Fir Tree Copse and Daisy Patch were finally in Allied hands. But the main Turkish line still had not been spotted, let alone attacked, and the New Zealanders were finished. The Wellingtons had made some ground on their left and the Canterburys pushed forward to link up with the Australians on their right, but other than these, any aspirations for a New Zealand advance had been smashed. Cecil Malthus had pushed forward with the Canterburys and was relieved that 'the enemy's fire, being distributed everywhere, was not nearly so deadly as in the morning, but our company's losses were heavy enough'.[38] Among the dead was Second Lieutenant

Alexander Forsythe, the much-loved officer who had been with
Cecil and his mates since training in Nelson. He went down
hard with a bullet in the head and didn't move again.

On the right of the Allied line, the French had once again
pushed forward against the strong Turkish lines in Kereves Dere.
One of the most lurid accounts of their advance comes from
an unlikely source – the diary of Lieutenant General Hamilton.
His headquarters position on Hill 114 gave him a grandstand
view of the action and he described the spectacle effusively.

> On the right, at first nothing. Then suddenly, in the
> twinkling of an eye, the whole of the Northern slopes of
> the Kereves Dere Ravine was covered by bright coloured
> irregular surging crowds, moving in quite another way to
> the khaki-clad figures on their left: – one moment pouring
> over the debatable ground like a torrent, anon twisted and
> turning and flying like multitudes of dead leaves before the
> pestilent breath of the howitzers. No living man has ever
> seen so strange a vision as this: in its disarray; in its rushing
> to and fro; in the martial music, shouts and evolutions![39]

The French advance might have made for an enlivening
spectacle for Hamilton, but to the men caught up in it, it was an
ordeal of blood and fire. Hamilton was briefly encouraged by
what he saw, but this rapidly turned to disappointment.

> My glasses shook as I looked, though I believe I seemed very
> calm. It seemed; it truly seemed as if the tide of blue, grey,
> scarlet specks was submerging the enemy's strongholds.
> A thousand of them converged and rushed the redoubt at
> the head of Kereves Dere. A few seconds later into it – one!
> two!! three!!! fell from the clouds the Turkish six inchers.
> Where the redoubt had been a huge column of smoke arose

> as from the crater of a volcano ... The puppet figures we
> watched began to waver; the Senegalese were torn and
> scattered. Once more these huge explosions unloading their
> cargoes of midnight on to the evening gloom ... Night slid
> down into the smoke. The last thing – against the skyline –
> a little column of French soldiers of the line charging back
> upwards towards the last redoubt. After that – darkness!

Against such impervious positions, the French attack was
doomed to fail, just as their previous efforts had been. The *poilu*
advanced bravely but made little ground and fell back, leaving
hundreds of dead and wounded on the field.

Joe Murray was much closer to this action than he would
have liked. His small party from the Hood Battalion of the
Royal Naval Division had dug in the previous day with a ragtag
assortment of soldiers from other battalions in the RND, and
even a handful of Senegalese troops who had lost their way
while fighting in the French sector. Joe and his comrades could
hear the cacophony of battle unfolding on both sides of them.

> Way over on the left fighting had begun again. Our men
> were attacking ... Many would be left to die of their wounds
> or of thirst, tormented by millions of flies. A few yards of
> scrub-covered ground had been wrested from the enemy
> but not enough.[40]

Back at Tommies' Trench, the Australians were still pushing
forward. As each wave of men arrived, they were urgently
rushed forward into the maelstrom. Men were dropping fast
both behind and in front of the trench, and their bodies soon
dotted the landscape.

A British officer watched the spectacle with horror from high
ground behind the lines.

> Through glasses at six o'clock I can see little figures running here and there on the high ground to the extreme right beyond the White House – now taking cover, now running forward, now disappearing on the other side; ugly black shells rain amongst them and make a sickening sight. Turkish artillery appears to have increased considerably. Their shells rain all along our line, but none come on the beaches. All their artillery seems concentrated on our trenches. Again and again I see shells fall right in the middle of men who seem to be running ... I watch till the sight sickens me.[41]

One of the men caught up in this sickening ordeal was Sergeant George Greig. He was out in front of his platoon, exhorting his men to keep pushing forward. He raised his head to get a clearer view of the Turkish line and was struck by a bullet between the eyes. He was dead before he hit the ground.

Private Frank Brent of the 6th Battalion was witnessing so much carnage all around him that he became fatalistic, accepting the fact that he had no chance of seeing out the day alive.

> You could see your mates going down right and left. And you were face-to-face with the stark realisation that this was the end of it. And that was the thought that was with you the whole time, because despite the fact that we couldn't see a Turk, he was pelting us with everything he'd got from all corners, and the marvel to me is how the Dickens he was able to do it after the barrage that had fallen on him. And sure enough, we got to within about a mile of Krithia village when I copped my packet. And as I lay down I said, 'Thank Christ for that.'[42]

After an hour of this carnage, Major Gordon Bennett of the 6th Battalion was now effectively the only officer still standing. He picked his way forward past the corpses, bent double to make himself as small a target as possible. He came across men in groups of twos and threes, the only survivors of the first waves to advance. He gathered them up and they pushed forward. But after another short advance, Bennett gave up and they all hit the ground. He now only had twenty men with him and could see that there were no Australians in front of his small group, alive or dead. It was pointless to continue, so he ordered the men to dig in.* They had advanced about 400 metres from Tommies' Trench – as far as any Australian would get in the battle. More men bravely crept forward and joined the digging. As the sun began to sink in the sky, a shallow trench line was forming as the men lay flat on their bellies and scraped away at the dry earth with entrenching tools and fingers, their packs stacked in front of their heads to offer a small measure of protection. One of them was Sergeant Cecil Eades of the 7th Battalion.

> Well we charged but what we charged, goodness only knows. I never ran so much in my life. Then the machine-guns started. That stopped our charging! We advanced by short rushes to within striking distance but were too decimated to complete the attack. Captain Heron and I happened to be alongside each other and there was a wretched Turk enfilading us with stray shots. Heron and I took turns with the rifle and entrenching tool until Heron got an enfilading bullet over the right eye. I then had to dig for the two of us. We got down to cover without any further mishap. Why the Turks never counter-attacked that night and wiped the lot of us out, God alone knows. Think of it – a little band of men,

---

* Bennett might have performed well at Krithia (and throughout the First World War) but as a major general in command of the 8th Division in the Second World War, he would earn notoriety for seemingly abandoning his men in the face of the Japanese invasion of Singapore and fleeing to Australia.

not more than 300, stuck right out in front of the army with
nothing to the right or left.[43]

The men were starving and had no prospect of receiving
supplies, so they raided the packs of the dead men all around
them for desperately needed rations and water. Some men of the
5th Battalion saw movement in the scrub to their right and fired
a few shots. Half a dozen Turks jumped up and bolted through
the bushes. These were the only enemy soldiers the Australians
saw during the entire battle. As the evening shadows grew,
more Australians pressed forward across the field strewn with
corpses and reinforced the line.

On their left, the New Zealand survivors were also digging.
Cecil Malthus was ordered to make a perilous journey to the
rear with four wounded men.

> I took the opportunity of getting a boot from a dead man,
> to replace the one that had been ripped open. No stretchers
> nor bearers were available. I spent most of the night
> searching for them, losing my way continually, till I could
> hardly stand. Once I came to with a start, to realise that I
> had been on the very edge of falling asleep while walking.
> Luckily I always managed to get back to my wounded, who
> required frequent attention.[44]

Cecil's bravery didn't amount to much; two of his wounded
comrades died within days. Dawn was breaking as Cecil made
his way back to the front line and began the wearying and
relentless job of digging in. 'I had to dig – for the fourth time –
a shallow grave for myself, just behind the line, and fell into it
exhausted.'[45]

And so ended the Second Battle of Krithia and, with it,
Allied hopes for a swift victory at Gallipoli. On the morning

of 6 May, Hamilton had expected that Achi Baba would be captured before nightfall. By the evening of 8 May, after three days of brutal fighting, the Allied front line had advanced less than 500 metres. This was an advance so insignificant it barely made contact with the most advanced Turkish posts. Except for a small section in front of the French, the main Turkish line had not even been located, let alone attacked. About 20,000 British, French, Australian and New Zealand troops had participated in the bloody advance. More than 6500 of them now lay dead or wounded.

The Australian attack had lasted little more than an hour; they had crossed about 900 metres of ground, both behind and ahead of the British front line, and had faced rifle and machine-gun fire that was as heavy as anything Australian troops would encounter for the rest of the war. Of the 2500 men who had entered the fight, nearly half were killed or wounded. The survivors continued to dig in, safe for the time being but shaken by what they had been through and seen. They settled in for a long night, haunted by the shouts of the Turks in the line out in front, and the visions of death that just wouldn't leave them.

The final action of 8 May occurred late at night, when two British battalions moved forward to link up with the Australian line and secure the right flank. To get to the front line, they had to cross the same stretch of ground that had cost the Australians more than 1000 men to capture during the day. Advancing under the cover of darkness, the British were completely screened from Turkish fire and reached the front line without suffering a single casualty.

15.

AFTERMATH

The Second Battle of Krithia resulted in the death of not just thousands of troops but also of hope. Prior to the battle, the Allies had been driven by the conviction that they would overcome the Turks at any moment, and that the way to Constantinople would miraculously open before them. After the battle, the crushing realisation that Gallipoli would now be defined by stalemate and attrition descended on the peninsula like a black veil. The orders issued before and even during the battle were filled with optimism and platitudes; the failure of the advances on 8 May prompted a string of orders from Sir Ian Hamilton's headquarters that promised nothing but hard graft and diminishing returns. The most fascinating aspect of this transition is how early in the campaign it came about and just how quickly things changed.

On 9 May, orders were issued from Hamilton's headquarters that basically dismantled the convoluted command structure and intermingling of units he had put in place for the failed attack at Krithia. Despite opening with the (completely false) assessment that 'the enemy are known to have suffered heavy casualties in yesterday's action',[1] the order simply spelled out which units would occupy various parts of the line and didn't even pretend that any new opportunities had presented themselves. The following day, Hunter-Weston issued a Special Order that demonstrated how little had been achieved in the bloody days preceding, by maintaining that 'vigorous and systematic attacks' must continue to be made by the British troops but without giving much clue as to how or when these would take place. It then gives an extraordinary directive:

> Infantry Commanders will also forward to Divisional Headquarters proposals for the attack of the particular portions of the enemy's position in their front, as well as any information they can obtain as to the localities held by the enemy which may affect such attacks.[2]

With captains and corporals in the front line asked to come up with creative attack plans for their own small section of front, as well as quizzed for any information about where the enemy actually was, it's painfully clear how blind Hamilton and Hunter-Weston were flying.

The order also details requirements for snipers and artillery cooperation and ends with a typical Hunter-Weston bit of completely untenable bravado.

> If the attack is systematically prepared on the above lines and the offensive against the enemy never relinquished for a moment, the final capture of the position now in front of us should be an easier task than the advance up to our present position has been. The Major General Commanding is convinced that this attack will be undertaken in the same fine spirit which has carried the division forward through the past heavy fighting to its present situation within reach

of the *first objective of the expedition*,* the capture of the Achi Baba line.³

Despite the fact that the order doesn't actually spell out what 'attack' should take place or how it should be carried out, Hunter-Weston is confident that through determination and 'fine spirit' the Turkish line will somehow magically be overcome. The order then inadvertently reveals what a fiasco the entire campaign has become by reminding the reader that the objectives for the *first day* have still not been achieved.

On 11 May – only sixteen days after the landing – Hamilton issued the astonishing Force Order 8, which basically threw in the towel on any prospects of a rapid advance and advised the troops to prepare for the long ordeal of trench warfare. It congratulated the troops on their 'magnificent work' of the past fortnight, then advised that this arduous work has 'necessitated a brief pause to recoup, refit and prepare for fresh exertions'.⁴ This must have come as a blessed relief to the exhausted and demoralised men who had been bleeding on the Krithia plain since the landing but even they must have been astounded to read that 'operations in the immediate future will approximate more to semi-siege warfare than open operations in the field'. It's extraordinary that Hamilton so readily used the term 'siege' to describe the situation at Helles. The operation here was supposed to be a swift advance, and now the Allies were admitting they were besieged only a few kilometres from where they had come ashore.

Over five pages, the order then spells out in detail exactly how the British and French should go about entrenching themselves at Helles, a process that would have been eerily and disturbingly familiar to any officer who had seen action on the

---

* My italics.

Western Front. Trenches should form 'one continuous line', support trenches should be dug behind the front line, machine guns should be placed carefully to provide flanking fire against enemy attacks, aggressive patrolling should take place at night, infantry commanders should coordinate with the artillery so that each sector of trenches is adequately covered and telephone lines should be laid underground in triple rows, so that communication can be maintained between the front line and headquarters. The most noteworthy aspect of this order is how defensive it is – mostly dedicated to ensuring the British solidify their position so much that the Turks won't be able to overwhelm them. Not only was Hamilton now not advancing on Constantinople – he wasn't advancing anywhere. In a single document, the entire Gallipoli campaign had been turned on its head.

Not only were the troops instructed to limit their offensives, two days later, they were also instructed to limit their shooting as well. On 13 May, Hamilton addressed his near-terminal paucity of shells by issuing Force Order 11, which instructed his artillery to become frugal to the point of delinquency. The order spelled out that for the foreseeable future, a period of 'comparative inactivity', artillery ammunition should only be used for 'what is absolutely necessary for the maintenance of our position or for the purpose of retaliation'.[5] The gunners were instructed to save their 18-pounder ammunition and fire their 15-pounder shells instead, a round so puny that it was effectively obsolete by the end of the Boer War. Howitzer shells were to be 'economised' even further and were only to be fired in support of infantry during an organised attack. The final point in the order carried a distinct whiff of panic, with instructions that even during an enemy attack, 'the expenditure of ammunition can only be governed by the one principle of the amount necessary to defeat the attack, but even at such a time the necessity for economy of ammunition should never be lost sight of'. If the artillery wasn't allowed to fire in anger, and even in defence to fire only the absolute minimum of shells, its role on the battlefield was effectively crippled.

When read collectively so many decades after the fact, this collection of orders paints a picture of a force that is stretched to breaking point. Given their limitations and repeated failures, it was clear that the Allies at Gallipoli stood no chance of capturing even Krithia or Achi Baba, let alone the Dardanelles forts and Constantinople. The Gallipoli dream was in tatters, yet no-one in command appeared to have the courage to acknowledge it. Dogged determination and wishful thinking replaced sound military strategy.

Hamilton had taken a deep breath and cabled Kitchener on the night of 8 May. For once, his correspondence was not cloaked in false optimism, painting a reasonably accurate picture of the results of the battle.

The result of the operation has been failure, as my object remains unachieved. The fortifications and their machine guns were too scientific and too strongly held to be rushed, although I had every available man in today. Our troops had done all that flesh and blood can do against semi-permanent works and they are not able to carry them. More and more munitions will be needed to do so. I fear that this is a very unpalatable conclusion, but I can see no way out of it.[6]

Hamilton was correct in his assessment that the attack had been a dismal failure, but his justification for why it had all gone so wrong was inaccurate and self-mitigating. Nowhere on the entire Turkish front could the defences be described as 'semi-permanent'. The Turks didn't even have a connected line of trenches. Regardless, the state of the Turkish main line had had no effect on the outcome of the battle – simply because the Allied forces hadn't gotten anywhere near it. They had been shot down by machine guns and rifles in forward outposts, which didn't really consist of trenches at all and were mostly sited in natural features such as gullies and creekbeds, or even simply behind clumps of scrub.

The main causes for the failure of the Second Battle of Krithia were much more straightforward and well within Hamilton's ability to overcome. Regardless of his desire to get on the move before the Turks could dig in, Hamilton had rushed the attack. Orders were sketchy and issued to the attacking units at far too short notice to be properly acted upon. In their rush to resume the advance, Hamilton and Hunter-Weston acted on hunches and optimistic guesses rather than detailed intelligence. They had no idea where the Turks were located or how many troops they were facing. They failed to use airpower to fill in the blanks* and launched the attack without giving their already meagre artillery force much clue as to where they should be shooting. In addition, instead of simultaneous attacks across a wide front, the British and Anzac advances had mostly been piecemeal, with individual units rushed into the fray without coordination with the troops on either side (a situation that the New Zealanders and Australians in particular could attest to).

But the main reason the attack was such a bloody failure is the simplest and most obvious. In 1915, any advance against machine guns in broad daylight without adequate artillery support was doomed. As stated by the British official history,

---

*   Only twenty-three air sorties were flown during the three days of the battle and most of those were to assist the navy with targeting enemy artillery batteries on the Asian shore of the Dardanelles. Not a single one was timed with an infantry advance or was effective in clarifying the position of the Turkish defences in front of Krithia.

'Sir Ian Hamilton's original intention of a night advance was, in all the circumstances of the case, the only plan with a reasonable prospect of success.'[7] Why Hamilton felt unable or unwilling to insist on a night attack is one of the frustrating mysteries of the Gallipoli campaign.

As for the Australians and New Zealanders, they emerged from the fighting at Krithia like men waking up in a daze. During the night of 8 May, they consolidated their front line, often working in the open to widen and deepen the trench line. The Turks fired scattered shots at them but casualties were very light. It was obvious that the ground they had captured with such horrific loss in daylight could have been taken with minimal casualties after dark. Understandably, the men were aggrieved and felt that their sacrifice had been for nothing.

Their first priority was treating their wounded mates. As darkness fell the cries of hundreds of wounded pierced the night sky, many coming from men who had been hit in the early stages of the advance and were now lying behind the new front line. The Australian official history grimly notes that:

> From every part [of the line] went up the thin wavering call
> of the wounded for stretcher-bearers. A large proportion had
> been hit in the stomach or intestines – the most painful form
> of wound, and one from which, under Gallipoli conditions,
> scarcely any man recovered.[8]

Stretcher-bearers and medical teams were overwhelmed; wounded men were forced to lie without treatment and in agony for most of the night before they could be carried back to a dressing station. Many died before treatment reached them. Charles Bean was carrying water forward to the front line and was overwhelmed by the plight of the wounded. He noted in his diary that:

The cries of the wounded were heart-rending. The Tommies' Trench was full of them. The poor chaps there badly wanted water. Although the water was for the men at brigade headquarters one could not help giving the poor chaps a drink. I told them I had very little to spare and they must be content with a little. We got a mess-tin and handed a little down to everyone in the trench or under the parapet. Each fellow took about two sips and then handed it back – really you could have cried to see how unselfish they were.[9]

This is another example of Bean's bravery and humility – he included this anecdote in the official history, but wrote that the water had been carried by 'some soldier', rather than crediting himself.

Although the stretcher-bearers did sterling work, it was impossible to clear the wounded quickly. More than one bearer collapsed from exhaustion after having lugged wounded Australian and British soldiers over the broken ground of Helles for over twelve hours. Their job was made even more difficult by the lack of cover on the plain – for safety's sake, the nearest dressing station had to be located under a shallow bank nearly two kilometres behind the front line; the larger hospitals on W Beach were a further three kilometres back. A British staff officer was roped into helping tend to Australian and New Zealand wounded in one of these hospitals and noted (perhaps with a touch of self-delusion) that:

When I got back to camp the wounded were already pouring in – those who could hobble. I never saw a less complaining lot. They bore their wounds stoically. 'But it was fine to see the boys charge!' was one comment.[10]

Private John Turnbull of the 8th Battalion had survived the ordeal of the advance but, just when he thought he was safe, was ordered to escort a wounded officer back to the dressing station near the beach.

> I was not anxious for the job. I thought of that bullet swept ground I had just come over ... It was an awful trip back. Passing men dead, some delirious crying for water, others crying for stretcher bearers. Some not badly wounded putting on field dressings to men worse than themselves. Then there were the walking wounded looking for the dressing station. Continuously the Krithia Road was swept by machine gun fire and our wounded would be hit again.[11]

It wasn't just the wounded who needed attention – the dead did as well. The Australians made a valiant effort to gather the bodies of their dead mates and give them a half-decent burial, but it was never going to be easy on this exposed battlefield, with Turkish marksmen keen to add to the tally.

> By morning we were fairly safe, as we had a bit of cover. You could count 39 of our boys dead in the back of the trench, just in the space we could see. A burial party went out and buried 86 in one grave. I am quite satisfied that I had an unseen guardian over me that day.[12]

The Australians and New Zealanders held the front line for another two days, before being withdrawn on 11 May. Even this seemingly straightforward procedure came with its own risks, as Cecil Malthus discovered when he was sent to the rear to locate the British battalion that would relieve the New Zealanders.

I got there somehow and found the Manchesters waiting, but happened to trip over a bush as I approached them and was pounced on with levelled bayonets and arrested as a spy. It seemed I was skulking in the bushes and tried to bolt, and nothing I could say shook their opinion. My trial must have lasted 20 minutes before a more sensible type of officer came along and was immediately convinced of my bona fides … By the time I had conducted them to the front line my battalion had already bolted. I lay down among the stray bullets and in pouring rain and slept the sleep of the just. Next morning I awoke and saw streams of stragglers in all directions, wending their way southward. It had been a glorious muddle.[13]

The Anzacs were exhausted but stoically proud of their achievements on the field at Krithia. The attack marked a crucial shift in the relationship between Australian and New Zealand soldiers, which had been strained since the chaos of training in Egypt. Both sides now knew the other could be trusted once the guns started firing and there was a marked desire to go into future battles beside each other.

The scale of the sacrifice of 8 May only became apparent when the Anzac battalions conducted roll calls, to try to work out who was still with them and who was not. As the names were read out, nearly half of them went unanswered – each silence hung heavily in the air. Among the thousands of names that received no reply was Lieutenant Colonel Robert Gartside, Private Harry Kelly, Sergeant George Greig, Private Sam Norris, Private Jim Bayne and Private Bill Buckingham, the old father figure of the 6th Battalion. No-one had seen him since he had been wounded early in the advance. The tortuous roll call finally ended and the men shuffled off. Few spoke.

The Anzacs remained in the reserve bivouacs at Helles for another five days, helping the British and French to carry stores and ammunition to the fighting lines and helping themselves to extra rations as military police turned a blind eye. They embarked for the return journey to Anzac on 16 May, having participated in the Helles fiasco for a mere eleven days. The Australian 2nd Brigade had left Anzac on 5 May with 2568 men. By the end of Second Krithia, 1056 of them had been killed or wounded. The New Zealanders had arrived at Helles with 2493 men. During the battle, 771 of them had been killed or wounded. It was a loss that the brigades would never recover from for the rest of the campaign.

Joe Murray and his comrades in the Royal Naval Division stayed in the reserve trenches in the French sector until relieved on 13 May. A roll call confirmed that in Joe's company only three officers and ninety men were still standing. They had lost more than half their strength in nine days' fighting. The survivors moved into an orchard near the beach and dug 'grave-like' shelters covered with a ground sheet – scant protection from Turkish shells that lobbed into the camp uncomfortably frequently. The following day, the battalion was addressed by the French commander, General d'Amade, who told them, 'Every French soldier who has seen your work renders homage.' Joe's response was blunt.

> Now, wasn't that nice. To lose more than half your pals, many lying disembowelled a few hundred yards away; those who had so far escaped, half famished, skulking in holes, waiting to fight again, had to listen to this international courtesy. *Every French soldier renders homage.* My answer would be brief: 'This is no good when having to write home telling a mother or a wife how my pal, their son or husband, had died bravely.'[14]

Back at Anzac, the Aussies and Kiwis struggled to fully convey to their mates in the other brigades what they had been through. There was pride that they had advanced in the face of such withering fire, but also anger – most of it directed at their brigadier. McCay had always been a polarising officer who often clashed with his superiors and ticked off his men. And although he had displayed extreme bravery at Krithia, leading the advance from the front, calling the men forward when they were pinned down at Tommies' Trench and late in the day getting his leg smashed by a bullet, he was an easy target for the fury of a brigade that had lost nearly half its men in a pointless advance. The Krithia debacle cost McCay the respect of his men and he never got it back for the rest of the war.

One bright spot on the return to Anzac was the news that the mounted brigades had recently arrived from Egypt as reinforcements. The overstretched and exhausted infantry were delighted to see them.

On May 12 the joy at Anzac was unbounded. The Mounteds had arrived! Every face on the beach was wreathed in smiles. Here they all were – without their horses, but keen, and spoiling for a fight – the Australian Light Horse; the New Zealand Mounted Rifles Brigade, consisting of the Auckland, Wellington, and Canterbury Regiments; the field troop to reinforce the overworked 1st Field Company in its sapping and mining; the signal troop, to help with the telephone and buzzers; and the mounted field ambulance, to assist their overworked confreres with the wounded.

Whatever the trudging infantry men had thought in Egypt as the mounted men swept by, to-day there was nothing but the good humoured banter of 'Where's your horses?' As the eager troopers climbed the goat tracks of

Walker's Ridge a great sigh of relief was heaved by the sorely tried garrison of Anzac. Never were troops more welcome.[15]

A couple of days after the mounted units arrived, Birdwood demonstrated that even generals weren't safe at Gallipoli. He was bravely – some would say foolishly – reconnoitring enemy positions through a periscope at Quinn's Post, only twenty-five metres from the Turkish trenches.

Stupidly enough I forgot the top of these parapets is often not bullet proof, and a rascal opposite sent a bullet along which got me on the top of the head, but only just made a furrow which the doctor tells me only goes just as far as the bone, and has not hurt it in any way, so I'm thankful to say I am quite alright.[16]

It was no doubt a painful wound but he was back at his desk the same day.

Once settled in back at Anzac, the exhausted officers of the Australian 2nd Brigade did what they could to work out exactly what had gone on during the attack. This was normally a simple matter – witnesses would be interviewed and a report would be compiled for the unit's war diary. But at Krithia, this system went very wrong. A century after the fact, the 2nd Brigade's war diary makes for interesting and disconcerting reading.

War diaries are typically a dry and clinical reporting of the unit's activities during a given month; the higher up the command chain you go, the drier and more clinical they become. For example, the unit diary of the 2nd Brigade from January 1915 deals with topics as uninspiring as the issuing of boots, the arrival in the depot of a coffee cart and the unexpected fogginess of the weather.

The diary for the brigade from May 1915 is a remarkable contrast. It begins with a unique and alarming note.

> During action of May 8th/9th the whole of the Brigade Staff became casualties and all documents appear to have gone astray.

The diary then begins from, astoundingly, 18 May, which was long after the brigade had returned to Anzac and presumably the earliest date the diarist could witness its operations first-hand.

As for the Second Battle of Krithia, with no officer alive and unwounded who could give an account of exactly what happened during the attack, the diarist valiantly attempts to piece the story together from whatever bits of communication he can lay his hands on. The unintended, but highly fortuitous, result is that the modern reader has a unique insight into the Krithia battle, which is relayed effectively in real time, with signals and handwritten orders quoted verbatim as the battle unfolds.

In other circumstances, the unit diary might simply have reported that the brigade went into action at 5.30 pm and within a couple of hours had been stopped by the enemy after sustaining heavy casualties. In this account, we get a somewhat breathless, live narrative of the battle as it occurred. The strain as things started to go disastrously wrong grows with each message.

Not much is said about the attack itself, as there was very little communication between the advancing troops and their headquarters while they were being shot to pieces. But once they had dug in, there is a constant stream of alarming messages between 2nd Brigade officers and their temporary headquarters, the Composite Division.

6.30 pm   *From Composite Division*
Push on till dark. Direct attacks on all points
which will secure you a good line for the night.
At night hold and entrench all ground gained.

7.35 pm   *2nd Brigade to Composite Division*
Brigade 350 yards in front of firing trenches and
starting to dig in. Unsupported on both flanks.

7.40 pm   *2nd Brigade to Composite Division*
Send reinforcements to meet possible counter
attacks.

7.55 pm   *2nd Brigade to Composite Division*
I shall be badly enfiladed on my left by daylight
unless reinforced.

8.10 pm   *2nd Brigade to Composite Division*
Satisfactory fire line established. Brigade is being
heavily attacked and is still unsupported.

8.20 pm   *2nd Brigade to Composite Division*
Ammunition urgently needed.
Send reinforcements.

8.33 pm   *2nd Brigade to Composite Division*
Still being heavily attacked.

8.35 pm   *2nd Brigade to Composite Division*
Send troops up on flanks.

9.31 pm   *2nd Brigade to Composite Division*
Heavily attacked. Send reinforcements.

9.50 pm   *From Composite Division*
During night get your trenches in order, in a
good continuous line with traverses to protect you
against flanking fire. Also if possible reorganise
your companies and form support to firing line
with some of your men.

10.51 pm   *2nd Brigade to Composite Division*
I think I can hold if my right is safe.

11.30 pm	*2nd Brigade to Composite Division*
	Food and water urgently needed.
5.20 am	*2nd Brigade to Composite Division*
	Provide artillery support by day, as brigade has been severely cut up and is rather disorganised.
8.30 am	*From Composite Division*
	GOC congratulates troops on their fine effort and orders all positions to be strengthened and units reorganised and careful reconnaissance to be made to assist in next advance.
9 am	*2nd Brigade to Composite Division*
	Our position is satisfactory.

In spite of the trauma it had undergone at Krithia, some of the greatest trials the 2nd Brigade would face at Gallipoli were still to come. Two days after the brigade returned to Anzac, the Turks launched a huge assault in an attempt to drive the Anzacs into the sea. The Turks were shot down in their hundreds as they charged across no man's land and the battered survivors of the 2nd Brigade were rushed forward to reinforce the Australian battalions in the front line. Turkish corpses were still cooling in no man's land when a truce was called to try to deal with them. For the first (and only) time in the campaign, the enemies came face to face, as they shared the gruesome and humbling task of disposing of the dead from both sides. Although most of the bodies were Turks, there were some Anzacs among them who had been killed early in the campaign, often on the day of the landing.

Very few New Zealanders were found unburied, but there was evidence that they died game. One Aucklander was found still grasping his rifle, which was – barrel and bayonet – firmly embedded in the body of his dead opponent.[17]

For much of June and July, the Australian 2nd Brigade was often in reserve – having lost so many men at Krithia, it would take time to bring it back up to fighting strength. The 6th Battalion's war diary for June, which would normally comprise forty or fifty pages describing in detail the daily operations of the battalion, consists of just a single page, which states baldly: 'During this period the Battalion, being some 500 below establishment, was in reserve at Anzac. Nothing worthy of note took place.'[18] The diary for July is much the same.

At about this time, in the midst of all the killing and dying, Hamilton found time to send Birdwood a telegram requesting that he send a selected list of names for 'about five Distinguished Service Orders, five Military Crosses, and 15 Distinguished Conduct Medals for each Division under your command'.[19] Contrary to popular belief, gallantry medals in the First World War were often issued by quota.

Meanwhile, back down at Helles, Hamilton and Hunter-Weston were determined to have one final go at seizing Krithia. By June, Hamilton had succeeded in getting more reinforcements for his besieged Helles garrison but so had the Turks. And now, instead of facing isolated Turkish outposts, the British and French confronted an effectively complete Turkish defensive line. Krithia and Achi Baba were now further away than ever.

By probing forward at night, the British had been able to advance their line close enough to the Turkish line to give them a shot at capturing it. At least this time the casualties would occur in a fight for the enemy positions rather than in advances behind their own front lines. Yet, inexplicably, the Allies once again attacked in broad daylight. At noon on 4 June, in an advance that came to be known as the Third Battle of Krithia, the British and French launched another major push, an attempt to finally secure the objectives they had been set for the first day of the campaign. As before, they were inadequately supported by artillery and were raked by enfilading fire from hidden Turkish machine guns. In the centre, the British succeeded in breaking into the Turkish line but efforts to reinforce this success ended in carnage. Lieutenant Leslie Grant of the 1/4th Royal Scots described a scene from a nightmare as he leapt into the Turkish trench.

> I sank in almost to my knees in the soft earth, the place was a fearful mess, blood everywhere, arms, legs, entrails lying around. It sounds horrible in cold blood but at this time all that is savage in one seemed to be on top. I remember two things distinctly, one was wanting to cut off a man's ears and keep them as a trophy, the other was jumping on the dead, hacking their faces with my feet or crashing my rifle into them. Men fought with their rifles, their feet, their fists, a pick, a shovel, anything.[20]

The British held on for a couple of days but the Turks eventually counter-attacked and drove them back. At one point, the British line was in danger of completely collapsing as hundreds of men fled in the face of violent Turkish assaults. Second Lieutenant George Moor of the Hampshire Regiment stepped forward and 'stemmed the retirement',[21] in the process earning himself one of the most ignoble Victoria Crosses of the war. What his citation doesn't mention is that he halted the British retreat by shooting dead four of his own men with his revolver. Unsurprisingly, this brought the remainder of the fleeing soldiers to their senses, and they returned to the line and held the position.

By the end of the battle, the British line had advanced less than 400 metres. The French had been mauled in Kereves Dere in precisely the same fashion they had been in the two previous battles. These meagre gains had come at a cost of 6500 British and Frenchmen killed or wounded.

Joe Murray's role in the battle was shocking and surreal. He had attacked with the Hood Battalion and, despite watching his mates get shot to pieces all around him, had broken into the Turkish trenches with a small group. A hand-to-hand fight broke out and Joe was wounded. His attempts to return to the British line read like something out of a boys' own adventure novel and included getting stabbed in the wrist, leaping over a trench full of Turks as they thrust bayonets up at him and spending hours cowering in a shellhole a few feet in front of the Turkish lines as the muzzle of an enemy rifle fired countless rounds just above his head. He finally made a mad dash for safety when he heard the Turks vacating the firestep to attend to their evening prayers. He tumbled into a British trench and safety but was met by a ghastly sight.

> The floor of the trench was three or four deep with bodies. They were slumped on the fire step and hanging over the parapet, some head-first as they had died of their wounds or been riddled with bullets as they were trying to make their escape. Of others, only their legs could be seen, their bodies lying over the parapet … Our trench, once cut through the soil, was now a narrow passage through human flesh, bones and blood. The communication trench was so full of bodies that it could not be used to get the wounded out. They had been patched up with all the available dressings, but a couple of bandages is not much use when an arm or a leg has been shattered and many would bleed to death.[22]

Joe was appalled by the loss of life and seeming senselessness of the attack, and he wasn't the only one. Throughout the preceding two months, the British public had been fed stirring accounts in the press of heroics and triumph at Gallipoli and it has often been stated that these inflated reports were accepted by the masses without question. But in reality, by June, the public was beginning to smell a rat. An opinion piece in *Stead's Review* sums up the attitude of a sceptical public after the Third Battle of Krithia.

> The cables are still indefinite, still contradictory. We hold Maidos, and then we do not; we have captured Krithia, and again we have not; we are progressing mightily at Achi Baba, and still the Turks cling to the position. We come almost to the conclusion that after all this sanguinary fighting, all this prodigal pouring out of the lives of our bravest, we have secured little more than a firm foothold on the peninsula at certain spots.[23]

Hamilton launched other attacks later in June and again in July, with the same disastrous results. In Whitehall, news of yet more bloody reversals at Gallipoli perversely prompted the British government to double its efforts – a large force of reinforcements was despatched to the peninsula. Hamilton reversed his previous thinking and abandoned efforts at Helles – his focus would now fall on the Anzac sector, with his last roll of the dice at Gallipoli: the August Offensive.

By August, the Australian 2nd Brigade was somewhat stronger, bolstered by reinforcements and by men who had been wounded at Krithia returning to the battalions. The brigade reoccupied the Anzac front line in the hotly contested sector facing German Officers' Ridge. In the August Offensive, the 2nd Brigade was tasked with supporting the 1st Brigade in its attack on Lone Pine. On the night of 6 August, the 6th Battalion charged from specially dug tunnels opposite German Officers' Ridge in a disastrous diversionary attack. In scenes painfully familiar to the veterans of Krithia, the Australians were mown down by machine-gun fire from the flanks.

The signal for the assault was given – a blast of a whistle. Men in the fire-posts jumped out and rushed forward. The moment they did, the enemy raked No Man's Land with machine guns, rifles, and bombs. The thin line melted away. Some were hit before they left the posts. Those who followed fell back wounded, blocking the saps and preventing the rest of the attacking force from leaving the tunnel. The wounded crawled back out of the inferno into the safe refuge of the tunnel and before many minutes it was realised that the attack had failed.[24]

A second wave was foolishly ordered forward and met the same fate. The attack was a pointless and bloody failure. Another 146 men, most of whom had survived the horror of the advance at Krithia, now lay dead or wounded. Roughly 1000 men had landed on Anzac Cove with the 6th Battalion on 25 April. Now, three months later, after the perils of the landing, the first ten days at Anzac, the Battle of Krithia and the attack on German Officers' Ridge, the 6th Battalion was down to 318 men.

Over the next couple of days, the 7th and 5th battalions (with elements of the 8th) were called into the line to support the 1st Brigade men who had captured the Turkish trenches at Lone Pine. The battalions faced waves of Turkish counter-attacks, spearheaded by bomb and bayonet, and the close-quarter fighting in the claustrophobic trenches was brutal. The 7th Battalion's commander, Lieutenant Colonel 'Pompey' Elliott, wrote to his wife describing his horror at what he had seen and done in the charnel house of trenches.

In one charge it was so hot that we had no time to remove the wounded and, horrible to tell you, we had to tread on these poor dead and dying men lying in the trench to keep the gaps in the line filled. All war is horrible but this trench warfare is awful. A large proportion of wounds were in the head. I cannot wear my tunic today because it is all soiled and stained with a poor boy's brains which were splashed all over it. I saw the whole side of this lad's skull simply ripped out and his brains splashed round. When we left yesterday the trenches were indescribable. You must remember that not only our dead but the dead of the two previous days' fighting, Turks and Australians often locked in a last death struggle, still lay there in large numbers in spite of all efforts. Moreover their poor corpses were continually smashed by the enemy's shells and torn with bullet wounds. It was all like a horrible nightmare. Fancy seeing a man you knew blinded and with hands blown off trying to get up on his feet.[25]

Private Reuben Hampton was tasked with attempting to clear the Turkish positions with grenades (or 'bombs' as they were called in the First World War).

Took over part of captured trenches in Lonesome Pine. Very heavy going. Turks within 10 yards of us, still no sleep. We shifted our position to a more dangerous one. The physical effect of the last four months has started telling on me as I collapsed in the trench. After a couple of hours' spell I was put on an important post as bomb thrower. Turks are about 15 yards away and after enjoying a little fireworks for a few hours Abdul landed one of his bombs just behind me. I was extremely lucky that I did not get more seriously wounded.[26]

Hampton may have considered himself lucky, but his wounds were so serious that he was evacuated from the peninsula and never returned to Gallipoli.

By the time the 2nd Brigade battalions were withdrawn, four members of the 7th Battalion had earned the Victoria Cross:

Lieutenant Fred Tubb, Lieutenant Bill Dunstan, Sergeant Bill Symons and Corporal Alex Burton (who was killed by a bomb during the action). Of the 700 men who had gone into the attack with the 7th, more than 350 had been killed or wounded.

Although the Australians had captured Lone Pine, overall, the August Offensive was a failure. British, New Zealand and Australians troops (led by Colonel John Monash, future commander of the Australian Corps) attempted a grand flanking manoeuvre north of Anzac through the same impossibly rough country that a Turkish platoon had fled across on the day of the landing. They became hopelessly lost and suffered heavy casualties in the tangle of thorny gullies. The New Zealanders valiantly captured the high point of Chunuk Bair, then held it through some of the fiercest Turkish counter-attacks of the campaign. The following day, they were relieved by British troops who were overwhelmed and slaughtered by a huge Turkish attack. The Anzacs and British dug in further down the slope and the heights were never occupied by them again.

A British landing at Suvla Bay became a replay of the Anzac landing, as Turkish reinforcements surged onto the high ground and hemmed in the British troops below them. And men from the Australian Light Horse died in their hundreds in an area the size of a couple of tennis courts, as they charged Turkish positions at the Nek, one of the most famous and futile Australian attacks of the war.

A final combined British and Anzac attack at Hill 60 and Scimitar Hill on 21 August was greeted with furious machine-gun and artillery fire. The scrub caught alight – wounded men who couldn't drag themselves away were burnt alive. The Allies withdrew with heavy losses and dashed hopes.

The failure of the August Offensive marked the end of Allied offensive operations at Gallipoli. For the rest of the campaign, the imperative switched to holding ground, with the vain hope of somehow restarting a campaign that had become mired by its own blunders and missed opportunities. The Gallipoli campaign began a slow and painful decline that only ended when Hamilton was belatedly sacked in October and the new commander, General Charles Monro, made the tough decisions that Hamilton couldn't.

His assessment of the state of the Gallipoli campaign pulled no punches and finally convinced the politicians in Whitehall and the general public that the campaign was dead on its feet – and that no amount of wishful thinking was going to revive it.

> The positions occupied by our troops presented a military situation unique in history. The mere fringe of the coast line had been secured. The beaches and piers upon which they depended for all requirements in personnel and material were exposed to registered and observed Artillery fire. Our entrenchments were dominated almost throughout by the Turks. The possible Artillery positions were insufficient and defective. The Force, in short, held a line possessing every possible military defect.[27]

Churchill was outraged and resigned from the government in protest. He later wrote in his memoirs about Monro that 'he came, he saw, he capitulated'.[28] But Monro was right – the Gallipoli campaign was a fiasco and it was time to pull the plug. After seven months of fighting and the loss of more than 250,000 Allied troops, the British line at Helles was still nearly *two kilometres* short of Krithia, the objective for the first day.

The Anzacs began to withdraw from Gallipoli in December 1915. Ironically, the evacuation was one of the most successful operations of the entire campaign and the 2nd Brigade played its part. Two men of the 7th Battalion, Lance Corporal William Scurry and Private Bunty Lawrence, developed the famous water-operated self-firing rifle (popularly known as the 'drip rifle', although Scurry always referred to it as the 'pop-off rifle'). This innovation was part of the elaborate ruse that enabled the Anzacs to disengage under the noses of the Turks and pull back to the beaches.

For the later stages of the campaign, the 2nd Brigade had held a rabbit warren of tunnels and trenches on Silt Spur, in the Lone Pine sector. On the evening of 11 December, the brigade formally handed over the position to the 1st Brigade and began an orderly withdrawal down Victoria Gully, Shrapnel Valley, Rest Gully and Reserve Gully to the rickety piers at North Beach. There, they boarded lighters and cast off toward a waiting destroyer. 'Not a single shot was fired,' the unit diary noted in the margins, 'till just after the last barge left shore. There were no casualties.'[29]

The men of the 2nd Brigade huddled low in the boats in the chilly night air and watched in silence as the dark silhouette of Gallipoli grew small behind them. Before long, it was lost in the darkness. The men sat alone with their thoughts. For the battered survivors of Anzac and Krithia, the campaign was finally over.

16.

REMEMBERING

The last British troops withdrew from the Gallipoli peninsula on 9 January 1916, leaving behind the battered battlefield of Cape Helles, more than 21,000 dead comrades and a field of shattered dreams. A labyrinth of deserted trenches snaked across the gullies and plateaus at the southern toe of the peninsula. Smashed artillery guns, too bulky to remove, sat forlornly in their abandoned gun pits. Canted crosses marking hurriedly dug graves crowded in conspiratorial groups in makeshift cemeteries. Unburied corpses – British, French, Australian, New Zealand and Turkish – littered the battlefield.

It stayed that way for a long time. The Ottoman Empire collapsed, the war came to an end, and in 1918, British troops returned to Gallipoli and reoccupied the entire peninsula in a matter of days. Keen to honour the sacrifices of 1915, they set to work converting the former battlefields into a place of pilgrimage and remembrance, and to build permanent cemeteries to hold the dead and memorials to remember the missing.

Charles Bean, officially the Australian war correspondent and unofficially the caretaker of the Anzac legend, was in

London when the war ended. For the first time in more than four years, he was free to walk any battlefield of the war without risking a bullet in the head – and there was only one place he wanted to go. He quickly got permission from the government, assembled a curious and diverse group of officers he dubbed the Australian Historical Mission and boarded the first ship he could find for Gallipoli. On 18 January 1919, the hardy bunch set off from London on a very special journey. As Bean himself noted: 'it is safe to say, a hundred thousand other Australians would have given a good part of their deferred pay to have changed places with them.'[1]

Bean's official mission was to find answers to the 'riddles' of the Gallipoli campaign. How far had the Australians penetrated into Turkish territory on the first day? What ground had they captured during the August Offensive? Had the Turks been aware of the Gallipoli evacuation? How much of the Allied line could the Turks see from their commanding positions? Where had the Turkish heavy guns, which had plagued the Anzac garrison day and night for eight months, been located? He was also there to collect relics for the future Australian War Memorial, an institution that at this stage was just an amorphous concept in his head and notebooks.

But Bean was also on a personal mission. He had been captivated by the Gallipoli story, and the men who had forged it, since the day of the landing, and was desperate to get back there and walk the ground. His account of the expedition, *Gallipoli Mission*, is one of the most intriguing Gallipoli books ever written and, in spite of Bean's notoriously dry writing style and his desire to appear professionally detached from his subject, he betrays his true feelings on returning to the peninsula with phrases such as 'excitement', 'strange thrill' and 'my heart bounded'.[2] Bean truly loved this place and he was delighted to be back.

He was accompanied by several officers and sergeants who would help with documenting and mapping the journey, but also by the enigmatic war photographer Hubert Wilkins and the archetypal Aussie larrikin, the artist George Lambert. Between Bean's writing, Wilkins' photos and Lambert's paintings, the Australian Historical Mission would provide one of the most thorough and absorbing investigations of a battlefield ever recorded.

A key part of Bean's investigation was the battlefield of Krithia. He 'knew that battlefield better than any in the war – except perhaps Pozières in France – having made the double journey over it, up and back, four times during the afternoon and night of the advance'.[3]

So, after spending a couple of weeks at Anzac, endeavouring to solve the mysteries of the famous Australian battles in that sector, the mission braved relentless snow and wind and headed south, arriving at Cape Helles on 7 March 1919. They climbed to the top of Achi Baba, the hill that had been the primary British objective since the day of the landing, and discovered, shockingly, that the waters of the Dardanelles are not visible from the summit. Even if the British had captured it, their plans for using the heights as a stepping stone for attacks on the Dardanelles forts would have amounted to nothing. What Achi Baba did provide, however, was a grandstand view of the entire Allied area of operations at Helles. Every trench, every gun position, every road, every tree was plainly visible to the Turks.

> Turning round to obtain the view of the southern battlefield which had been enjoyed by the Turkish defenders throughout the campaign, we found the toe of the Peninsula exhibited like a raised plan. We could pick out every detail, Seddel Bahr [sic], the Hadji Ayub mound, the Krithia road,

the olive-trees by the Tommies' Trench, the patch of little firs, the Vineyard, and Krithia close below us.[4]

Bean was starting to get a clear idea of why the Battles of Krithia had been such a disaster. But he got an even clearer picture when the group rode down to the former Allied lines and began tracing on foot the advance of the Australians on 8 May 1915. They identified the start line, Tommies' Trench and the final redoubt line where the Australians had dug in (noting in the process that a map of the battlefield prepared by the French had not accurately marked the line reached by the Australians). But it was what they found behind the final Australian line that caused the breath to catch in their throats. The battlefield was still strewn with dead Australians.

> Searching in an extended line forward of the Tommies' Trench, [we] found the remains of Australians everywhere on the plain, as far forward as the two trenches of the Redoubt Line, 400 and 500 yards ahead respectively. We found Australian kit, and the arm patches of the 6th Battalion, red and purple, and the bronze 'Australia' from the shoulder strap, right up to the front Redoubt Line.[5]

George Lambert was so moved by the sombre scene that he requested a quiet moment to sketch the battlefield, to be used as a basis for a future painting. He later wrote that:

> Achi Baba makes a fine contour in the background and the plain is covered with bushes of heather and sage-brush, with a few small thorn-trees and olives ... The whole landscape is a dull mauvy grey with a sage green admixture and very delicate if sombre in tone. The dead, or rather their bones, spoil it, of course. I got ... a panel ready to get a quick shot

at the evening light ... made a very carefully considered landscape from which I can do a big one, if necessary. I was left alone and didn't really mind it; the work was very absorbing and the weather perfect.[6]

Bean collected some relics from the battlefield, including a tattered scrap of fabric from an Australian uniform, bearing the colour patch of the 6th Battalion and an 'Australia' shoulder badge, a sad reminder of the lonely fate of an Australian killed at Krithia. It is still in the collection of the Australian War Memorial today. He chatted briefly with Lieutenant Cyril Hughes, an Australian engineer who had been tasked with planning permanent cemeteries at Gallipoli, and pointed out to him a collection of graves the mission had discovered near Tommies' Trench. Then Bean and his comrades in the Australian Historical Mission mounted their horses and slowly rode away, leaving Krithia, and the ghosts of the 2nd Brigade, behind them.

— —

Cyril Hughes was a meticulous operator and the right man for the job of bringing order to the chaos of the old Gallipoli battlefields. Born in Tasmania, he had worked as a civil engineer and surveyor prior to enlisting in the Australian Light Horse at the outbreak of war. He landed at Gallipoli in May 1915 and served there, minus a couple of stints in hospital, for the duration of the campaign. In October 1915, his engineering talents were recognised and he was transferred to the Field Engineers, where he served in various roles in the Middle East until the end of the war. A couple of days before the Armistice, Hughes, now a lieutenant, received orders to report to the fledgling Graves Registration Unit in Salonika, and from there was despatched to Gallipoli to represent Australia's interests in the mammoth task of building permanent cemeteries and shifting bodies into them.

Hughes did more than just represent Australia. During the crucial early phases of the planning of Gallipoli's military cemeteries, he was the de facto officer in charge of cemetery planning on much of the peninsula. Most of what the modern visitor sees when they tour the cemeteries in the Anzac sector is the result of Hughes's work. He located old cemeteries and built new ones, and personally discovered hundreds of missing graves, usually by simply poking a metal rod into the ground to determine whether the earth was hard or soft.

His remit included dealing not only with the acres of bones and unmarked graves at Anzac but also with the remains of Australians killed at Cape Helles – he travelled down there at about the same time as Charles Bean and the Australian Historical Mission. Hughes discovered that the British were in the process of concentrating all their graves into six permanent cemeteries, one of which was coincidentally and conveniently being built just behind the final Redoubt Line where the Australians had dug in after their painful advance at Krithia. Graves units had already begun moving Australian bodies into the new cemetery and Hughes found that Lieutenant Colonel Robert Gartside, who had commanded the 7th Battalion in the advance and had been killed by machine-gun fire, had been buried along with about fifty other Australians in the new cemetery.

The remains of a fair number of Australians were scattered over the line of advance made on May 8th, which reached from what is known as Clapham Junction to within about 400 yards in front of the vineyard near Krithia, the total area covered by the advances being around 1000 yards by 2000.

I have arranged that all remains were to be collected and placed in the cemetery made on the site where Colonel Gartside and other members of the AIF are buried.[7]

And so the remains of hundreds of Australians who lay out on the former battlefield, either unburied or in shallow graves, were carefully gathered together and reburied in Redoubt Cemetery. Today, the cemetery is still there, sitting forlornly in the middle of the Krithia plain, permanently marking the spot where the Australians dug in on their final line in May 1915. It's a curious place – a visit there leads to mixed emotions. Less than two kilometres away is the village of Krithia, now known as Alcitepe, which can be reached in a leisurely five-minute drive – the cemetery is almost on the village outskirts. But to the Australians who dug in here over a century ago, the village was so unreachable it might as well have been on the moon. To the northeast, the ground rises sedately to the hump of Achi Baba, just over four kilometres away. To the southwest, the parched ground is covered in olive trees and clumps of gorse – it's not thick but it's thick enough to obscure the view of the battlefield leading back to the Helles landing beaches. This was the ground where, in 1919, Charles Bean and Cyril Hughes discovered the lonely bundles of bone and cloth lying where they had fallen more than three years earlier.

These are the men who now lie in Redoubt Cemetery. They couldn't be identified, of course – after three years in the baking summer sun and icy winter winds of Gallipoli, there was little left to distinguish them – so they were buried as unknown soldiers, alongside more than 2000 of their comrades from Britain and New Zealand. Redoubt is a big cemetery but, like all the cemeteries at Gallipoli, it's an iceberg – there's much more going on beneath the surface than is immediately apparent when you walk through the gate. Of the 2027 men buried here, only 637 have headstones. The rest lie under a wide expanse of lawn, their identities unknown, their graves unmarked.

In a corner of the cemetery, a large tree throws a welcome patch of shade over the graves. Unexpectedly, the tree is an English oak, planted by the parents of Second Lieutenant Eric Duckworth of the Lancashire Fusiliers, who was killed near here in a diversionary attack launched as part of the August Offensive. It's a living memorial – the only private memorial in a Commonwealth cemetery on the peninsula.

Most of the Australians who were killed in the murderous advance at Krithia lie in this cemetery, but they aren't formally remembered here. To read their names, we must travel south, to the Helles Memorial on the southern tip of the peninsula. This graceful stone obelisk is both a battle memorial and a place of commemoration and grieving. Alongside more than 20,000 British soldiers commemorated here are the names of 249 Australians – the missing of the Second Battle of Krithia. It's fitting that they are here – they fell beside their British comrades far from the battlefields of Anzac and now they are forever remembered beside them. The 179 New Zealanders missing from the battle are commemorated on a memorial in Twelve Tree Copse Cemetery, close to where they fell, although administrative confusion has resulted in several of the New Zealand missing from Krithia being commemorated on the Chunuk Bair Memorial at Anzac.

In the decades that followed the First World War, the Second Battle of Krithia slipped through the cracks of Anzac history. Although well remembered in Britian, to Australians and New Zealanders, the name 'Krithia' means little. An online search of Australian street names reveals 178 Anzac Streets (or variants such as Avenue, Lane, etc.), forty-one Gallipolis, 191 Kitcheners, 155 Monashes, 107 Birdwoods, twenty Lone Pines, even nine Dardanelles – but only one street in Australia is named 'Krithia' (in Coburg North, Victoria, in the heart of the region where the 2nd Brigade was raised). But to the men who fought through it, the Second Battle of Krithia was one of the most harrowing ordeals they faced in the entire war and they never forgot it.

The battle briefly and intermittently rose in prominence as the key players in the campaign released their memoirs in the post-war years. In 1920, Sir Ian Hamilton published his diaries from the campaign in two volumes (imaginatively titled *Gallipoli Diary*). The desire to salvage his tarnished reputation and shift some of the blame after the disaster that was Gallipoli was acute. Hamilton naively believed that getting his side of the story out there would earn him some points in the court of public opinion. It didn't work.

To Hamilton, the key architect of the Gallipoli failure was Kitchener. In the words of historian Jenny Macleod, 'Hamilton's *Gallipoli Diary* is a subtle but continuous attack upon Kitchener.'[8] The release of his diary revealed that Hamilton felt he hadn't done anything wrong at Gallipoli and that he was simply let down by a failure to properly supply and support him. It was a tenuous position but one that he defiantly stuck to for the rest of his life.*

— -

---

*   In 1916, with the announcement of a special commission into the conduct of the campaign, Hamilton and Churchill conspired to shift the blame for the Gallipoli debacle to Kitchener. But just as they were ready to stick the knife in, Kitchener inconveniently drowned when his ship hit a mine off the Orkney Islands. Sensibly, Hamilton and Churchill determined that attempting to besmirch the reputation of a national hero who had just been killed in action was inadvisable, so they were forced to shoulder more of the burden of responsibility for the Gallipoli disaster than either of them would have liked.

The men who fought at Krithia all came from different places and led very different lives until history conspired to bring them violently together on this small patch of turf in a far-flung corner of Türkiye. Some of them survived the ordeal and some didn't, but they were all forever changed by what they experienced on that baked plain in front of the village of Krithia.

Private Cecil Malthus survived several near misses at Krithia, and several more during the rest of the Gallipoli campaign. Back at Anzac, he fought with the Canterburys at Quinn's Post and Rhododendron Ridge. He survived the fighting but was felled by scarlet fever and was sent to hospital. He arrived back at Gallipoli just in time for the evacuation. On the Western Front, he fought in the Battle of the Somme and was wounded by a bomb in September 1916. During his recovery, he had two toes amputated after gangrene set in. This ended his military career and he was invalided back to New Zealand. He married in 1919 and taught as a professor of modern languages at the University of Canterbury for more than twenty years. He published his memoirs, *Anzac: A Retrospect*, in 1965. Cecil died in 1976, aged eighty-six.

After the Gallipoli evacuation, Able Seaman Joe Murray continued to serve with the Hood Battalion of the Royal Naval Division on the Western Front. He was wounded during the closing days of the Battle of the Somme in 1916, and again during the Battle of Arras in 1917, this time so severely that he was sent back to England and never returned to the front. After the war, he worked in an eclectic range of jobs that included painting theatres in England, growing tobacco in China and prospecting for gold in Spitzbergen. He married in 1920 and had a son. In 1965, Joe published *Gallipoli: As I Saw It*, his bestselling memoir, and he became one of the most celebrated Gallipoli veterans in the UK. He appeared in numerous interviews and television programmes until he died aged ninety-seven in 1994. He had outlived both his wife and son by several decades.

Private Harry Kelly's war was a short one. The shoulder wound that he received at Krithia was so severe that he was evacuated to Egypt and then sent home. By the end of July, he was back in Australia, only eight months after having left. He was discharged from the army and never served again. He returned to Victoria, married in 1916 and had five children. He worked as a clerk and lived a quiet family life in Coburg until his death in 1957. He was sixty-two.

His good mate Private Harold 'Nick' Nicholls, who was wounded at the same time as Harry and helped him limp back to a field hospital, also never returned to the war. His arm wound was serious enough to have him sent to hospital in England and, eventually, back to Australia. He remained good mates with Harry for the next four decades and lived near him in Coburg until his death in 1975, aged eighty-nine. The Turkish bullet that had hit him at Krithia was still in his arm when he died.

Private Bill Buckingham, the resplendently moustachioed cooper from Melbourne who had been a father figure to his platoon in the 6th Battalion, was reported wounded and missing after the Battle of Krithia. For eighteen months, his wife Catherine pleaded with the War Department for information about his fate. As he was officially considered missing, she was not eligible for a pension and could only support her five children with assistance from Carlton Breweries, her husband's former employer. She lived in a house she dubbed *Mailliw* – 'William' spelt backward. Bill was finally reclassified as killed in action in April 1916 and, soon after, his oldest son Jack enlisted in the AIF. Jack Buckingham was killed in action in the Ypres Salient in October 1917, aged nineteen. Neither father nor son's body was ever recovered. Today, Bill is remembered on the Helles Memorial and Jack is remembered on the Menin Gate in Ypres.

Lieutenant Colonel William Malone, the brusque and brazen commander of the Wellington Battalion, returned with his New Zealanders to Anzac after the Battle of Krithia and continued to inspire his men and infuriate his superiors in equal measure. Three months after Krithia, the Wellingtons played a pivotal role in the August Offensive; on 8 August, Malone personally led them in a bold attack to secure the heights of Chunuk Bair, the New Zealand objective. For the next twenty-four hours, the battalion faced an onslaught of Turkish counter-attacks, which they fought off with bomb and bayonet. Late in the day, a salvo of shells from an Allied battery fell short and landed squarely in the Wellington trench. Malone and half a dozen other men were killed. He was fifty-six. The Allies were forced from the summit of Chunuk Bair the next day and Malone's body was never recovered. Today, he is commemorated on the Chunuk Bair Memorial, along with 309 of his men who have no known grave.

George Greig, Company Sergeant Major in the 7th Battalion, who had led the search for the missing sergeant back in Albany and who had a strange premonition about his death on 8 May, was killed close to the final line where the Australians dug in at Krithia. His body was never identified and his name is recorded on the Cape Helles Memorial. He was twenty-three.

The magnificently named Reuben Lucius Hampton, private in the 5th Battalion, survived Krithia but was wounded in the thigh and buttock at Lone Pine. He was evacuated to Malta and never returned to Gallipoli. On the Western Front, he served in various units and was promoted to sergeant but suffered from ill health and was frequently hospitalised. He was sent back to Australia suffering from tuberculosis in September 1918. He died from the disease in April the following year. He was twenty-seven.

Sergeant Jim Parker, the artilleryman whose sharp eye and pen painted a vivid picture of the Helles operations, survived the Gallipoli campaign and fought with distinction on the Western Front. He was wounded on the Somme in 1916 and earned a Military Medal at Ypres in 1918 for rescuing a group of men who had been buried by a shell burst. One of the men he saved, Sergeant Bill Fulton, would serve as Jim's best man at his wedding in 1919. Jim Parker worked as a saddler until he died suddenly at his Brighton home in 1950, aged sixty-five.

Corporal Clarrie Roberts returned with the 8th Battalion to Anzac after the Battle of Krithia. He was wounded at Lone Pine and died in a hospital in Malta on 13 August 1915, aged twenty-one. He is buried in Pieta Military Cemetery in Malta.

Private Jim Bayne kept a detailed diary of his experiences serving in the Wellington Battalion from his enlistment in 1914 until the Battle of Krithia. His last entry was made on the morning of 8 May and describes the battalion being ordered to march to the front line after breakfast. He was killed in the attack soon after, aged twenty-eight, and the diary was found on his body five months later. His body was subsequently lost and he is remembered on the Chunuk Bair Memorial.*

Lieutenant General Sir Ian Hamilton was recalled to London after being sacked as commander of the Mediterranean Expeditionary Force, a humiliation that effectively ended his military career. After the war, he championed the rights of returned servicemen and served as the Scottish president of the British Legion. In 1920, he published *Gallipoli Diary,* a two-volume facsimile of his 1915 diaries and one of the greatest attempts at arse-covering in military history. He courted controversy in the lead-up to the Second World War by publicly

---

*   Confusingly, his date of death is listed as 4 September 1915, which appears to be the date he was officially declared dead after having been missing since Krithia.

stating his admiration for the up-and-coming Adolf Hitler and was accused of being an antisemite and Nazi sympathiser. He died in London in 1947, aged ninety-four.

Major General Sir Aylmer Hunter-Weston continued serving as the commander of the 29th Division at Gallipoli throughout the bloody advances of June and July. At the end of July, he was suddenly sent back to England and it's never been clear exactly why. Official accounts state that he was suffering from sunstroke or enteric fever (or possibly both) but Sir Ian Hamilton later referred to Hunter-Weston's 'breakdown' as the reason for his removal. Regardless, by 1916, he was fit enough to return to command and led the VIII Corps during the disastrous Battle of the Somme. He continued to lead the corps with varying degrees of success until the Armistice and is considered one of the most controversial British commanders of the war. On 18 March 1940, he died after falling from a turret at his home in Scotland in mysterious circumstances. He was seventy-five.

Colonel James McCay, commander of the Australian 2nd Brigade at Krithia, continued to forge an unenviable reputation as the wrong man in the wrong place for the rest of the war. After Gallipoli, he was promoted to command the Australian 5th Division and oversaw a disastrous desert march in March 1916 that nearly broke the 14th Brigade. In July 1916, he played a leading role in the near destruction of his division at the Battle of Fromelles, the most costly twenty-four hours in Australian military history. Even though Krithia, the desert march and Fromelles were not entirely McCay's fault, he had a unique knack for losing the trust of both his men and his superiors, and he was squarely and loudly blamed for all three. He was relieved of frontline command in January 1917 and spent the rest of the war overseeing the Australian depots in England, during which time he managed to alienate just about everyone he came in contact with. He died in Melbourne in

1930, aged sixty-five, having never succeeded in redeeming his sullied reputation.

General William Birdwood, commander of the ANZAC Corps at Gallipoli, forged a reputation for serene courage and steadfast concern for the welfare of his men throughout the campaign. After the evacuation, he commanded the I Anzac Corps on the Western Front and, although he was British, he genuinely liked and understood the Australians he commanded. He astutely appointed Australian commanders to key positions and nurtured the fighting capabilities of the Australian soldier that he had first witnessed at Gallipoli. He was responsible for building up Australian training bases in England and for uniting all five Australian divisions as the Australian Corps. In May 1918, Birdwood relented to pressure to hand over command of the corps to an Australian and was succeeded by Lieutenant General John Monash, whose reputation was made on the back of Australian successes in late 1918. But Birdwood deserves much of the credit for refining the Australians into an elite fighting force. He remained an extremely popular figure in Australia and received a hero's welcome when he toured the country in 1920. Ten years later, he unsuccessfully petitioned to become governor-general. He died aged eighty-five in 1951. Since 1915, he had signed his name as 'Birdwood of Anzac'.

Lieutenant Colonel Mahmed Sefik, who had commanded the gritty defence of the Anzac Cove sector on the day of the landing, was one of the best Ottoman regimental commanders of the war. Despite being an outspoken critic of Turkish leadership and tactics, Sefik's exceptional abilities were well recognised and he was promoted to command the 19th Division in August 1915. After success at Gallipoli, the division was deployed to reinforce the flailing Austro-Hungarian army in Galicia. Although Sefik did a sterling job training and leading his division, he clashed with his German and Austro-Hungarian superiors about the way his Turkish troops were being deployed and was recalled at the end of 1916. He served the rest of the war as a commander of local garrison and home-guard units. He fought during the War of Independence but again clashed with his superiors and was transferred to rear duties. He resigned from the army in 1931. He never received the credit he was due for his role in the success of the Gallipoli campaign and died a 'broken man'[9] in 1964. His memoirs give a rare insight into Turkish operations during the campaign and are one of the most important Ottoman sources for modern scholars.

Lieutenant Colonel Mustafa Kemal would become the most important leader in modern Turkish history. His reputation was forged by his successes at Gallipoli and he was hailed as the 'Saviour of Constantinople'. In 1916, he was promoted to general and fought on the Eastern Front, becoming the only Turkish general to achieve victories over the Russians. For the rest of the war, Kemal served as an army commander, eventually overseeing the collapsing Ottoman forces in Syria. After the Ottoman defeat, he returned to Constantinople in late 1919, in time to see Allied ships sailing triumphantly up the Bosphorus, a humiliation that he was determined to redress. From 1919 to 1922, he led the liberation army in the Turkish War of Independence, eventually succeeding in overthrowing the sultan and ousting the Allies. In 1923, the new Republic of Turkey was established with Kemal as its first president. For the next fifteen years, he transformed Turkey from the 'Sick Man of Europe', as the Ottoman Empire had been called, to a thriving modern republic. He introduced reforms to government and education that made Turkey a secular state, gave equal rights to women and modernised agriculture, industry and science. Kemal's reforms saw, amongst many other things, the introduction of a Latin alphabet, the promotion of the arts and the modernisation of the Turkish economy. In 1934, the country introduced the

Surname Law, which abandoned the former Ottoman practice of generic titles and required that all citizens of Turkey adopt fixed, hereditary surnames. Following the law, Kemal was renamed Kemal Atatürk ('Father of the Turks'). He died after a short illness in 1938 and his body was interred in a mausoleum in Ankara. He remains a beloved figure in modern Türkiye.

— —

On the plains in front of Krithia, a hot breeze sings through the branches of a grove of spindly olive trees. A tribe of wiry goats scratches at the baked earth, the tin bells around their scrawny necks clanking half-heartedly. The goat herder wears a dusty suit coat and a three-day stubble, and wanders behind the tribe, content to follow it where it leads. He's doing pretty much what his father did before him, and what goat herders have done here for hundreds of years.

No-one much comes to this corner of the Gallipoli peninsula. This place is for goat herders and tomato farmers – the tourists all head further north, to sites with romantic-sounding names like Anzac Cove and Lone Pine.

There's not a lot to suggest that anything important happened here, no clue that tens of thousands of men died in these insignificant fields. The shallow trench that snakes through the nearby pine copse could just as easily be a drainage ditch. The metal pickets that once supported barbed-wire entanglements could be mistaken for fence posts – about the only thing that reveals this as a former battlefield is Redoubt Cemetery, with its neat rows of headstones laid out like soldiers on parade.

In one corner of the cemetery lies Corporal Archie Odgers, a 25-year-old plumber from Melbourne who, for reasons unknown, enlisted, fought and died under the alias 'Mark Wraith'. We don't know much about Archie Odgers, except that he joined up within two weeks of the outbreak of war and that he did well as a soldier in the nine months he served with the Australian 7th Battalion. He fell in the horrendous Australian advance on Krithia but, unlike most of his fallen comrades, his body was identified after the war and he now lies beneath a headstone. That headstone bears an inscription that was composed by his family back in Australia, who never had the chance to visit his grave: *Still Living, Still Loving, Still With Us*. It's an apt sentiment – Archie Odgers and his comrades from the Battle of Krithia *are* still with us, if only we make the effort to seek them out.

ACKNOWLEDGEMENTS

Thanks to the team at Hachette Australia including Sophie Hamley, Matthew Kelly, Annie Zhang and Jeremy Sherlock.

Peter Hart provided invaluable input into the direction of the narrative and sources that brought the story to life. Thanks also to his partner in crime Gary Bain; their *Pete & Gary's Military History* podcast was a great source of inspiration and distraction!

My immense gratitude to the many outstanding historians who provided advice and direction during the writing of the book: Hugh Dolan, Brad Manera, Bernard de Broglio, Andrew Bellamy, Peter Smith, Jo Hook, Lambis Englezos, Craig Roach, Stephen Chambers, Richard van Emden and many others.

Two diligent researchers helped uncover the stories of the soldiers featured in the narrative: Kristen Alexander and Lorraine Newland. Thanks also to Tom Buckingham for the information he provided about his relative Bill Buckingham, who died at Krithia.

Thanks to my amazing team at Mat McLachlan Battlefield Tours for the hard work that enables so many people to walk in the footsteps of the Anzacs: Bree Cracknell, Rosanna Gelonesi,

Aphra Carroll, Greg Lee, Kath Barry and Dianne Overton. And a special shout-out to my tireless producer and publicist Jess Stebnicki – little of the work I do would happen without you!

And finally, to my family. Thank you for all that you've done to encourage and support me. My three children, Brooke, Heath and James, are the light of my life, and my ever-patient wife Jess is my co-pilot in life who I couldn't do without.

ENDNOTES

1. The New Zealander
1   Unless otherwise noted, all quotes associated with Pte Cecil Malthus
     are drawn from: Cecil Malthus, *Anzac: A Retrospect*, Whitcombe &
     Tombs, 1965.
2   Diary of William Malone, quoted in Crawford and Cooke, *No Better
     Death* (ebook).

2. The Englishman
1   Unless otherwise noted, all quotes associated with Seaman Joe
     Murray are drawn from: Joseph Murray, *Gallipoli: As I Saw It*,
     William Kimber, 1965.

3. The Australian
1   Unless otherwise noted, all quotes associated with Pte Harry
     Kelly are sourced from: Diary of Private HV Kelly, 7th Battalion,
     Australian War Memorial.
2   Diary of GF Greig, 7th Battalion, Australian War Memorial.
3   CEW Bean, *The Official History of Australia in the War of 1914–1918*
     (vol. I), Angus & Robertson, 1939, p98 ('Australian Official History').
4   Ibid, p128.

4. The War in 1915
1   Diary of Rifleman William Eve, 1/16th (County of London) Battalion
     (Queen's Westminster Rifles), 7 January 1915, National Army
     Museum.
2   Australian Official History (vol. II.), p2.
3   Peter Hart, 'Sir Ian Hamilton', *Britain at War*, 27 April 2017.

5. Landing at Helles: The Turkish Perspective

1   Harvey Broadbent, *Gallipoli: The Turkish Defence,* The Miegunyah Press, 2015, p127.
2   Ibid, p126.
3   Ibid, p473.
4   Mahmut Sabri, quoted in Broadbent, p130.
5   Ibid, p131.
6   Ibid.
7   Private Robert Martin, quoted in Stephen Chambers, *Krithia: Gallipoli*, Pen & Sword, 2020, p15.
8   Chambers, pp16–17.
9   Edward J. Erickson, *Gallipoli: the Ottoman Campaign*, Pen & Sword, 2010, p70.
10 Peter Hart, *Gallipoli*, Profile Books, 2011, p132.
11 Ibid, p134.
12 Lieutenant Douglas Talbot, Royal Navy, quoted in Chambers, p12.
13 Broadbent, p474.
14 Ibid, p136.
15 Ibid, p139.
16 1/KOSB war diary, quoted in Chambers, p4.
17 CF Aspinall-Oglander, *Military Operations Gallipoli* (vol. I.), William Heinemann Ltd, 1929, p210 ('British Official History').
18 Sir Ian Hamilton, *Gallipoli Diary*, George H. Doran Company, 1920 (ebook).
19 Ibid.

6. Landing at Anzac: The Turkish Perspective

1   Richard van Emden and Stephen Chambers, *Gallipoli: The Dardanelles Disaster in Soldiers' Words and Photographs*, Bloomsbury Publishing, 2015.
2   Australian Official History, p260.
3   Adil Sahin, quoted in Kevin Fewster, Vecihi Basarin and Hatice Hurmuz Basarin, *Gallipoli: The Turkish Story*, Allen & Unwin, 2003, p63.
4   Second Lieutenant I. Hayrettin, quoted by Haluk Oral, *Gallipoli 1915: Through Turkish Eyes*, Bahcesehir University Press, 2012, p49.
5   Australian Official History, pp268–69.
6   Mucip Bey, quoted by Sefik, 'The Dardanelles: The Ari Burnu Battles and 27 Regiment', Imperial War Museum.
7   Ibid.
8   CEW Bean, *Gallipoli Mission*, ABC Books, 1991, p117.
9   Diary of Private Reuben Hampton, 5th Battalion, 25 April 1915, Australian War Memorial.

10   Ibid.
11   Bean, *Gallipoli Mission*, p153.
12   Sefik, 'The Dardanelles: The Ari Burnu Battles and 27 Regiment, Imperial War Museum.
13   *Atatürk Memoirs,* Imperial War Museum, pp6–7.
14   Ibid, pp8–9.
15   HW Murray, 'The First Three Weeks on Gallipoli', *Reveille*, 1 April 1939, p60.
16   Malthus, p46.
17   Diary of Corporal Clarrie Roberts, 8th Battalion, 25 April 1915, Australian War Memorial.

7. Helles: The First Ten Days
1   29th Division Unit Diary, 26 April 1915.
2   Hamilton, 25 April 1915.
3   British Official History, p278.
4   Ibid, p286.
5   Ibid, p287.
6   Ibid, p289.
7   Hamilton, 28 April 1915.
8   Ibid.
9   Ibid.
10   British Official History, p295.
11   Ibid, p304
12   Ibid, p295.
13   AH Mure, *With the Incomparable 29th*, W&R Chambers, 1919, pp80–81.
14   Ibid, pp87–88.

8. Anzac: The First Ten Days
1   Captain CG Dix and historian Frank Cain, quoted in Erickson, footnote 21.
2   PC Fenwick, 'Reminiscences of Anzac', *Reveille*, 31 March 1932, p39.
3   Malone; Crawford and Cooke, *No Better Death* (ebook)
4   Kelly diary.
5   Malthus, p47.
6   Diary of Private James Parker, 2nd Field Artillery Brigade, Australian War Memorial.
7   Kelly diary.
8   Ibid.
9   Malthus, p48.
10   Kelly diary.
11   Malthus, p48.

12   Hampton diary, 25 April 1915.
13   Mesut Uyar, *The Ottoman Defence Against the Anzac Landing: 25 April 1915*, Big Sky Publishing, 2015.
14   Malthus, p49.
15   Private Sydney Powell, 4th Battalion, quoted in van Emden and Chambers.
16   Ibid.
17   War Diary, General Staff, Headquarters, Australian and New Zealand Army Corps, 27 April 1915, Australian War Memorial.
18   Australian Official History, p529.
19   Malthus, p55.
20   Australian Official History, p531.
21   Ibid, p532.
22   Malthus, p60.
23   Australian Official History, p535.
24   'Marsova' (pseudonym), '"Nerves": A Gallipoli Panic', *Reveille,* 31 March 1931, p58.
25   Malone; Crawford and Cooke, *No Better Death* (ebook).
26   Greig diary, 29 April 1915.
27   Diary of Private James Bayne, National Library of New Zealand.
28   Malone; Crawford and Cooke, *No Better Death* (ebook).
29   Diary of Private Sam Norris, 6th Battalion, 3 May 1915, State Library of NSW.
30   Malthus, p56.
31   British Official History, p299.

9. The Turkish Response
1   British Official History, p317.
2   Ibid.
3   Hans Kannengiesser, *The Campaign in Gallipoli,* William Brendon and Son, 1927, pp131–32.
4   British Official History, p317.
5   Chambers, p32.
6   Ibid, p33.
7   Kannengiesser, p132.
8   Ibid, p133.
9   Murray, p57.
10   Chambers, p38.

10. Resuming the Advance
1   Australian Official History (vol. II), p2.
2   Hugh Dolan, *Gallipoli Air War*, Pan MacMillan, 2013 (ebook).

3 Letter from Sergent Pilote Henri Dumas, quoted in 'La Guerre en Orient', *La Vie Aérienne*, 8 and 15 April 1920; English translation available at: aegeanairwar.com/articles/souvenir-sportif-henri-dumas-at-the-dardanelles.
4 George Bertram Horridge, oral history interview, Imperial War Museum, 7498, Reel 2.
5 Australian Official History, p601.
6 4403 Cipher, 4 May 1915, General Staff, General Headquarters, Mediterranean Expeditionary Force.
7 British Official History, p326.
8 Force Order 5, General Headquarters, Mediterranean Expeditionary Force.
9 Murray, pp67–68.

11. The Anzac Move to Helles
1 Operational Order 106, 3 May 1915, General Staff, Headquarters, Australian and New Zealand Army Corps.
2 Cable from ANZAC to GHQ, 1.53 pm, 4 May 1915, General Staff, Headquarters, Australian and New Zealand Army Corps.
3 Cable from ANZAC to GHQ, 6 pm, 4 May 1915, General Staff, Headquarters, Australian and New Zealand Army Corps.
4 Malthus, p61.
5 'Embarkation of 5/6 May, 1915', General Staff, Headquarters, Australian and New Zealand Army Corps.
6 Malone; Crawford and Cooke, *No Better Death* (ebook).
7 Malthus, p61.
8 'Embarkation of 5/6 May, 1915', General Staff, Headquarters, Australian and New Zealand Army Corps.

12. 6 May
1 AW Keown, *Forward with the Fifth*, The Specialty Press, 1921, p106.
2 Malthus, p64.
3 Norris diary, 6 May 1915.
4 Kelly diary.
5 British Official History, p343.
6 Diary of Sergeant Leslie Goldring, 6 May 1915, Australian War Memorial.
7 Diary of Charles Bean, 6 May 1915, Australian War Memorial.
8 Ibid.
9 Malone; Crawford and Cooke, *No Better Death* (ebook).
10 Malthus, p65.

11   Fred Waite, *Official History Of New Zealand's Effort In The Great War*, Whitcombe & Toms, 1919, p123 ('New Zealand Official History').
12   Kelly diary.
13   British Official History, p333.
14   Ibid.
15   Arthur Behrend, *Make Me a Soldier: A Platoon Commander in Gallipoli*, Eyre & Spottiswoode, 1961, p66–67.
16   British Official History, p331 (footnote).
17   Parker diary, 6 May 1915.
18   Private Charles Watkins, 6th Lancashire Fusiliers, quoted in van Emden and Chambers.
19   Lieutenant Henri Feuille, quoted in Peter Hart, 'The French at Gallipoli', *The Gallipolian*, no. 137, Spring 2015, p44.
20   Hermann Lorey, quoted in Chambers, pp46–47.
21   Murray, pp68–69.
22   Joseph Murray, oral history interview, Imperial War Museum.
23   Australian Official History, p6.
24   Malone; Crawford and Cooke, *No Better Death* (ebook).
25   Hamilton, 9 May 1915.
26   British Official History, p336.
27   29th Divisional Operation, Order No. 5, 6 May 1915, National Archives.

13. 7 May
1   British Official History, p336.
2   Ibid, p341.
3   Ibid, p338 (footnote).
4   Ibid.
5   Malthus, p67.
6   Goldring diary.
7   Horridge, oral history interview, Reel 2.
8   Ibid.
9   Ibid.
10   Ibid.
11   British Official History p340 (footnote).
12   Murray, p76.
13   New Zealand Official History, p123.
14   Ibid.
15   British Official History, p343.
16   Sketch map, 'Situation 7th/8th May 1915', Appendix XIV, 29th Division Unit Diary, National Archives.
17   British Official History, p341 (footnote).

14. 8 May

1   Cable 207, 7 May 1915, General Staff, General Headquarters, Mediterranean Expeditionary Force.
2   Force Order No. 6, 7 May 1915, General Staff, General Headquarters, Mediterranean Expeditionary Force.
3   British Official History, p343.
4   Malone; Crawford and Cooke, *No Better Death* (ebook).
5   Malthus, p67.
6   Parker diary.
7   Malthus, p68.
8   Malone; Crawford and Cooke, *No Better Death* (ebook).
9   Captain Kenneth Gresson, Canterbury Battalion, quoted in 'The Second Battle of Krithia', *Pete & Gary's Military History* podcast, 8 May 2020.
10   Malthus, p68.
11   New Zealand Official History, p125.
12   Malthus, p70.
13   Ibid, pp70–71.
14   Australian Official History, p18.
15   British Official History, p344.
16   Malthus, p71.
17   Australian Official History, pp19–20.
18   2nd Infantry Brigade War Diary, May 1915, Appendix A.
19   Ibid.
20   Letter attached to diary of GF Greig, to Mrs Greig from Hector E. Bastin, 21 August 1917, Australian War Memorial.
21   Parker diary.
22   Goldring diary.
23   Private Frank Brent, 6th Battalion, *BBC Four* television interview, 1964.
24   Australian Official History, p26.
25   Bean, *Gallipoli Mission*, pp290–91.
26   Australian Official History, p26.
27   Roberts diary.
28   Australian Official History, p27.
29   Norris diary.
30   Kelly diary.
31   Bean, *Gallipoli Mission*, p293.
32   'FJS', *The Bulletin*, vol. 36, no. 1866, 18 May 1915, p28.
33   2nd Brigade monthly notes, vol. 1, no. 11, April 1919, p6.
34   Kelly diary.
35   Australian Official History, pp29–30.
36   Ibid, p31.

37   Les Carlyon, *Gallipoli,* Bantam Books, 2003 (ebook).
38   Malthus, p71.
39   Hamilton, 9 May 1915.
40   Murray, p77.
41   John Graham Gillam, *Gallipoli Diary*, George Allen & Unwin, 1918, pp77–78.
42   Brent, television interview, 1964.
43   Sergeant Cecil Eades, 7th Battalion, quoted in 'The Second Battle of Krithia', *Pete & Gary's Military History* podcast, 8 May 2020.
44   Malthus, p72.
45   Ibid.

15. Aftermath
1   Force Order No. 7, 9 May 1915, General Headquarters, Mediterranean Expeditionary Force.
2   29th Division Special Order, 10 May 1915.
3   Ibid.
4   Force Order No. 8, 11 May 1915, General Headquarters, Mediterranean Expeditionary Force.
5   Force Order No. 11, 13 May 1915, General Headquarters, Mediterranean Expeditionary Force.
6   Hamilton cable to Kitchener, 8 May 1915, quoted in British Official History, p349.
7   Ibid, pp350–51.
8   Australian Official History (vol. II), p39.
9   Bean, *Gallipoli Mission*, p298.
10   Rev O Creighton, *With the Twenty-Ninth Division in Gallipoli*, Longmans, Green & Co, 1916, p84.
11   Diary of John Turnbull, 8th Battalion, 8 May 1915, Australian War Memorial.
12   Ron Austin, *The White Gurkhas: The Australians at the Second Battle of Krithia, Gallipoli*, RJ & SP Austin, 1989, p118.
13   Malthus, pp73–74.
14   Murray, p81.
15   New Zealand Official History, p134.
16   Telegram from Birdwood to Hamilton, ANZAC Headquarters, 14 May 1915, Australian War Memorial.
17   New Zealand Official History, p146.
18   2nd Brigade War Diary, June 1915.
19   Copy of telegraph message No MFA86/1, 20 May 1915, Australian War Memorial.
20   Nigel Steel and Peter Hart, *Defeat at Gallipoli*, Macmillan, 1994, (ebook).

21   *The London Gazette* (Supplement), 24 July 1915, p7282.
22   Murray, pp103–04.
23   *Stead's Review of Reviews*, 11/6/1915, p440.
24   Major Gordon Bennett, quoted in Steel and Hart (ebook).
25   Letter, Lieutenant Colonel Harold Elliott, 7th Battalion, 8 August 1915, Australian War Memorial.
26   Hampton diary, 9 August 1915.
27   *The London Gazette* (Supplement), 7 April 1916, pp3777–78.
28   Winston S Churchill, *The World Crisis: 1911–1918*, Free Press, 2005, p532.
29   Unit Diary, 2nd Brigade, 11 December 1915, Australian War Memorial.

16. Remembering
1   Bean, *Gallipoli Mission*, p13.
2   Ibid, pp45–48.
3   Ibid, p286.
4   Ibid, p304.
5   Ibid, p299.
6   Amy Lambert, *Thirty Years of an Artist's Life: The Career of GW Lambert, ARA*, Australian Artist Editions, 1977, pp113–14.
7   Cyril Hughes, *Report of Australian Representative with Graves Registration Unit, Gallipoli*, 1919, Australian War Memorial, pp3–4.
8   Jenny Macleod, 'General Sir Ian Hamilton and the Dardanelles Commission', *War in History*, vol. 8, no. 4, November 2001, footnote 52.
9   Uyar, p65.

INDEX